NAPOLEON
AND HIS
MARSHALS

NAPOLEON
AND HIS
MARSHALS

A. G. MACDONELL

PRION

This edition first published in Great Britain 1996 by
PRION
32-34 Gordon House Road,
London NW5 1LP

Originally published by Macmillan and Co. 1934
Copyright Macmillan Publishers Ltd and A. G. Macdonell.
All rights reserved.

A catalogue record of this book can be obtained from the
British Library

ISBN 1-85375-222-3

Cover design by Bob Eames
Cover image the Battle of Zürich, 25th September 1799,
by François Bouchot (1800-1842) courtesy of the Bridgeman Art
Library/Giraudon/Château de Versailles
Printed and bound in Great Britain by
Biddles Ltd., Guildford & Kings Lynn

To
MONA AND JENNY

LIEUTENANT-COLONEL A. H. TEED,
FONTCREUSE,
CASSIS,
BOUCHES DU RHÔNE.

MY DEAR COLONEL,

IT was in your Sunny Provencal Vineyard that I first got the notion of writing this book. You had lent me the *Memoirs of Baron de Marbot*, had talked learnedly and wisely about the tactics of Waterloo, and had refilled my glass with your glowing *vin rosé*. For the threefold inspiration, I owe you much thanks.

Yours,

A. G. M.

HASCOMBE PLACE,
GODALMING,
SURREY.

CONTENTS

LIST OF THE MARSHALS CREATED BY THE EMPEROR NAPOLEON

NAPOLEON, Emperor of the French, by a Decree of May 19th, 1804, appointed eighteen officers of the French Army to be Marshals of the Empire. Four of these were honorary Marshals from the Senate. The other fourteen were on the active list.

The four honorary Marshals were:

KELLERMANN, aged sixty-nine, son of a merchant.
LEFÈBVRE, aged forty-nine, son of a miller.
PÉRIGNON aged fifty, son of a landowner.
SÉRURIER aged sixty-two, son of an officer of the
    Household Troops.

The fourteen Marshals on the active list were:

BERTHIER aged fifty-one, son of a surveying
    engineer.
MURAT, aged thirty-seven, son of an innkeeper.
MONCEY, aged fifty, son of a lawyer.
JOURDAN, aged forty-two, son of a doctor.
MASSÉNA aged forty-eight, son of a tanner and
    soap-manufacturer.
AUGEREAU, aged forty-seven, son of a working
    mason.
BERNADOTTE, aged forty-one, son of a lawyer.
SOULT, aged thirty-five, son of a lawyer.
BRUNE, aged forty-one, son of a lawyer.
LANNES, aged thirty-five, son of a peasant farmer.
MORTIER, aged thirty-six, son of a farmer.
NEY, aged thirty-five, son of a barrel-cooper.
DAVOUT, aged thirty-four, son of an officer.
BESSIÈRES aged thirty-six, son of a surgeon.

Eight were subsequently added:
In 1807:
VICTOR, aged forty-three, son of a soldier.
In 1809:
MACDONALD, aged forty-four, son of a soldier.
MARMONT, aged thirty-five, son of an officer.
OUDINOT, aged forty-two, son of a brewer.
In 1811:
SUCHET, aged forty-one, son of a silk-manufacturer.
In 1812:
ST. CYR, aged forty-eight, son of a tanner.
In 1813:
PONIATOWSKI, aged fifty, son of a prince.
In 1815:
GROUCHY, aged forty-nine, son of a marquis.

CHAPTER I

The Army Of Italy

MODERN warfare dates from the first campaign in which General Bonaparte was in chief command of an army, the French Army of Italy in 1796. The tactics and strategy of the professional soldiers of the pre-Revolution years of the eighteenth century had been cast in a stiff and narrow mould. The Marlborough wars had been, with four classic exceptions, a matter of endless jockeying for position, covered by entrenched lines or based upon the great fortresses of the Low Countries. Condé, and Turenne, and Frederick of Prussia had conformed in general to the accepted theories of marching to and fro with, from time to time, a head-on collision. But the ragged armies of the Sansculottes in 1793 introduced the whirlwind advance upon the enemy, which in absurd, amateurish fashion swept away the professional precision at Fleurus and Neerwinden and Jemappes, and took as their watch-word 'Attack, attack, attack.' But in spite of their brilliant successes they were amateurs after all, and it was only their wild exaltation of soul that made them invincible, and when they had won their victories they knew as little how to use and exploit them as Turenne or Luxembourg. All that was changed in 1796. But though men knew that a change had come, very few understood what the change

1

was and how the new magic was worked, either in 1796 or for years afterwards, and of all the fighting-men who watched the new art in the hands of the master, and tried to learn their trade from him, only one appreciated and understood the secret to the extent that he was able to use it himself, and he, Marshal Davout, had only two opportunities in all his twenty years of service.

* * *

On March 26th, 1796, the veteran generals of the Army of Italy were sitting at the Army Headquarters at Nice, waiting for the ridiculous little gunner-general whom political intrigue and, many said, petticoat-influence had hoisted into chief command. Schérer, the superseded Commander, was there, waiting to hand over his command to his successor. Schérer was sixty-one, a ripe age for a general in those strenuous days, and he had seen much service in Flanders in '93 and '94, but he had neither the energy nor the ability to crack the Austro-Sardinian nut which lay in wedge-form across the Ligurian hills, and he was glad to resign. The three commanders of the divisional groups were there also. Sérurier, once Count Sérurier, was a man of fifty-four. A militia lieutenant at thirteen, an ensign in the regiment of La Beauce at seventeen, he had reached the rank of major after thirty-four laborious years of service when the Revolution broke out. He became an ardent Republican and soon reached the command of a division. Sérurier, in every thought, every word, every movement, was a soldier of the old Royal School. He was slow and brave and precise and cautious. He was a stern disciplinarian but a thoughtful commander. If his men maintained their dressing by the right in columns of fours, that was all he asked, and he would reward them by working himself, slowly and methodically, to a standstill in looking after their rations and their billets. On active service he was incessantly making the round of his outposts, examining everything with his own eyes and taking the gloomiest view of everything he saw. No wonder he was incessantly in a fog. The military art had gone past him and left him stranded. There was a perfect example of his notions of warfare in this campaign of '96. When he was ordered to attack the Piedmontese at Mondovi, he could conjure up no better tactical formation than an assault of three equal and parallel columns, equidistant from each other, in perfect alignment, in perfect step, with himself sword in hand, ten paces in front of the centre column. (Unfortunately for those who were ready to laugh at the honest fellow, the attack was a complete success.) He was honest financially and straightforward morally, and if he had years ago lost all initiative and if he was utterly bewildered by the new rushing tactics, and the lightning marches, and the lamentable neglect of the geometric alignments, and the rest of the principles of war so dear to his heart, nevertheless Sérurier's solidity, and his sterling, universally recognized, worth of character, and his old-fashioned traditions of service, made a valuable link between the old order and the new. He was a tall, stern, gloomy man with a heavy, stolid face, and a big scar on his lip, and he could never have been mistaken for anything but what he was, a rather stupid soldier.

Augereau, the second in age of the group-commanders, was a very different sort of man. The son of a poor working-mason in the St. Marceau Faubourg of Paris and a German fruit-stallseller, he remained to the end of his extraordinary life a gamin of the Parisian gutters. His first employment was as a footman to the Marquis de Bassompierre, but he was discharged for seducing the maid of the Marquise. He then got work as a waiter in the Café de Valois, a gambling-house in the Palais Royal, and was discharged for seducing a waitress. Augereau decided thereupon that civil life was altogether too complicated and he enlisted in the cavalry regiment of Burgundy, but was promptly discharged for indiscipline.

Soon after, however, his magnificent figure, his huge hawk-nose, his athletic reputation, and his invincible braggadocio, attracted the attention of the Marquis de Poyanne, colonel of carabineers, who enrolled him in his regiment without inquiring too closely into his past. This time young trooper Augereau managed to control himself a little better, and he quickly made his name as an efficient soldier, a boon companion, a ready quarreller, and the best swordsman in all the Royal cavalry.

General Marbot has some stories about him at this period. The famous coloured fencing-master, St. Georges, was sitting in a café one day when Augereau came past. 'There goes the best blade in France,' said St. Georges. Immediately the sergeant of a heavy cavalry regiment, who was famous for his truculence and his fencing, challenged Augereau to a duel, and was run through the body for his pains. On another occasion a famous bully of the gendarmes of Lunéville fought Augereau and, before engaging, inquired whether his opponent would prefer to be buried in the town or in the country.

'In the country,' replied Pierre Augereau. 'Very well,' said the gendarme, 'we will put you beside the two sergeants I fought yesterday.'

The last thrust of the duel was delivered by Augereau with the words, 'You will be buried in the country.'

But the life could not last. A young puppy of an officer struck the redoubtable trooper with his cane on parade. Augereau seized the stick and flicked it away. The lad in a gust of petulance whipped out his sword, but Augereau was the best blade in all the Royal cavalry and he fled to Switzerland on a stolen horse while they buried the young officer with full regimental ceremony.

From Switzerland he went as a traveller in watches and clocks to Constantinople and as far afield as Odessa. There he found a first-class war in progress and he enlisted in the Russian Army, and was present as a sergeant at Suvorov's capture of Ismail. The Paris street-boy, however, decided that the Russians were little better than savages, and he worked his way north through Poland into Prussia, where his magnificent figure and military experience readily brought him admission into the famous Guards. Unhappily for the new guardsman, a short time after he enlisted Frederick gave instructions that no Frenchman in his army should get reward or promotion. This did not suit Augereau, and he decided to desert. But the penalty for desertion from the Prussian Army was death, and the reward for capturing deserters was very high, so that it was an unusually risky proceeding. Augereau therefore came to the conclusion that if it was to be done at all, it must be done in the grand style, and placing himself at the head of sixty others, he fought his way out of Prussia into Saxony sword in hand. Once across the border he gave up military affairs for a time and earned his living as a dancing-master. He then drifted south again to Athens, where he fell in love with a beautiful Greek girl and eloped with her to Lisbon. But by this time the French Revolution had broken out and he was thrown into jail by the Portuguese Government as a Revolutionary. He might have remained months, or even years, in prison, but his wife managed to board a French merchant ship which had anchored in Lisbon harbour, and implored the captain to take the news to Paris that a Frenchman was unjustly imprisoned. The merchant captain was one of those obscure heroes whose name even has not come down to posterity. Instead of returning to France with the news, he instantly went ashore and announced to the Portuguese Government in a loud voice that unless the prisoner was handed over to him immediately, he would take the responsibility on behalf of the French Republic of declaring war upon the Kingdom of Portugal. The terrified Portuguese immediately gave up Augereau to the gallant captain and the ship sailed triumphantly back to France.

On his return, in 1792, the ex-street-boy joined a volunteer battalion and fought in the Vendée with such distinction that he was unanimously elected chief of the battalion. His promotion to a divisional-commander, via an adjutancy-general in the Pyrenees in '93, was as quick as was usual in these early days, and it was at about this time that Augereau performed a feat of bravery that was more gallant, and vastly less common, than fifty desperate deeds under fire. He actually stood up against a Representative of the People, one of those terrible, all-powerful plenipotentiaries from Paris, who had come down to accuse General Dagobert, an old officer of the Seven Years' War, of that deadliest of crimes – *Incivisme*. Greater men than Augereau had cringed before a Representative of the People, but nothing, neither physical threats nor moral threats, could daunt the huge gutter-snipe, and General Dagobert was saved from the guillotine. (Little good it did poor Dagobert in the end, for he died the following year of fatigue in front of San Miguel in the valley of the Segne, after he had struggled across the Pass of Perdue.)

General Augereau was no ladies' man, and the vivacious Madame Junot calls him in her Memoirs a blockhead and a cypher, and is shocked by the breadth and profundity of his swearing. He was, in fact, a soldier and nothing else. A buffoon, a brute, and a *bonhomme*, these three words cover most of his character; and military instinct covers the rest. For whatever can be said against him, he was the best tactician in the Army of Italy. His division was always deployed at the right moment, his attacks were timed for the right moment, and his supports and reserves were always at hand. He maintained order and discipline, he never ceased looking after the welfare of his men, by whom he was adored, and he was a loyal colleague both as a general and, later, as a Marshal. And, like all old soldiers, there was never a moment when he was not on the lookout for something to annex (in the language of the War of 1914-18, to 'scrounge'), and there was never a moment, even after a victory, when he was not tired, grumbling, and fed-up. It was characteristic of Augereau that though he was the loudest laugher of all the generals at Nice in 1796 at the imminent arrival of Bonaparte, the *gringolat*, the hop-o'-my-thumb, yet he was the first to write a soldierly letter of loyalty to his new commander, even though the tough veteran was then thirty-nine and the hop-o'-my-thumb only twenty-seven.

The third of the trio at Nice was André Masséna, the strangest and one of the two ablest (Davout being the other) of all Napoleon's men. Born at Nice in 1758, he ran away to sea as a cabin-boy at the age of thirteen and made several voyages in the Mediterranean, and even one as far as Cayenne, retired from the sea and enlisted as a private, when seventeen, in the Royal Italian regiment, and quickly rose to be sergeant-instructor and, later, company-sergeant-major. But after fourteen years' service he became disgusted with the impossibility of further advancement, and in August 1789 Le Sieur Masséna was certified as having served for fourteen years with distinction, and was given his discharge. Retiring to Antibes, he ostensibly set up a dried fruit and provision shop, but actually conducted a thriving trade in contraband over the wooded hills of Savoy into Italy, thus gaining an intimate knowledge of the by-paths and tracks of a country that was so soon to be of terrible importance to the Republic.

But in 1792 the ex-sergeant-major saw that there were better opportunities of fame and fortune, especially fortune, in the new democratic military life than were ever to be found in smuggling, and in that year Masséna, not Le Sieur this time, but *le citoyen*, was elected to command the second battalion of the Var, and by April, 1795, he was a general commanding the first division of the right wing of the Army of Italy.

André Masséna was a dark, thin man, with dark eyes and a long nose (there is no evidence for the story that he was a Jew and that his real name was Manasseh) and he was a very dry, silent, dour man. He very seldom spoke ill of others, and very seldom lost his temper. Off the field of battle, his mind seemed sluggish: on it, he was a blaze of fire, and energy, and brilliant, swift decision. His two over-mastering passions were women and money. He was so skilful in his pursuit of the former that a contemporary could write, 'He adored all women without ever failing in his regard for his wife,' and he was so able in his pursuit of money that he left forty millions of francs at his death. Masséna and Augereau were lifelong friends from 1796.

These three, then, the stiff old pedant, the swash-buckling gamin, and the silent understander of the human heart, waited at Nice for the hop-o'-my-thumb. The little gunner arrived on March 27th, 1796, bringing with him a handful of friends, only three of whom need be mentioned here, and a carriage full of history-books, and on April 12th the first cannon-shots of the New Warfare were being fired in front of the village of Montenotte.

The three men who came down with Bonaparte to Nice were Alexandre Berthier, a staff-officer, Joachim Murat, a cavalryman, and Marmont, a gunner, and Bonaparte's oldest friend.

Berthier was the son of a surveying engineer who built the Ministries of War, Marine, and Foreign Affairs at Versailles for Louis XV and was duly rewarded with a patent of nobility, a heritable pension of 12,000 livres, an infantry colonelcy, the Command-in-Chief of the Corps of Surveying Engineers, and the Orders of St. Louis and of St. Michael, all of which vanished at the Revolution. Berthier himself naturally became a military engineer, and went as a captain in 1778 to fight for American Independence with Rochambeau, performed gallantly upon the banks of the Ohio, became a colonel, and returned in time to be made, by Louis XVI, major-general of the National Guard of Versailles. He kept his head and his post during '89 and '90, but lost merit with the Revolutionaries by conniving at the escape of the King's aunts, and it was only his extraordinary aptitude for staff-work — already becoming well known – that kept him in high rank. He was Chief-of-Staff successively to such diverse leaders as the terrorist Ronsin in the Vendée, the brilliant ex-aristo Biron, and the workman Rossignol. The Terror drove him to ground for two years – he was too moderate and prudent for the Terrorists' liking – and then he mysteriously re-emerged from obscurity as Chief-of-Staff to old Kellermann, the Valmy Kellermann, in the Army of the Alps in '94.

Alexandre Berthier was an exceptionally ugly little man, with a huge, ungainly head, and movements so clumsy that they were almost pathetic. His hair was frizzy; his great red hands, in which a pencil moved as delicately and as truly over the maps as if it was guided by a touch of thistledown, were made uglier still by the stumps of finger-nails which were bitten and bitten till they bled; and whenever he talked he spluttered and stammered a mass of brusque, egotistical, tactless gaucheries. 'If he conceded a request he did it without affability; if he refused, he did it with harshness.'[1] As a staff-officer he was in a class by himself. There has, perhaps, never been a staff-officer in any army to excel Alexandre Berthier. His mind was clear, his grasp of detail apparently illimitable, his capacity for work colossal. It is recorded that on one campaign he went without sleep for thirteen days and nights. An emergency, at whatever hour of the day or night, always seemed to find him fully dressed and ready for work, and he knew at any hour of the twenty-four the name of the commander and the fighting strength of each of the units to which he was sending orders, and the exact position that each of them ought to be occupying. But outside his bureau, away from his maps, Berthier could think of one thing only, and that was his immense, his unbelievable, his God-given luck in being allowed to live on the same planet as the beautiful Madame de Visconti.

---

[1] *Bourrienne.*

Joachim Murat was a very different card. A Gascon of the Gascons, he was born in '67 at La Bastide, near Cahors, where his father combined the professions of innkeeper and estate-agent to the Talleyrand family. Joachim was in early life designed for the Church under the patronage of the great Talleyrand, the one-time Bishop of Autun. But Joachim was not cut for the cloth and he ran away from home at the age of twenty and enlisted in Captain Neil's company of the Horse Chasseurs of Champagne. Before the opening of the campaign of '96 he had only come into prominence once, but it was a brilliantly selected moment to choose for prominence and it led the innkeeper's son to a European throne. For General Bonaparte could not have blown away the Revolution in 1795 with his celebrated 'whiff of grape-shot' if he had not had guns to fire the grape-shot out of, and on that wild, clamorous, terrible night in Vendémiaire, 1795, all the world was on the prowl for guns. And if it was General Bonaparte who remembered the forty pieces of the National Guard that were parked in Les Sablons, it was Captain Murat, temporarily in command of the 21st Chasseurs, who galloped off at midnight to bring them in. Five agonizing hours of waiting followed for General Bonaparte and his friends in the Tuileries, and then the watchers heard at last the rattle of the gun-carriages on the *pavé* streets, and at half-past nine that morning the Revolution was over. From that moment the Master-Gunner never forgot the young cavalryman who sharked up the tools of his trade for him in that October darkness, and when, in 1796, Captain Murat gasconaded up to Bonaparte on the eve of his departure to command the Army of Italy and said, 'General, you have no Colonel A.D.C. I propose to accompany you in that capacity,' Bonaparte smiled and accepted the audacious offer.

Only in their love of wonderful clothes did handsome Murat and ugly little Berthier resemble each other. Of Marmont there will be more later.

Of the original creation of Marshals in 1804, these five held high commands in the Italian Campaign – Masséna, Berthier, Murat, Augereau, and Sérurier. A sixth, Brigadier Lannes, commanding a brigade in Augereau's division, first appears in military history at the assault on Dego in the first tempestuous ninety-six hours of the campaign. Jean Lannes was another Gascon, a farmer's son from Lectoure and once an apprentice dyer, and he was a great talker and swearer, the words in broad Gascon tumbling out in a thunderous vocabulary and his eyes flashing fire all the while. Lannes was a small man, not particularly handsome but neat and elegant, and was called 'The Roland of the Army.' It was always a source of vexation to Napoleon that Lannes up to the end steadily declined to cut his hair short in the modern fashion, and stuck to his short, thick queue which he loaded with powder and pomatum.

On April 11th, 1796, the Army of Italy was flung at the point of the wedge, the junction of the Austrian and Sardinian armies. In ninety-six hours of marching and fighting the wedge was split, the armies driven apart, and the line of the Alps had been turned. Nine days later the Sardinians threw up the sponge, and the tattered, shoeless, passionately uplifted Army of France was in full cry for Milan and Mantua, and North Italy was ablaze with welcome for the Liberators.

But the great campaign was all Bonaparte's. The divisional commanders appear in history from time to time, but only for fleeting moments. Sérurier's one conspicuous achievement was to get malaria in the marshy districts round Mantua while the siege was dragging on. Augereau, whose division quickly became what in these days would be called the storm troops, had his great moment at the battle of Castiglione when, in front, the Austrian Marshal Wurmser was coming over the Brenner, 50,000 strong, and Mantua was still holding out behind them. It was the only time in that campaign that Hop-o'-my-thumb's nerve failed him and he summoned a council of war and seemed about to accept their advice to throw up the siege and retreat upon Milan. But the huge gutter-snipe adventurer, the Commander of the storm troops, was all for standing and fighting.

At the Council of War at Roverbella Bonaparte was despondent and nervous. Augereau shouted against the idea of retreating. 'Attack first,' he exclaimed, 'and then if we are beaten it will be time to think of retreating.'

One of the lesser generals asked, 'How are you going to support the right wing?'

'With bayonets,' was the simple reply. Then turning to Bonaparte he said, 'We shall be attacked tomorrow; 20,000 Austrians are within an hour of us; but it isn't that that worries me; it is that I would like to see you a bit calmer. Fight here and I will answer for victory. Besides,' he added, with the sly grin for which he was famous, 'if we do lose I shall be a deader, so I will be all right either way.' Bonaparte accepted the advice, and the outcome was the five days of marching and fighting which are usually called the Battle of Castiglione, in which the two Austrian columns were beaten in detail and harried back into the hills. It was Augereau who led the final desperate attack of the reserves which won Castiglione. For many years after that council of war Napoleon answered all complaints against Augereau with the words, 'Ah! But remember what he did for us at Castiglione.'

But apart from this one great day, Augereau's part was confined to hard fighting, looting with such success that his 'plunder-wagons became as familiar as his sword' (his taste in jewels was impeccable, and his experience as a traveller in watches came in very handy), and suppressing local insurrections with rope and firing-squad.

Masséna's great day was at the Battle of Rivoli, the last and greatest of the victories of the campaign, when the six converging columns of Austria were flung back from the Rivoli plateau, and Bonaparte greeted Masséna upon the battlefield as the *enfant chéri de la Victoire*. It was at Rivoli, also, that Captain Bessières, formerly a hairdresser at Preissac in Languedoc, distinguished himself in a minor way and was promoted major.

Brigadier Lannes' part in the campaign consisted mostly in the leading of infantry attacks. With Berthier he led the second rush which in the end swept the bridge of Lodi, and captured the artillery which had devastated the first assault with its point-blank volleys of grape. After the battle at the bridge of Arcola, Bonaparte sent a captured flag to Lannes with the message:

> At Arcola, there was a moment when the fortune of the day was so uncertain that nothing but the utmost bravery on the part of the leaders could have saved the situation. Thereupon, bleeding from three terrible wounds, you left the field-hospital, resolved to conquer or die. You were the first to cross the Adda. Yours must be the honour of owning and guarding this glorious flag.

It was at about this period, too, that Lannes gave a sample of that cool, Gascon impertinence, so typical of the land of d'Artagnan, which he was to display years later in a vastly more important crisis. Sent after the fall of Mantua in February, 1797, to force the Pope into carrying out the armistice terms, he was riding alone in front of a dozen troopers, when he came suddenly round a rocky corner of the road near Ancona on a squadron of three hundred Papal horse-men.

'Draw swords,' shouted the Papal officer.

'How dare you draw swords?' cried Lannes instantly. 'Sheathe them at once.'

'Very good, sir,' replied the crestfallen officer.

This was excellent and the Gascon tried again. 'Dismount,' was his next venture.

'Very good, sir,' and the squadron dismounted.

Lannes tried once more. 'Lead your horses to my Headquarters.'

'Very good, sir,' and off they went.

Lannes said afterwards, 'If I'd bolted, some clumsy fool would have had a shot at me, and I thought it would be less risky to try a bit of cheek.'

But though these flamboyant soldiers had their moments in '96, all the rest was Bonaparte's.

**

After the fall of Mantua, Bonaparte did not rest for an instant upon his laurels. He threw himself with all his devastating energy into the pursuit of a new objective which was neither a fortress nor a victory on a field of battle. It was nothing less than the nerve-centre of the huge organization which was waging war against the French Republic from the flat plains of the Netherlands to the Kingdom of Naples and the marshes of Calabria, and this nerve-centre was Vienna itself, the Imperial City of the Holy Roman Emperors. A fine new division had arrived from the Army of the Rhine, commanded by another young Gascon, Bernadotte, and 70,000 victorious veterans went swarming up into the Carnic Alps, Masséna leading with faultless brilliance. But there was a deadly menace that haunted Bonaparte day and night, even when he was winning all along the line by expert and unerring manoeuvres, and Vienna was almost in sight. The menace was this. If the French Army of the Rhine made no demonstration in the north, the Austrians might detach an overwhelming army against his left flank and rear, while he was hundreds of miles from his base, still more hundreds from France, and entangled in the snowy passes of a rocky, barren, hostile land. He sent courier after courier to Paris imploring the Directory to order at least a demonstration on the Rhine, if they could not rise to a full-blooded offensive. The first answer he got was unsatisfactory enough – that the Army of the Rhine would not be in a condition to undertake active operations for some time. The second answer was devastating. Augereau had been appointed to the command of the Rhine, the great veteran Army of the Rhine, 120,000 strong.

When the despatch arrived, Bonaparte took Marmont aside, his earliest friend of subaltern days, and pointed to the Alpine panorama that lay before them, and said, 'Marmont, the campaigning season is far advanced; the snows are beginning; the country is difficult for offensive warfare. But never mind. We could have got over all that. But there is one obstacle that we cannot get over, the appointment of Augereau to command the Rhine,' and a few days later he signed the preliminaries of peace at Leoben, only sixty-five miles from Vienna. On the very next day Hoche crossed the Rhine and Moreau was preparing to follow, but Bonaparte did not get this crucial news till weeks later.

Augereau, of course, was delighted at this chance to show his real talents, and he astonished the Rhine officers with his superb uniform, which was laced all over, even to his boots, with gold embroidery, and with his conversation that was mainly about loot in Italy and not at all about General Bonaparte. And when General Bonaparte, in the same year, 1797, passed through Offenbourg, the Rhine General-Headquarters, on his way to the conference at Rastatt, he received a casual, word-of-mouth message from General Augereau, the commander of the Rhine, offering to provide a bed for General Bonaparte, the commander of Italy. It was not for seventeen years that the gamin addressed his old chief like that again.

* * *

The Campaign of '96 shook Europe to its foundations. A twenty-seven-year-old gunner had opened a campaign at Nice and closed it within sixty-five miles of Vienna, and the world understood vaguely that a portent had arrived, and that though the Revolution was over in the streets of

Paris, the Three Colours might yet be seen upon the battlefields of Europe and Asia and Africa.

This campaign also marked an epoch in the history of the French Army. The Revolution had swept away the stiff and stupid formalism of the Royal Army, and had substituted a wild exaltation for discipline, unorthodox victory for text-book defeat, and a passionate idealism for a weekly wage. The Italian campaign of '96 was the first return to professionalism since the Revolution. There was no room in Bonaparte's schemes for men like Carnot, leading an attack in civilian clothes and conquering because he had a profound conviction that Right always must conquer. Bonaparte preferred the man whose knowledge of supply-work and transport enabled him to fetch up an extra brigade when the pinch came. So the amateurs dropped out, and brilliant professionals took up the leading, and the rank-and-file were inspired by continuous victory and unlimited chances of promotion and loot, rather than by the inner belief that the Rights of Man were in danger, and that self-sacrifice for the Revolution was the noblest act in life.

CHAPTER II

THE OLD REPUBLICANS

WHEN General Bonaparte introduced his new whirl-wind methods into the art of warfare in 1796, the only real changes which he made at first were the furious marching and the imposition of a Will of genius upon his men. The reorganizing, the corps system, the standardization of the artillery types, the lozenge formation, the giant batteries, the pivotal battle, the cavalry screen, all these came later. But in 1796 Bonaparte won his startling victories with an army that was a legacy from the past. He did not create the fierce Spirit of Attack; he inherited it from the Sambre-et-Meuse. He did not create the tradition of Glory; it came from Condé and Turenne and Luxembourg and the thousand victories of France. He did not invent the infantry Attack in Column with a cloud of skirmishers in front, for it was forced upon the Revolutionary armies by the lack of training which made the Attack in Line, so dear to Frederick the Great and his super-trained soldiers, an impossibility for amateurs. The close Column was easier to handle than a long, perfectly dressed Line, and the cloud of skirmishers gave full scope for the natural individualism and *élan* and intelligence of the Frenchman.

17

Bonaparte's early armies, their spirit and tradition, their tactics and their weapons, and their incomparable array of officer-talent, were armies of the Revolutionary wars in Italy, in the Pyrenees, and especially in the Low Countries and on the Rhine, and no one knew it better than Napoleon himself. When the first creation of Marshals was made, six out of the eighteen were men who could not remotely be described as brilliant soldiers. They were not young, they were not dashing, and they were not talented. Their elevation to the rank of Marshal of the Empire was due solely to Napoleon's intense desire to weld three regimes into one and call it France. He wanted to preserve the balance between past, present, and future, and so he took six strong Republicans and gave them the great old Royalist title and set them to serve the Empire. The survivors of Jacobinism were to wear the glories of Louis Soleil at the court of the new Dynasty. The six were Kellermann, Jourdan, Lefèbvre, Pérignon, Moncey, and Sérurier. Sérurier's career has been sketched in the chapter on the Army of Italy. Pérignon's career need take up little space. Born in 1754 of an old family near Toulouse, he was a pre-Revolution soldier of the Royal Grenadiers of Guienne, a moderate Republican in 1789, Deputy in the Legislative Assembly, and he served as a divisional commander with distinction in the Pyrenees in '94 and '95. In 1799 he took a somewhat unfortunate part in the disastrous battle of Novi in North Italy against the Russian Suvorov. Stationed on the left wing of the French Army, he began the day in a feeble and hesitating manner, and, after much incompetence, came to the prudent conclusion that it would be wiser to surrender than to fight; and further, that it would be wiser still to be the first to surrender. Accordingly he and his friend Grouchy of the cavalry, later of Waterloo fame, sent their troops back to the rear and waited in an inn courtyard to give themselves up. Unluckily for their comfort, but luckily for their fame, the Austrian hussars of the advance-guard mistook them for an ambuscade and attacked and wounded them both before the situation was explained. The two generals were thus able to figure as heroic officers, 'wounded and taken while fighting desperately to cover the retreat of their beloved troops.' Pérignon was not employed again on active service. It might have been better if Grouchy had not been either.

Lefèbvre was the complete sergeant-major and throughout his life remained the complete sergeant-major. He was the son of an Alsatian miller, who had himself been a trooper of hussars, and young Lefèbvre joined the French Guards at eighteen, became senior sergeant in fifteen years, and so, in 1789, belonged to one of the three proverbially honest classes in Paris, curés, notaries, and guard-sergeants. In 1791 it was Lefèbvre who commanded the company of grenadiers that protected the King and Queen from the mob-violence on their return from the flight to Varennes. Later he fought on the Moselle and the Rhine, without acquiring any great distinction. In 1797 he was with Augereau on the Rhine, and seldom can any army have contained two rougher diamonds. At a performance at headquarters of Voltaire's *Death of Caesar*, Lefèbvre was enthralled by the play and applauded loudly, exclaiming repeatedly, 'I say, who is the chap who wrote this? What's his name? Is he here?' His fellow-countryman Rapp observed once sardonically, 'Lefèbvre looks an even bigger fool than I do.'

Kellermann was the fourth of the Old Republican Marshals. He was born in 1735 at Strasburg of a distinguished merchant family. In 1753 he became an ensign in the Royal-Bavière regiment, and served in the Seven Years' War. He was made a Marshal because he commanded the French line at the most trivial and yet the most important, the smallest and yet the greatest, battle that ever changed the destinies of the world. As a battle the Cannonade of Valmy was a joke; as an event it was portentous. Dumouriez, an excellent general who afterwards deserted to the enemy, was Commander-in-Chief of a rabble. The disciplined troops of Prussia, the legacy of the terrible Frederick, were rolling into France like a steady and ponderous iron machine, and their Austrian allies, if a little handicapped by having to take all their orders from Vienna, were puffing along manfully beside them through the rain. Dumouriez had only one chance, to hold the passes through the densely wooded hills of the Argonne. 'I will hold them like Thermopylae,' were almost his last words before he evacuated two of them in a great hurry and took up a position of almost unbelievable audacity by the mill of Valmy, with his back to the Argonne and Germany, and his face to Paris. 'I think,' said Napoleon years afterwards, 'that I was probably the boldest general who ever lived, but I wouldn't have dared to take post there.'

The iron machine rolled through the mud of the evacuated passes, and swung round the doomed army, and came to the assault on September 20th at Valmy. Kellermann commanded the line on the hill, Dumouriez the reserve behind the hill. For hours the Prussian artillery thundered at the timorous Sansculottes; for hours the Republican artillery thundered hack, and, to the astonishment of everyone on both sides, the Sansculottes held firm. Kellermann himself was immovable. At last the Prussian general estimated that his time had come, and he launched Frederick's irresistible engine – the line-attack of Prussian infantry – down into the valley to climb the low ridge to the Valmy mill. Steadily and slowly the infantry went down, and then something went wrong with the engine. Whether the clockwork got clogged up with mud, or whether the Commander-in-Chief lost his nerve, at any rate the line-attack wavered, halted, and then with complete precision and dignity turned itself into a line-retreat, and the battle was over. Next day the enemy was gone.

> With 36,000 men and forty guns the French had arrested the advance of Europe, not by skilful tactics or the touch of steel, but by the moral effect of their solidity when they met the best of existing armies. The nation discovered that the Continent was at its mercy, and the war begun for the salvation of monarchy became a war for the expansion of the Republic. It was founded at Paris and consolidated at Valmy.[1]

Moncey was born in 1754. He was the son of a lawyer in Besançon, and had been originally designed for his father's profession. But he was determined to be a soldier, and at an early age ran away from home and enlisted in the infantry regiment of Conti. Bought out by his parents after six months, he ran away again and re-enlisted in the regiment of Champagne, and was bought out again and persuaded to return to his legal studies. But when in 1774 he enlisted for the third time, in the Gendarmerie of Lunéville (the regiment which provided the unfortunate opponent in Augereau's famous duel), Moncey's parents gave up the struggle and allowed him to remain in the army. At the Revolution he became a strong Republican, and played a distinguished part in the fighting in the Pyrenees in 1792-93. He was an honest, slow, prudent, cautious soldier, very reliable and very stupid.

Jourdan's military career was long and varied. He was a doctor's son from Limoges, and at sixteen he enlisted in the Auxerre regiment of infantry and fought with them in the American War of Independence. After obtaining his discharge, lie settled down as a peddling-draper and haberdasher and married a modiste. The wife kept the shop while the husband travelled from fair to fair with his stock-in-trade on his back.

The usual swift Revolutionary promotion for men who combined ability and personal popularity swept Jourdan from the command of a battalion of volunteers of Haute-Vienne to the rank of divisional-general, and the

1 Lord Acton.

victory at Wattignies in 1793 which Carnot, the Minister of War, practically forced him to win, with the resulting relief of Maubeuge, placed him with Dumouriez and Pichegru in the front line of the defence of the Revolution. Fleurus was his great victory, on June 26th, 1794. On that day the terror of invasion which had loomed so desperately near, and for so agonizingly long, was rolled away from the soil of France for twenty years, and at Fleurus the vital link was forged in the chain of victory which began beneath the mill at Valmy and came to an end for ever in 1815 at the village of Ligny between Charleroi and Brussels. At Fleurus Jourdan was fortunate in his first pitched battle, for not only did Carnot, the Organizer of Victory, come up to the army just in time to overrule Jourdan's plans, but he led the attack himself, on foot, with his civilian hat on the end of a sword. In 1794 the Army of the Moselle was joined to parts of the Armies of the Rhine and Maubeuge, and became the immortal Army of the Sambre-et-Meuse, 90,000 strong, with Jourdan in command. The Army of the Sambre-et-Meuse made a brilliant advance through the cockpit of Europe, and Mainz, across the Rhine, was its easternmost capture, in September, 1795. Thereafter its fortunes, and its commander's, declined, and the Archduke Charles of Austria struck them a deadly blow at Stockach in 1799. It was years before Napoleon considered Jourdan fit to command an army in the field again – it would have been better for both if he had never considered him fit again – but nevertheless he made him a Marshal, because in his person the ex-peddling draper represented something of the glories of '93 when the ragged men carried the Three Colours and sang the terrible song of Marseilles from Fleurus to the Rhine, and captured the fortresses of Flanders and the fortresses of Holland and Brabant, and crossed the Lys, and the Scheldt, and the Dendre, and the Senne, and the Dyle, and the Meuse, and the Leek, and entered Antwerp and Rotterdam and Amsterdam and the Hague, and thundered on their horses across the ice to capture with naked swords the battle fleet of Holland.

CHAPTER III

EGYPT

THERE are four episodes between 1798 and the creation of the Marshalate in which many, if not all, the future Marshals played their parts. The first is the expedition to Egypt, the second is Masséna's defence of France in the bastion of Switzerland, the third is the *coup d'État* by which the Directory was overthrown and the Consulate set up, with Bonaparte as First Consul, and the fourth is the campaign and battle of Marengo. These four must be briefly described, for Napoleon, throughout his career, regarded Marengo as his touchstone, and just as he was apt to divide his life into pre-Marengo and post-Marengo years, so he was always inclined to give honours, promotions, and, on occasions, leniency to soldiers of whatever rank who had fought with him on or before the day of that famous victory.

* * *

In 1798 the two implacable enemies, the English Oligarchy and General Bonaparte, simultaneously decided to strike each other in unexpected quarters, the former selecting Italy and the latter Egypt. Nelson took his fleet to the Mediterranean and Bonaparte took his army to the Bay of Aboukir. With him were Berthier, Murat, Lannes, and Marmont of the Army of Italy, and a fifth officer, who became a Marshal in 1804, who now appears in prominence for the first time, Louis Nicolas Davout. Davout was either the first, or the second to Masséna, of all the fighting men of the Empire. Some historians, and almost all contemporaries, give the first place to Masséna because of Zürich and the saving of France in '99. Others give it to Davout because, if he had no victory that had such immense repercussions in Europe as that of Zürich, at least he suffered no such defeat as Masséna did on the ridge of Bussaco in 1810, where he met for the first time the power of British musketry, defending in line against an attack in column. Two recent French historians have been emphatic about Davout's place in the hierarchy of military skill. 'The only member of the Napoleonic School,' one calls him. 'The only pupil that Napoleon ever had.' While the other says, 'Davout was the only one who understood Napoleon, and who was admitted to discuss with him the great operations. He alone grasped the high conception of Napoleonic War.' Against this view, on the other hand, is the undoubted fact that Napoleon on three separate occasions did not make the fullest use of Davout's talents. Once, in 1809, he let the mere fact of Berthier's technical seniority – they were created Marshals on the same day – jeopardize the entire campaign against the Archduke Charles on the Danube, and it needed all Napoleon's genius to extricate the army from Berthier's blundering. In 1813 he gave the command of the Army of the Elbe to the Viceroy of Italy, over Davout's head, simply because the Viceroy was one of the Family, and in the last campaign of all, Davout was left at the War Office in Paris, and the right wing of the last attack, that might have changed history, was entrusted to the miserable Marquis de Grouchy.

Davout was born at Auxerre, Yonne, in 1770, of an old, aristocratic but untitled, Burgundian family of soldiers, of which it was said that 'Whenever a Davout is born, it is a sword that has come out of its scabbard.'

Before the Revolution, as a sub-lieutenant in the regiment of Royal-Champagne, he caused grave scandal in the officers' mess by openly professing himself a partisan of the 'new ideas' that were simmering so menacingly throughout the country from Marseilles to Dunkirk, and in 1790 he organized and led a successful mutiny against his brother-officers, and took a revolutionary deputation of his regiment to Paris. (One of the members was a vehement, hotheaded, republican sergeant, named Victor, who became a Marshal in 1808.) The only result of all this activity was six weeks' imprisonment in the citadel of Arras and the enforced resignation of his Royal commission because of his Republicanism. Davout was soon lieutenant-colonel of a Republican regiment which is said to have been the one that fired on General Dumouriez as he was deserting. But he was soon forced to resign his Republican commission because of his nobility of birth. This might have seemed to make the prospects of a military career somewhat gloomy for young Davout, if neither side would have him, but those were odd times in the world of promotion, and the line of demarcation between the guillotine and high rank was very narrow, and the twice-cashiered youth re-emerged mysteriously into history in the very next year as a brigadier-general in the Army of the Moselle.

In 1798 Davout left the Rhine army, where he had been serving under Moreau, and joined the Army of Egypt and thus served under Bonaparte for the first time.

He was a strange character; a cold, hard man; an iron disciplinarian; a stubborn man, and utterly incorruptible. He combined a ceaseless care for the men under his command, who loved him, while they feared him, with a ruthless severity towards his officers, especially his colonels and, when he became a Marshal, his generals, all of whom detested him bitterly. His only friends throughout his life were Marceau the brilliant, who was mortally wounded at Altenkirchen above Coblenz in 1796; the generous Desaix, shot through the head at Marengo; Leclerc who died of fever in L'île de la Tortue near Saint Domingo in 1802; the universally beloved Duroc, Grand Marshal of the Palace, whom a shell struck down in 1813 at the Emperor's side; Montbrun, the big, black-bearded cavalry-man who was at last, after a thousand exploits, killed in '12 at Borodino, and Marshal Oudinot. Oudinot was his oldest friend and comrade. They called each other 'thou' even in the most formal of despatches, and the end of their friendship, which will be told in due course, was characteristic of Davout's strange coldness. Davout's three lifelong enemies were Murat and Bernadotte (the Gascon Kings) and Berthier, the ugly little paragon among staff-officers. The only person whom Davout loved, besides the Emperor, was his wife. His love-letters to her are charm-ing and full of tenderness. 'I am sorry you will not spend the money I send you in diamonds for yourself,' or 'I send you some tulip-bulbs for your garden,' or, in the midst of the desperate campaigning in Saxony, 'I send you some Saxon linen; they are famous for it and I think you will like it.' Never throughout his life did he allow any single one of his relatives to have the faintest intimacy with him except his adored wife.

When he landed in Egypt, General Davout was dirty and slovenly in appearance; he grumbled incessantly; the rare smiles on his cold, handsome face were invariably sar-donic, and he inspired Bonaparte, whose natural instincts impelled him in any case to dislike the Rhine-army men of his rival Moreau, with the most profound antipathy, an antipathy which was steadily increased by Davout's care-fully cultivated habit of associating with all the officers in Egypt who were notoriously hostile to the Commander-in-Chief.

* * *

On July 1st, 1798, the first landing was made in the Marabout roadstead, and the veterans of Italy made hay in no time of the defence of Alexandria, and then began the sandy march, through the blazing days and chilly nights, from Alexandria to the Nile. 'Forty centuries looked down upon them' as they swept the Mamelukes away by the Pyramids. Cairo was captured. The flying columns went south and east and the conquest of Egypt had been completed, when the deep boom across the desert and the sudden glare, as the flagship *L'Orient* blew up under the salvoes of Nelson, brought in a moment the grim news that the *conquistadores* themselves were caught.

The generals were flung instantly into despair, for France, the gentle land of their homes, seemed cut off for ever, and the parching, brazen sands of Egypt were a poor substitute for the long vineyards of Burgundy, and the cornlands of La Beauce, and the street-cries of Paris, and the shadow of the dark trees upon the Garonne. But though they despaired, which was bad, they learnt, which was good, for the first time that they were serving under a Commander who never despaired.

The wreckage of dead Admiral Bruix's Line of Battle was still drifting in the Bay of Aboukir when Bonaparte flung himself buoyantly into a thousand details of orgnization. Nine days after the news of the Nile he was establishing the Institute of Egypt in Cairo, accepting its vice-presidency under the presidency of the great mathematician Monge, and setting a number of little problems to the savants at their first session. (A new regime was beginning, under which even professors had to mingle the practical with the abstract.)

'Can the baking-ovens of the army be improved?' he demanded of the men of science. Could any substitute for hops be found for the brewing of beer? Was the windmill or the water-mill the more suitable for milling at Cairo? How could the army establish a powder-factory, and did

Egypt possess any of the ingredients for the manufacture of gunpowder?

On the less utilitarian side, the demoniacally energetic Commander set the professors to work to study and measure ruins, decipher hieroglyphics, and make drawings of statues.

It was inconvenient that Nelson should have destroyed the French fleet, and severed all communications between 40,000 Frenchmen and France, but that was no reason why the Sphinx should not be measured, the Rosetta stone deciphered, the land surveyed, the soils analysed, and the inundations of the Nile determined. At Suez Bonaparte himself found the canal of Sesostris, half as old as time, and followed Mahomet and the great Saladin in signing his name in the visitors' book of the monks of Sinai.

But the generals grumbled, and the men died of the plague, and the English blockade stopped the love-letters from France. The only sport available was fishing in the Nile for the bodies of the Mamelukes who had been killed in the fighting. For the Mamelukes always carried their valuables with them into battle, and a Gascon private of the 32nd Regiment of the Line hit upon a notion of hammering his bayonet into the form of a hook and fishing for them. But even that amusement petered out when the supply of Mamelukes was exhausted.

The hospitals were crowded with sick. When the plague was in full blast there were no other epidemics; when the plague disappeared it was succeeded by yellow fever, scurvy, elephantiasis, and leprosy. Tetanus and ophthalmia were rampant. The main hospital diet was camel's-meat broth, and the water was brackish.

The generals frankly detested the whole business. Even before the disaster to the fleet, Lannes had shaken the tricolor cockade out of his hat, trampled it in the sands and declared that he was fed-up. Murat was emphatically in favour of a protest or even a mutiny, and Bessières, already his faithful understudy, agreed with him. Lannes, Murat, and Bessières had been severely reprimanded by Bonaparte for acting as seconds to General Junot in a duel on the banks of the Nile, and their pride was still hurt. Bonaparte had rather unkindly compared them to silly crocodiles fighting in the reeds. But Murat and Bessières were soon more than hurt. They became seriously alarmed when the Commander-in-Chief hinted very plainly that he knew all about their intrigues, and Murat went about openly asserting that – Lannes had sold the cocoanut.[1] Even the faithful Berthier complained incessantly. Poor Berthier was wasting away. He loathed Africa and Asia and the Sphinx and the Nile and the Pyramids and everything. Less than a year ago he had been thoroughly enjoying himself in Rome. Campaigning in the horrible sand was a very different thing from looting the gold *plaques* of the Treasure from the chapel of Notre Dame de Lorette, and holding the fifty richest families in Rome to ransom and plundering their palaces. He remembered bitterly that Masséna, who had come down in a hurry, but too late, for a share in the loot, was now probably enjoying a free hand in Italy. There was no loot in Egypt except those stupid hieroglyphics that the Commander-in-Chief seemed to think so much of, and all the time Masséna was probably making a fortune. And there was the exquisite Madame de Visconti also. Berthier had hated the way in which Masséna had looked at that beautiful lady when he took over the command in Rome, and Masséna was as famous for his conquests in the boudoir as for his exploits on the plateau of Rivoli. Berthier had put a spoke in Massénsa's wheel when he advised him so craftily to confiscate all the church plate that he himself had missed, so that the

[1] *Vendu la calebasse.'*

unpaid troops had instantly mutinied. But all that was now wasted craft, for here he was stuck in the beastly desert, and Masséna was having the time of his life. The ugly little chief-of-staff was so desperate to get back to the beautiful Visconti, and he spent so much of his time in imploring Bonaparte to let him take his chance with the English blockade and slip off home, and in praying on his knees to a picture of his adored lady, that his staff-work went all to pieces, and Bonaparte at last frigidly handed him his passport and his ticket. Berthier was in ecstasy, but on hearing that the marvellous youth whom he served was likely to set out for Asia at any moment, he changed his mind and handed back his passport. The result was the instant thawing of the frigidity, and a warm reconciliation. But even the warmth of the reconciliation did not cloud the eyes of Bonaparte. 'Look at Berthier,' he said to General Kléber, 'pouting and grumbling, and that is the man with his old woman's temper, whose flatterers call him my Mentor. If I ever get into power, I'll put him so high that everyone will see his mediocrity.'

But the grumblers were not given much time for disgruntled reflection. There were revolts of Egyptians to suppress, such as the one in the Bahiré district which was led by no less a person than the envoy of the Angel Elmodi and the One and Only Prophet Mahomet, a gentleman who could produce fire out of his beard, and could be killed but not wounded. (Fortunately for the French the Angel Elmodi's representative happened to get a slight wound fairly early in the revolt, whereupon his disgusted and disillusioned followers at once went home.)

There was also the return journey to be considered, and Bonaparte, having rejected both the march on India and the march along the north of Africa to Ceuta, opposite Gibraltar, chose instead the route to Paris via Syria and the Taurus Mountains and the dreary uplands of Anatolia and the Bosphorus and the Golden Gate and the Holy Church of Santa Sophia. So the army started off, and

marched in the bitter cold of winter, through the treeless
desert where the only fuel to be had were the innumerable skeletons which crackled with a macabre merriment
under the pots. They crossed three hundred miles of
desert, and passed Gaza, from which Berthier, somewhat
cheered by the prospect of getting home, even via
Constantinople, wrote to Marmont, 'We have a country
here which is like Provence, and the climate is like
Europe.' In March, 1799, they captured the town of Jaffa
with its walls and towers and orange gardens and cedar-
trees, and marched on to the north. The next town, or
rather townlet, which they attacked was St. Jean d'Acre,
and here the adventure came to an end. The Star of
Bonaparte never failed him in these early days, and
it came to his rescue when the wild and brilliant Sidney
Smith, helped by a French *émigré* engineer named
Phélippeaux, defended the town so stubbornly that the
expedition had to turn hack. All the desperate escalading
of Lannes with his grenadiers was unavailing against the
British navy, the French engineer, and the fanaticism of
the obscure Mahomedan soldiers. Lannes received a
severe wound at St. Jean d'Acre, or rather the wound
would have been severe for anyone else. But apparently
there was something queer about Lannes' bones. They
did not break on the impact of a bullet, but somehow
only bent so that the bullet glanced off them. In the
final assault he was struck on the temple and given up
for dead. A captain of grenadiers, however, ran forward
with five or six men to rescue him. All were shot down
except the captain, who dragged Lannes back by the leg
to safety. (Lannes never forgot that captain of grenadiers,
and later set him up in a posting-hotel in the Midi, and
often visited him.) It was found that the bullet had run
round to the back of his head without doing any damage
and was easily extracted. It left only a stiffness, a sort of
kink of the neck, so that Lannes thereafter always carried
his head a little on one side. Later, at Aboukir he was hit

at point-blank range on the hip-bone, and again the bullet glanced round the bone and finished up in the back of his leg.

The expedition to Paris via Constantinople was called off, and Bonaparte had his men back in Cairo, three hundred miles away across the long, heavy, burning sands, in twenty-six days. Sidney Smith's erratic, chivalric genius had given Europe another sixteen years of warfare.

Soon after the return from Syria in midsummer '99, the Turks took a hand in the game and landed an army of 10,000 men from the sea at Aboukir. But the Turks did not quite understand what sort of a game it was, and how it was played. Within four days they had left the land again, the entire 10,000 having been killed or driven into the sea to drown or be killed by the guns of their own navy. Lannes led the right wing of the whirlwind attack, while Murat set the stamp upon his growing reputation by a superb charge on the left. It was the first and last time that this great horseman found himself leading not only a cavalry charge but a dromedary charge as well. He galloped sensationally after the flying enemy challenging individual fugitives to personal combat and waving his sword on which was engraved 'L'honneur et les dames,' and was hit in the jaw by a pistol-bullet for his trouble. When it was all over, Bonaparte rode up to Murat and asked, 'Did the cavalry take an oath to do the whole business today?' Lannes, hot and dusty and tired, was furious at this eclipsing of his exploits.

There was a curious incident after the battle. Davout, the slovenly and troublesome, was left in reserve with a detachment, and after the battle demanded an interview with Bonaparte in order to complain bitterly of his unfair treatment. The interview was granted, and the two men met in private for the first time. No one knows in what words Davout put his grievance, nor how the great psychologist answered him, hut from that moment to the end of his life Davout was the most completely devoted of all the Imperial soldiers. Thenceforward he modelled himself on Napoleon for everything, for hard work, for study of his profession, for personal cleanliness and smartness, for energy, manner, and the carefully acquired trick of being brusque and gracious in bewildering alternations, in the same breath.

Lannes went to hospital with a wound in the leg and was disgusted to find himself in the next bed to Murat. He was still more disgusted to hear from France that his wife, from whom he had parted fourteen months before, had just given birth to a bouncing boy.

In the whirlwind battle of Aboukir Bonaparte consolidated his position in Egypt, but a few hours later Sidney Smith shot it all to pieces with a newspaper. For that chivalrous opponent, while exchanging prisoners, sent ashore as a compliment a packet of back numbers of the *Journal de Francfort*, and Bonaparte, who had heard nothing of France and Paris for months, closeted himself with Berthier for four hours to study the news. At the end of it he said, 'Send for Admiral Ganteaume.' Ships were wanted and wanted quickly. A few nights later the Commander-in-Chief of the Army of Egypt slipped away with a couple of Venetian-built frigates, the *Muiron* and the *Carrère*, taking with him one or two of the scientists of the Institute, and of his fighting men the indispensable Berthier, Lannes of the escalading infantry, the brilliant Murat, Marmont the gunner and oldest friend, and the gentlemanly Bessières.

They embarked at midnight, and were a little uneasy at the sight of a mysterious corvette which was lying off the harbour, with all lights out. But in the early morning when a breeze sprang up they were relieved to see that it had vanished, and nothing more was ever heard of it. Bonaparte himself chose the route along the north coast of Africa. Rather than fall into the hands of the English, he was prepared to land and fight his way with his party of officers from Tunis to the Straits of Gibraltar.

For twenty-one days the two frigates struggled against wind and current along the deserted coast. At night the warm land-breezes helped them a little until, after three dreary weeks, they reached Cap Bon and the wind at last went round to the east. It turned only just in time, for the first critical stage of the voyage, the Cap Bon-Marsala Cordon of English cruisers was just ahead, and there would not have been time in the short night to run the gauntlet with only the breeze off the land. On the night that the strong wind blew up from Asia Minor, the frigates turned to the north-east, extinguished all lights, and the little party put their faith in Bonaparte's Star. All that night they ran silently on, watching from the darkened decks the bright lamps of the English cruisers around them. And when the summer dawn came up there were no ships in sight, and they were abreast of Carthage, and the Cordon had been run. Then, turning north, they reached Ajaccio at last, and the officers were astounded at the number of citizens who came aboard and claimed to be cousins of the Commander-in-Chief.

At Ajaccio they heard the news of Novi, in North Italy, where on August 15th, 1799, Suvorov, the Russian, had routed the French. Joubert was dead, and Pérignon and Grouchy had ingloriously surrendered.

After four days' hunting in the Corsican hills, the party embarked again for the final dash, and once again their luck was so perfect that when they were within sight of France and saw directly in front of them a squadron of fourteen war-ships, probably Russian, it was already evening. The two frigates turned north-east and were soon lost in the gathering twilight and the shadows and the flying foam, and after thirty-four days at sea, the party reached Fréjus. The luck had held to the end, for if the fourteen ships had not appeared and driven them off their course, they would have landed at Toulon and been put in quarantine, and Bonaparte's enemies would have had forty days in which to rally. But at Fréjus the people went mad, and refused to allow their hero to be worried by regulations. It was a narrow escape, even as it was, for Murat, Lannes with his crutches, and Marmont, had to ride from Fréjus to Toulon to pick up their carriages, and, sleeping the first night at Vitauban, they heard the rattle of horses' hooves as the quarantine officers from Toulon went galloping through to arrest the ships. But Bonaparte was already on the high road to Paris.

The army that was left behind in Egypt split itself into two factions. General Menou led the Bonapartists, and the unfortunate Kléber, who was thrust into the command by the Commander-in-Chief's surreptitious departure, and thrust out of it a few months later by the knife of an Egyptian assassin on the day of Marengo, led the anti-Bonapartists. Kléber had always hated the whole expedition from the very beginning, and had been heard to mutter about Bonaparte in front of the breach of St. Jean d'Acre, 'There goes the little scoundrel; he's no bigger than my boot.' Davout, the brand-new Bonapartist, threw himself on to the side of Menou, not even flinching when that representative of Republican France made himself and his country somewhat ludicrous by turning Mahomedan, by marrying a plain and middle-aged Mahomedan because she was the daughter of the Shireef and thus a descendant of the Prophet, by taking the name of Abdallah, and only escaping the ceremony of a public circumcision by humiliating himself before his fat and leering prospective father-in-law.

CHAPTER IV

MASSÉNA AND SUVOROV

AT the beginning of 1799 the French Republic was in great danger of being overthrown by force of arms. Not since Dumouriez and Kellermann made their desperate stand at Valmy had the threat been so serious, and they at least had the backing of passionate enthusiasm. There was very little enthusiasm in 1799, and indeed there was very little to enthuse about. On all sides the friends were falling away and the enemies were gathering round. England and Russia had formed an alliance and were busily preparing for a combined descent upon Antwerp and the Low Countries. Portugal had entered the lists. Naples was fermenting with rebellion. Piedmont, her churches, palaces, museums, and even private houses pillaged by Generals Joubert and Grouchy, and her treasury robbed of more than ten million francs in three months, had risen in active revolt against the French. And on March 12th, 1799, the Austrian Emperor declared war on the French Republic, and within a fortnight the Archduke Charles of Hapsburg was smashing Jourdan at Stockach in Swabia, and harrying the Republicans back through the Black Forest to the Rhine. A Russian army, subsidized by England, marched under the command of Korsakov towards the Rhine to co-operate with Charles; a second

Russian army descended into northern Italy to help the Piedmontese and stir up revolt in Naples, and it was commanded by no less a personality than the great Suvorov, sacker of cities, the terror of Turkey and Poland, the ruthless, ever-victorious lieutenant of the Tsar. The Republicans cracked under the strain. The line of the Adige was lost, then the line of the Mincio. Mantua, the key fortress of the north of Italy, which had cost so much marching and so much fighting and so much genius when young Bonaparte was gripping it with one hand and fending off the relieving armies with the other, less than three years before, fell without a blow.

The tide came rolling westward across the plains. Turin fell and Milan fell. Moreau, the famous Republican general who afterwards won the victory of Hohenlinden, tried to stem the rush and was thrown back into Genoa leaving Sérurier and 3,000 men behind as prisoners. General Macdonald, the French son of an old Scottish *émigré*, came pounding up to the rescue from Naples with an army, and was met and so hammered by Suvorov in three days' fighting on the Trebbia that the survivors barely struggled across the Apennines to join Moreau's fragments in Genoa. The new fretwork republics, Cisalpine, Roman, Parthenopean, crumbled into the sawdust that they were made of and on August 15th Suvorov led a combined Austro-Russian army to an overwhelming victory over the Republicans at Novi. Joubert, the French Commander-in-Chief was killed at the outset of the battle. General Grouchy and General Pérignon had so lost the spirit of '93 that they were the first to surrender when the day began to go against them, and only the icy General St. Cyr preserved a remnant of order and discipline in his divisions, when the rout went streaming in the twilight through the narrow gorge of Pasturana, the southern heights of which were ablaze with the enfilading fire of the Hungarian infantry.

This, then, was the position of the Republic in July, 1799. The Rhine army, defeated and dispirited, was back on the Rhine. The Army of Italy had been destroyed. North Italy, Rome, Naples, all had been lost. England and Russia were landing in Flanders. From north and east and south the victorious columns of the Allies were converging upon the frontiers, and General Bonaparte with 40,000 veterans was locked up in Egypt, and the fleet of Nelson was intercepting not only his return, but almost all news of his farings and his fightings.

One army remained to France in Europe and only one, the Army of Switzerland, under General Masséna, the ex-cabin-boy and smuggler. This army was spread out in a vast semicircle on the northern, eastern, and southern frontiers of Switzerland from Bâle to Lake Constance, and from Constance to the Stelvio and by the Splügen round to the St. Gothard, and thence to the St. Bernard and the Simplon. Switzerland, if held by a French army, is a gigantic bastion in the long line of the defensive frontiers of France which are the Rhine from Antwerp to Bâle, and the high hills of Savoy, and the Pyrenees. And so long as Masséna's Army of Switzerland held the bastion, the Archduke Charles did not dare, could not dare, to cross the Rhine, and even Suvorov, desperate fighter though he was, hesitated about pushing into France along what is now called the Riviera, and thus leaving his communications at the mercy of a French irruption from the Alpine passes. So all depended on Masséna's army. It was the last.

But although this army was a forlorn hope, nevertheless there were certain things in its favour. The rocky mountainous country which it occupied was ideal for defensive warfare, and the tough veteran soldiers had grown accustomed to the hardships, and were experts in the technique, of Alpine warfare. And what was probably even more important, it was magnificently officered. If ever an army of the eighteenth century was blazing with military talent it was that last army of the Republic in 1799.

Oudinot was chief-of-staff – not that Oudinot earned great fame as a Marshal except as a stubborn aud trustworthy leader of grenadiers, but he did great things at Zürich in 1799. Suchet, who later became one of the ablest of all the Marshals, was commanding a brigade. Drouet better known to Englishmen as the d'Erlon of Waterloo – was adjutant-general of a division, and among the subordinate generals were Molitor, Gazan, Mesnard, Chabran, Loison, Lorge, the swashbuckling Vandamme, Souham, Laroche, Lecourbe, and Mortier; of these, Mortier became a Marshal in the original creation. He was a big, pleasant man, kind-hearted and popular with his inferiors and his superiors, a loyal colleague, and not a particularly brilliant soldier. 'A big mortar has a short range,' was a current epigram on the disproportion between his size and his talents. As a young general, he was inclined to let his easy sense of humour run away with him, and his loud and frequent laughter was thought to be unseemly for a senior officer of the Republic. He was a brave man, but in war-time was entirely run by his staff and in peace-time by his wife. He was partly English, and spoke English almost as fluently as French. His first name was Edouard.

But, more important in Masséna's army than all these distinguished names were those redoubtable soldiers, Michel Ney and Nicolas Jean-de-Dieu Soult. Ney was the son of an old soldier who had retired to become a barrel-cooper at Saarlouis in Lorraine. Young Ney was a hussar trooper before the Revolution and a hussar captain after it, with the army of the Sambre-et-Meuse. His first battle was Valmy, and in the great rush across the Low Countries to the Rhine, it was Captain Ney who led the advance-guard. He was a man of middle size, very strong, very brave, with blue eyes and red hair, and he was a first-class swordsman and horseman. His native language was German, and he had no other thought in his mind but the acquisition of military glory.

Soult was a very different type. He was the son of a small notary in the village of St. Amans-la-Bastide in the valley of the Tarn near Albi. While still in his teens he joined the regiment of Royal Infantry as a private. He must have been a good soldier from the start, for he soon became a sergeant. But Soult, all his life, was a man of ambition, although the objects of his ambition varied very considerably as time went on. His first, to become a soldier, was soon followed by his second. For, returning on leave to St. Amans, he was seized with an overwhelming desire to obtain his discharge from the army and become a baker. To wear a white cap and white apron and be covered, morning, noon, and night, with flour was the ideal life for Nicolas Jean-de-Dieu Soult. Fortunately, however, his family over-persuaded him, and he went back to the army. After the Revolution he went up the military ladder at the same speed as his other illustrious contemporaries. All his service up to the campaign of Zürich had been done in Flanders and on the Rhine, and he did not meet General Bonaparte until after Marengo.

* * *

There was only one course open for the Austro-Russian allies in 1799, and that was to join hands and eject Masséna from his bastion. They were in a magnificent position for doing so. For a bastion, or a salient, is a double-edged weapon; it may threaten the enemy's communications, but it may also, if the enemy is in superior force, be attacked simultaneously on three sides, and it was this that the allies proceeded to do.

A simultaneous, quintuple attack was launched; from the north against Vandamme and Oudinot; from the north-east across the Rhine (south of Lake Constance) against Lorge; from the east a double attack into the Grisons by way of the valley of the Thal and the Stelvio where Lecourbe, the great mountain fighter, was on guard; and from the south past Lake Como up to the Splügen. The only bright spot for the Republic, and it was not particularly bright, was that so far there was no news of Suvorov coming up out of Italy by way of Bellinzona to the Gothard. But even without him the pressure was much too strong. The Imperialists quickly overran the Grisons, forced Loison back over the Splügen, crossed the upper Rhine at all points, and by the second half of June had captured Zürich, and reached the Lake of the Four Cantons, and were almost into the Gothard from the north. The game was in their hands. All they had to do was to fetch Suvorov up from the south, and pull in the main armies of the Archduke Charles down from the north, and the bastion of Switzerland would be captured, the Rhine frontier thrown open at a dozen places, and the white cockade of the Bourbons mounted again upon the Tuileries.

The position of the Republicans was desperate, and Masséna might well have thought it his whole duty to save his army from the closing pincers, and escape as swiftly as possible from a Switzerland which had been converted so suddenly from a bastion into a trap. But Masséna took the larger view. He had France to think of. It was he, and he alone, who was defending Flanders, and the Rhine, and the line of the high hills of Savoy, and the coast-road to Nice. It was only in the bastion that Paris could be saved. In Switzerland he might possibly maintain the defence even with a crippled army; if he retreated into France and saved his army, he could play nothing but a minor part against the overwhelming odds. So he determined to hold on at all costs outside Zürich and wait for something to happen. He massed the bulk of his army on his left, opposite Zürich, facing the Austro-Russian army under the Russian Korsakov. Soult was posted in the centre, south of the Lake of Zürich, to watch the Austrians under Hotze, while Lecourbe was strung out in a long thin line of posts, with his left in touch with Soult, and his right holding the

Gothard and watching for the advance of the great and terrible Suvorov.

Almost at once the allies made their first strategical error. They assumed that Masséna was done for, and ordered the northern arm of the trap, the Archduke Charles and his 50,000 men, to make a right-turn and march off to keep an eye on the Netherlands, where the Anglo-Russian expeditionary force was nearly due to land, and to be ready to storm the Rhine as soon as the old fox was out of his bastion. The old fox watched them go, and held his ground, and waited.

For almost a month the fate of France depended upon the moral courage of that one man who sat on the hills outside Zürich and silently watched the trap closing upon him from the south. The north was now comparatively free. The deadly danger was coming up from Italy.

Four men held the stage at this moment of ominous calm, when all Europe was awaiting the fall of the Republic. The Archduke Charles, who played such an important part in playing no part at all, was a fine soldier, a strategist and a tactician, able but cautious, and much harassed by the grotesque and blind incompetence of the politicians of Vienna. Korsakov, commanding in Zürich, was a vain and foolish man, a reputed lover of the great Catherine, a gourmand, and a gambler. In a conference with the Archduke he laid down his two main principles of warfare: 'Where you put an Austrian battalion, a Russian company will suffice,' and 'Russians never retire.' Korsakov was a fanatical adherent of Imperialism, and often boasted over the gaming-tables that he was going to send Masséna to Petersburg as a specimen of the Republican type. In the intervals of his loving and his dining, he packed Zürich more and more tightly with men and horses and wagons, which ought to have been strung out far to the rear on the lines of communication. But as Russians never retire, lines of communication are not so important with them as with other armies.

45

The third actor was Suvorov himself, that weird cross between a baby and a moujik, sometimes clown, sometimes spartan, 'hero, buffoon, half-demon, and half-dirt,'[1] passionate lover of war, hysterical, egotistical, now grovelling to Patiomkin for a command, now rushing to the front line to encourage an assault. As a strategist he relied upon maps and prayer indiscriminately. As a tactician his method of warfare was the simple one of 'march at the enemy and attack him,' and the terrible victories which he won on the field of battle, and the sack of Ismail, and the appalling butchery of civilians in the Praga suburb of Warsaw, made the name of Suvorov into a half-legendary demon. The illusion of unearthly terror was increased by his unbelievable ugliness of face. Tsar Peter III promoted him from captain to colonel in order to remove the monstrosity from the Imperial Guards, and all looking-glasses had to be covered up wherever he went. This was the man who was coming up from Italy. He knew something about fighting against the French, for he had only just finished smashing and hammering them at Novi, in front of Genoa, and on the Trebbia, and all men, save one, trembled at his name. In the middle of the closing trap lay the fourth actor, who did not tremble at anyone's name, Masséna, cold, watchful, silent, cunning.

This, then, was the position at the end of August, 1799. The cautious Charles had gone; the old fox lay listening to the goose cackling in Zürich; and the demon of the Slavonic hordes was plunging up the Gothard from Bellinzona.

It was on September 8th, 1799, that Suvorov parted company with his allies in Italy and started up the pass on his way to join Korsakov at Zürich and close the trap. On the 24th he was at Airolo, at the foot of the pass, and there the troubles began. Lecourbe commanded the defence,

---

[1] *Byron.*

and Lecourbe was the most skilful of all the mountain-fighters. The resistance was stubborn, and the everlasting snows of Gothard seemed, to the appalled plainsmen from the steppes, to reach perpendicularly into the planets themselves. Even when the pass was won by an attack of converging columns, the troubles were only half over. There were valleys and rocks, rushing streams with broken bridges, and unfordable gorges and precipices to be crossed and passed, and always Lecourbe was in front, or on the flank, or behind, harassing, counter-attacking, and delaying. By the 26th Suvorov was already a day behind his time-table, and snow, mist, and biting winds were on the side of the defence. But the volcanic Russian commander would halt neither for man nor weather, and the advance staggered forward over the mountain paths. The junction with gay Korsakov at Zürich was everything and the comfort of the soldiers, only a few weeks out of the Italian plains in midsummer, was nothing. Besides, on the 28th Suvorov's Army of Italy would have reached the valley of the Muotta and the town of Schwyz, and there Suvorov would find supplies sent him by Korsakov and Hotze. At Schwyz he would make contact with his colleagues and hear the latest news of the situation. On the 28th the advance-guard duly reached the valley of the Muotta, and on that day Suvorov found that he had been wrong on the one point and right on the other. There were no supplies, but there was news, plenty of news. The goose in Zürich had cackled a little bit too long, and the fox had got it.

Masséna had timed his stroke to perfection. He had watched Korsakov pushing his line out to the west of Zürich, pushing it further and further so that finally a great part of it was actually posted with its back to the Lake, and the communications of the whole of the Russian's left wing and centre lay through the bottle-neck of the town's crowded and narrow streets. Masséna watched and watched, silently, impassively The couriers came posting up from Lecourbe with news of Suvorov's advance, and still he made no move. And then suddenly the moment came and Masséna sent his whole army up to the attack. He himself pinned Korsakov against the Lake of Zürich and the town, while Oudinot swept through Korsakov's right wing and hemmed him in from behind. For two days the darling of the Empress Catherine struggled in the trap, and then, forming his infantry into a solid wedge, he cut his way through the lines of Oudinot and fled pell-mell out of Switzerland, heaving 8,000 prisoners, a hundred guns, all he had, and all his treasure and all his stores. On the same day, further south, Soult fell upon the Austrian Hotze and pitched him over the frontier in rout and disaster, and on the days following Molitor dealt with the Russian corps-commander, Jellacic, in exactly the same way. The great pincers were destroyed, and there was nothing for the surviving southern jaw to do except to bolt for home instantly and precipitately. Suvorov's allies were destroyed. Lecourbe was behind him, victorious Masséna was on his flank, and there was no way out but to abandon guns and wagons and march his 15,000 starving, ragged veterans across the mountains into the Grisons.

Suvorov escaped, but Masséna was left in triumph in the bastion of Switzerland. The Rhine was safe and Savoy was safe, and the Republic had got a breathing-space.

CHAPTER V

THE GREAT COUP

ALL through the summer of 1799, while Bonaparte was cut off in Egypt, Paris was bubbling with intrigue and whisperings and discontent. The government of lawyers was falling deeper and deeper into disrepute, and all men longed for a change, and all men knew that a change was coming. But no one could see how, and by whom, and when, it would come. The Royalists were active and full of confidence, and it was even rumoured that the young Duke of Enghien was in Paris, waiting his chance to seize the country for the Bourbons. The new Jacobins had founded a Club in the Riding School of the Palace of the Council of the Ancients, and Generals Augereau and Jourdan were its enthusiastic patrons. Fouché was at his Police-bureau, trying hard to suppress both Royalists and neo-Jacobins. Talleyrand and Siéyès were stealing from group to group, probing, sounding, hinting, and learning. In the provinces there was disorder and brigandage and seething discontent. The State was bankrupt, the Government of Directors was detested, and the armies had been ignominiously defeated, and the Italian conquests of Bonaparte dissipated. But how was the Government to be hounded out, and what was to take its place? The Abbé Siéyès had an answer ready for the second question. He himself would take its place. The first one was not so easy of solution, for violence might be necessary, and the Abbé was no fighting-man. And he knew it. So he began to cast around for a sword that would do the work for him while he did the thinking, and while he stayed in the background till the sword-play was over and he could reap its harvest. There were plenty of swords in Paris in 1799, but it was not so easy to get the right one, and the wrong one would be a disaster, if not certainly for France, at any rate certainly for the Abbé.

Augereau and Jourdan were no use. They were red-hot Jacobins – it was rumoured that Jourdan had been toasting the Return of the Pikes; Lefèbvre, Military Governor of Paris, was an old booby. Moreau was too staunch a Republican, and besides he was a timid politician, and Masséna was too busy holding Switzerland against five armies, and young Bonaparte was in Kamschatka for all anyone knew. Joubert would have been a possibility, but then Joubert had put himself out of the running by letting himself be killed at Novi in August, and really there was no one available for the work except Bernadotte, the Minister of War. Siéyès shook his head doubtfully. He did not care very much about Bernadotte and he did not trust him very much. The man was inclined to Jacobinism, and there were persistent stories that Jourdan and he had been putting their heads together on the subject of a *coup d'état* of their own, in which the first act would be, not the elevation of the Abbé Siéyès to be Head of the Government, but his arrest and consignment to the dungeons of the Conciergerie.

But there was no one else, so Bernadotte it had to be.

***

Bernadotte was a Gascon of the Gascons. He was born in Béarn, the land of Henri Quatre. He was twenty-six years of age when the Revolution closed the first part of his career, in which he climbed to the dizzy pinnacle of the rank of regimental sergeant-major. Death closed the second part fifty-five years later, but in the meantime the Béarnais had climbed to the rank of King.

He was a strange man, a mixture of cool subtlety and torrential swashbuckling, of prudence and folly, of rhetoric and silence. General Caffarelli could describe him as a 'flatterer of people likely to be useful, a treacherous and dangerous enemy,' and at the same time General Desaix, the hero of Marengo, could say that he was 'full of fire, of vigour, of fine enthusiasms, above all of character; very estimable.' Desaix also added the singular sentence, 'He is not popular, because he is supposed to be mad.'

But whatever his colleagues thought of him – and none of the Marshals was more whole-heartedly detested by the others – he was immensely popular with all his subordinates. He was very thoughtful to his junior officers; he looked after the welfare of his men as devotedly as Augereau or Davout; and he invariably went out of his way to be kind and friendly to wounded, prisoners, and all civilians, especially in conquered territory.

Bernadotte was a general in the Army of the Sambre-et-Meuse under Jourdan in 1793, and he graduated in the art of handling soldiers beside Ney and Soult in Flanders and the Rhineland. When Bernadotte commanded Jourdan's vanguard in its sweep through Brabant to the Meuse, it was Colonel Ney of the light cavalry who rode in front of the vanguard, and a warm friendship sprang up between the Gascon and the German-speaking Saarois, which lasted until Bernadotte left the Army of France and in 1813 turned his hand against the tricolor.

Bernadotte remained with the army until September, 1796, gaining such a reputation as a divisional commander that many thought he would be appointed to succeed Jourdan as Commander-in-Chief when Jourdan's nerve began to fail him and he was dismissed. But when the time came he was passed over, and he seriously contemplated resigning from the army altogether and settling down quietly in Pau. The transfer of his division, however, to share in the glories and the sun of Italy with the new and dazzling rocket, General Bonaparte, came in the nick of time, and he marched his men down to Milan. The reinforcement was welcome so far as the campaigning was concerned, but in every other way it was a perfect nuisance, for the arrival of this splendid division, strong, disciplined, and well-equipped, was the cause of endless friction between the ragged rascals of the 'citizens' army', the army of victories and lightning marches, and the smart men from the 'gentlemen's army', the army of the placid warfare of the Rhineland.

Trouble began almost at once, and the officers of Italy made no secret of their dislike of their new colleague's gasconading rhetoric. Bernadotte and Bonaparte met for the first time in September, 1797, and never at any time was there cordiality between them. Bernadotte was doubtful from the start about Bonaparte's fidelity to the Republic, and Bonaparte soon grew tired of hearing praises of the smart new division. Matters were not helped by the furious antipathy which burst out, at first sight, between the newcomer and Berthier, Bonaparte's chief-of-staff, and twice within a few months the Gascon had challenged the other to a duel.

The campaign into the Carnic Alps, in the rush to Vienna, threw together the two brilliant Gascons who climbed from obscurity to thrones, for Murat, the inn-keeper's son from Cahors, was given the command of Bernadotte's advance-guard. Murat very soon began to educate his new commander in the campaigning methods of the Army of Italy. For, on hearing that a certain cavalry general named Dugua had been given permission by Bonaparte to loot Trieste, Murat slipped off and, by hard riding, a thing that he was an expert in, managed to get into Trieste, loot it himself, and get out again just as Dugua entered the town. Bernadotte, to whom this sort of thing was new, was a quick learner, and a few days later he annexed for himself and his staff a large amount of quicksilver from the Idrian mines.

As soon as the campaign was over, the brawling and bickering between the polished Messieurs of the Rhine and the scallywag Citoyens of Italy broke out again furiously; at Laybach, Brune, temporarily commanding Masséna's division, called on Bernadotte's chief-of-staff and asked him to forbid the use of the word Monsieur in his division. The chief-of-staff flatly refused and offered to fight Brune instead. Officers and men instantly took up their leaders' quarrel, and within twelve hours fifty men had been killed in duels and more than three hundred wounded. Masséna and Bernadotte hated each other all their lives after Laybach. Augereau also forbad the use of the fatal word and had the mortification of seeing his order cancelled by Bonaparte.

Then came a duel of intrigue between Gascon and Corsican. Bernadotte went back to Paris, lay low in the crisis of Fructidor '97, and, when the cat jumped, jumped after it and angled for the Ministry of War. Bonaparte, in great alarm, fetched him back to the Army of Italy, and the coolness between the two men increased, especially as the Commander-in-Chief took great pleasure in praising to the other's face the military skill of Masséna, Joubert, and even Augereau, whose strategical abilities he was known to regard as comic. Another device for increasing the friction was the breaking-up by Bonaparte of the 'Gentlemen's Division' and the distribution of the units throughout the Army. Bernadotte, who had led it and loved it through four years of campaigning, was furiously angry and showed it. Bonaparte replied by getting him appointed to the command of the outlying posts in the Ionian Islands, a satisfactory distance from Paris. Bernadotte countered this with a devastating thrust. He wriggled out of the Ionian business somehow, and secured no less a dazzling appointment than the High Command of the Army of Italy itself, which Bonaparte had just given up. Bonaparte gave a howl of rage and dismay. That the plum of all the Commands, Italy, the army of '96, his army, his very own and no one else's, should go to the one man whom he wanted out of the way, was unthinkable. A frenzy of intrigue followed, and at the last moment Bonaparte managed to get the appointment cancelled, and exregimental-sergeant-major Bernadotte was sent, instead, to the Court of His Most Apostolic Majesty, the Emperor of Austria, as Ambassador of the French Republic.

It was a delicate mission, for there had been no French Ambassador at Vienna since General Bernadotte's Government had cut off the elegant head of the Austrian Antoinette, and Vienna was crowded with grand French *émigrés* who were waiting for the three-coloured storm to blow over so that they could return to their estates, their incomes and their privileges. The sudden appointment of an ill-bred Gascon adventurer to this reactionary, proud, aristocratic, Imperial city led to loud and bitter protests from the Ballplatz, in the middle of which the new Ambassador, with a suite that was singularly made up of two young civilian secretaries, four dashing subalterns of the Sambre-et-Meuse and an elderly Pole who was an expert in pro-Polish propaganda, unexpectedly arrived and presented his unwelcome credentials.

The story of that embassy is a lively one. On the one hand Bernadotte's easy manners, handsome appearance, and southern affability made him popular (he was a big handsome man, with a huge pointed nose, and a mass of black hair that waved in the wind, and dazzling teeth), but on the other it requires something more than affability and good looks to carry off such tasks as trying to prevent *émigrés* from wearing their decorations, or trying to blackmail the Foreign Minister of a great Empire into resigning office, by threatening to publish the story of a youthful peccadillo. It is not surprising that Bernadotte's Embassy came to an abrupt end, with the Ambassador

standing on his official staircase, sword in hand, defending his Chancery with steel and rhetoric against an
invading mob of populace.

That was an end, for a time, of diplomacy as a career
for Bernadotte. But when he came back from Vienna,
Bonaparte had gone to Egypt and Sidney Smith's cruisers
were preventing him from interfering in the internal politics of France, and in 1799 Bernadotte got the Ministry
of War that he had hankered after, and had full scope for
thundering out his wild rhetoric in an endless series of
letters, proclamations, orders, speeches, and denunciations.
While he was engaged upon these verbal activities, he
found time to bombard Masséna in Switzerland with
a whole series of madcap schemes of strategy which, luckily for France, that crafty and far-sighted Commander
flatly refused to obey.

This was the man whom Siéyès reluctantly chose to be
his sword in his *coup d'état*, chose because there was no
other, and time was running short. The People would
not stand the Government much longer, and a People's
discontent is the Jacobin's chance, as Lenin knew so well
in 1917. Siéyès had to strike before the Jacobins used
their chance. So he put the scheme before the Gascon,
and the Gascon hesitated. When politics and gambles
were afoot there was one place that he liked to occupy,
and that was a seat upon the fence. If there was jumping
to be done, let the cats show the way. So Bernadotte
shilly-shallied and shuffled and hesitated, and Siéyès saw
that his last man was no use. In a *coup d'état* the man
who hesitates is bound to he strung up on a gallows
before the day is out, whichever side he is on, and if he
happens to be a military leader, all his side gets strung
up with him. Bernadotte was no good, and he had to
go. A few days later he threatened to resign from the
War Ministry — he was a great hand at threats of resignation — and his bluff was promptly called by the Abbé
and out he went.

But still Siéyès was lacking his sword. He tried Moreau again. After all, Moreau was not in with the Jourdan-Augereau crew of the Riding School Club, and he was a great soldier. On October 13th the two men met and dined together in the Luxembourg, and while they were dining a messenger came in with a despatch. General Bonaparte had landed at Fréjus. 'There is your man,' said Moreau. 'He will manage your *coup d'état* much better than I.'

***

For a fortnight, from the 16th of October to the 29th, 1799, Paris held its breath and stared wonderingly, suspiciously, hopefully, adoringly, fearfully, at little General Bonaparte as he strolled about in his frock-coat, with his hands in his pockets, discussing the stars, and the higher mathematics, and the hieroglyphics, and the possibility of a Suez Canal, and the immortality of the soul, and the height of the Sphinx, and everything under the sun except politics and wars. All the politicians and intriguers were after him, dangling round Joséphine's house in the Rue Chantereine, re-christened the Rue de la Victoire, and Jourdan and Augereau and their Jacobin friends were in a fever of agitation.

On October 30th Bonaparte threw off the aimlessness which had concealed a penetrating and exhaustive summing-up of the political situation and joined Siéyès, and the intensive work began. For 'even a discredited constitution cannot safely be exploded into the air without a nice attention to detail.'[1]

Joséphine's house was crowded all day now, not with intriguing politicians but with soldiers, tough, wiry officers from Egypt with their sun-tanned, dried-up faces,

[1] H.A. Fisher.

Lannes, who carried weight with the infantry, still hob-
bling about on his crutches from his Aboukir wound;
and Murat, hero of the cavalry, with his pistol-wound
in the jaw; and Berthier, ecstatic at being out of that
pestilential Egypt at last; and young Marmont, influential with the gunners, all good men in a *coup d'état*. They
were not like Bernadotte. There would be no hesitating
about any of these when it came to a street-fight.
Sérurier also was there, stiff and soldierly, and Macdonald,
the Scotsman, and the sabres clanked all day and into the
night on Joséphine's polished parquets. All these were
key-men in the coming coup, trustworthy and utterly reliable.

Against them were Jourdan and Augereau. The doubtful ones included Moreau and Lefèbvre. Lefèbvre was the
most important of the doubtful ones, not because of his
influence, for he had none, nor because of his brains, for
he had none of them either, but because he was Military
Governor of Paris and thus was the holder of a key position. So poor old Lefèbvre was lured to the Chantereine,
and bluffed by Bonaparte, and sirened by Joséphine into
acquiescing in something which he did not in the least
understand. He agreed to help, and went away distressed
and ill-at-ease.

But all these were small-fry in comparison with Bernadotte.
What would the crafty Gascon say? Which way would
he jump? Would he jump at all? Long and anxious were
the consultations in the Chantereine. Siéyès and Roger
Ducos, the Directors, and Talleyrand and Bonaparte, went
over and over the vital questions: Would Bernadotte
come in? and if not, could it be done without him? He
was sounded discreetly without result. From every angle
the baits were gently laid upon the surface of the water,
but the water ran deep.

At last a new line was suggested. Political dry-flies were
abandoned and feminine influence brought to bear. For
Bernadotte had married Désirée Clary, a pretty, simple,

vivacious little bourgeoise from Marseilles, and everyone knew that he was devoted to her, though perhaps not quite so devoted as she to him. Poor little Désirée used to weep when her handsome husband left her, if only for an hour, and wept again when he came back because he might have to go away again, say, in a week or two for another hour. There were several very good reasons why Désirée might be disposed to help. One reason was that Joseph Bonaparte had been in love with her and had wanted to marry her. Another was that Joseph had married, not Désirée, but Désirée's sister, Julie, and so was Bernadotte's brother-in-law. Bernadotte might be made to understand through Désirée that he was practically one of the Family, the Inner Ring, and that he ought to be moved equally by the call of sentiment and the certainty of reward. And what might be more important than all the rest, in the estimation of Désirée herself, was the knowledge that General Bonaparte himself had wooed her once, before the days of Joséphine. She might well be disposed, maternally, to help the little man whom she had rejected years ago.

The manoeuvring began again from this new domestic angle, and Joséphine and Julie Clary, Joseph's wife, were brought into action. But the Gascon was too crafty to be caught like that. He was delighted to come to all the parties, and the excursions into the country, and to invite the entire family to dine with him in his fine house in the Rue Cisalpine, and to entertain them with the gay and amiable chatter of a host. But though he adored his little Désirée, he was level-headed enough to keep his adoration and his politics apart, and in politics he did not trust her an inch, and when it came to business, he took refuge against the assaults of femininity behind a great nebulous cloud of long words and lofty principles.

At last the conspirators saw that they could waste no more time in the effort to decipher the meaning of

Bernadotte's smiles and evasions. The game must be played without him. Before dawn on the 18th Brumaire (November 9th), 1799, the streets of Paris were noisy with the clattering of dragoons and the tramp of infantry. Joséphine's house was crowded by breakfast-time with a mass of excited officers in uniform. Berthier did the honours, for the host was toiling in his office, and the hostess, whom great events moved far less than trivial ones, was in bed. Amid the rattle of sabres, the clinking of spurs, and the chatter of conversation, Lefèbvre arrived in a great hurry and agitation. The Governor of Paris was only trying to do his duty, and his duty clearly was to find out what was up. Bonaparte took the simple fellow aside, presented him with the sword which he had won at the battle of the Pyramids and, with a brief and brilliant word-picture of the glorious Republic in the grip of a miserable crew of attorneys and profiteers, reduced him to a flood of sentimental tears, coupled with a sobbing declaration, in the vilest Alsatian accent, of profound loyalty to the man who was going to save the country. (All the same, Bonaparte, who knew his man, as he knew most men, took the additional precaution of keeping Lefèbvre by his side all day under the pretence that he was his confidant and right-hand man.)

Suddenly Bernadotte appeared in the Chantereine, in plain clothes, gesticulating, pouring out masses of sonorous platitudes, and fencing at the air with his cane to drive home non-existent points. Bonaparte tried the same game as with Lefèbvre. He took him aside and told him the whole plot, implored his assistance, and urged him to run home and put on the uniform which he had rendered so glorious, and to rally in defence of the Republic which they all loved so much, and for which they were all ready to die, etcetera, etcetera, etcetera. But Bernadotte was not a simple, sentimental Alsatian. He was not the one to be caught by phrases. He used them enough himself to know how worthless they were. He remained, therefore, on his accustomed fence and would neither help nor hinder, and off he went to lunch with brother-in-law Joseph.

But in any case it was too late to bother about him now. The hunt was up and the conspirators hurried to their posts. Murat, always ready for excitement, galloped off with the cavalry to the Palais Bourbon; Marmont commanded the guns (this time the guns were at hand and there was no need to send a Captain Murat galloping off to the Sablons Park at dead of night to fetch them, as in '95); Lannes hobbled off on his crutches to command the Tuileries; Moreau, who had come in during the morning with an offer of help, took three hundred men to surround the Luxembourg; Macdonald went to Versailles to watch the Jacobins, and old Sérurier went first to the Point de Jour, and afterwards to St. Cloud. Bonaparte himself rode on a great black horse at the head of a glittering column of cavalry down to the Tuileries. Soon afterwards Jourdan turned up at the Tuileries and was given a friendly warning to keep quiet, and later Augereau swaggered in and embraced the man of the hour, and pretended with clumsy heartiness to have been on his side all the time.

By the evening of November 9th the Directors had been either forced to resign or imprisoned in their official residence. There now remained three obstacles: the Council of the Ancients, the Deputies of the Five Hundred at St. Cloud, and General Bernadotte. Late that night the Jacobin Deputies met and feverishly tried to work out a plan of campaign for the next day at St. Cloud, and Bernadotte proposed that they should elect him as joint military commander with Bonaparte.

On the next day the celebrated drama took place at St. Cloud, when Bonaparte lost his head and the Deputies sprang to their feet and stabbed at him with daggers and howled for his blood. It was the last flicker of the

Revolution. In the gathering twilight of the winter evening, Lefèbvre, his simple, disciplined soul revolting at the sight of soldiers being manhandled by civilians, drew his sword, and Murat formed a column of grenadiers, ordered the drums to beat, and led them into the Council Chamber against 'the attorneys and the profiteers'. For a moment or two there was a wild exchange of insults and party slogans, such as 'Down with the Jacobins', 'Long live the Constitution of the Year Three', 'The laurels of the soldiers are being tarnished,' 'Citizens, the Council is dissolved'. But the young cavalry general sounded a note of realism when he turned to his grenadiers and said, 'Throw me these blighters out of the window'.

So was fulfilled the prophecy of Mirabeau, that the Deputies would be flung out by bayonets.

That night the Republicans scattered and fled, all except Augereau, who was supremely able to tackle any situation, and get himself out of any scrape. He simply repeated with perfect *sang froid* and complete geniality that he had been on Bonaparte's side all the time. Jourdan found asylum in a friend's house, and Bernadotte, who twenty-four days earlier had offered to arrest Bonaparte for breaking the quarantine at Fréjus when the people were crying, 'We prefer the plague to the Austrians', hid in the forest of Senart, near Villeneuve St. Georges, with poor little Désirée, disguised as a boy, beside him.

At two o'clock in the morning of November 11th, 1799, the new Government was inaugurated in the Orangerie at St. Cloud, when the three Consuls, Bonaparte, Ducos, and Siéyès, swore fidelity in alphabetical order, to 'the Republic One and Indivisible, founded on Liberty, Equality, and the Representative System'.

The sword of Siéyès had done its work. It was now for the Abbé to govern.

Exactly one month after the *coup d'état*, General

61

Bonaparte became First Consul, and his colleagues were two gentlemen named Cambacérès and Lebrun.

The Abbé had chosen the wrong sword after all.

CHAPTER VI

MARENGO

DURING the last six weeks of 1799 and the first four months of 1800 the First Consul was frantically busy, working sixteen or eighteen hours a day, seven days a week, beginning the great reorganization of the internal affairs of France. The wheels of administration had creaked their way to an almost complete standstill under the Directorate, and they had to be started again. But although Bonaparte, during these months, was engaged on matters of peace, the enemies of France were engaged on matters of war, and the First Consul, among his thousand other tasks, had to get together some sort of an army. It was his first experience of army-raising, and he had to be quick about it, for the enemy were near the Rhine, and were almost everywhere triumphant in Italy. The First Consul had both frontiers to guard. He therefore chose Dijon as the Headquarters of his new Army of Reserve, as a good central point from which a disaster on either frontier might be repaired.

Three of the officers who afterwards became Marshals of the first vintage were employed on military operations during these months. One was Brune, who was sent down to the west with full authority to suppress the Royalist rebels of the Vendée, and as he was given 60,000 men to do it with, it was impossible even for Brune to make a failure.

The other two had somewhat more difficult work. For once again Masséna, with Soult as his second-in-command, was holding the pass for the Republic. This time it was at Genoa, where he was hemmed in on the land by the overwhelming strength of the Austrian army, and on the sea by the fleet of Lord Keith, which swarmed in the Gulf of Genoa, intercepting supply-carriers and despatch-pinnaces, and standing-in frequently to bombard the water-front. Inside the city was a hostile, sullen, starving population, the enfeebled, unpaid, disgruntled, typhoid-ridden remnants of the Army of Italy, and Masséna himself wearing, night and day, a ribbon of Madame de Récamier's as a mascot. It was impossible to hold out, and yet Masséna held out. Supplies went lower and lower until the daily ration was a handful of flour mixed with sawdust, starch, hair-powder, oatmeal, linseed, and cocoa.

Soult was wounded and captured in a disastrous affair in the difficult country outside the city.

Week after week of starvation and despair went by, but the ex-cabin-boy was unshakable. His orders were to hold the Austrian army till the First Consul was ready. Strategically, Masséna's position in Genoa was the same as it had been in the bastion of Switzerland the year before. The frontier of the Riviera was defended only by a weak army under Suchet, which the powerful forces of Austria could have brushed aside without difficulty. But they dared not leave Masséna behind in Genoa to cut their lines of communication across North Italy. Genoa, therefore, had to be captured before the final rush into France could be ventured upon, and the Republic at last overthrown.

The siege went on and on, and there was no sound of the guns of the First Consul coming over the Ligurian Hills. Every man in the city prayed hourly for surrender, every man except Masséna. Then on May 27th, Cavalry-Captain Franceschi, who afterwards died horribly in a Spanish dungeon, rowed a boat by night along the coast, slipped through the blockade, and finished the journey by swimming ashore with his sabre in his mouth amid the volleys of musketry and salvoes of cannon of the English, who had at last detected him. He brought the news that the Army of the Rhine had won at Biberach, and that the Army of Reserve, with the First Consul himself in command, was not coming over the Ligurian Hills to the relief of Genoa, but had already crossed the Great St. Bernard, and was, at that very moment, pouring down into the plains of Lombardy far away to the eastward. The one thing which had terrified the Austrians had happened and their communications had been cut. For Lannes had driven them in at Montebello, and the First Consul was lying with his army near the little village of Marengo between the Austrians and Vienna. The trick was done, whether by the general's tenacity or Madame de Récamier's ribbon, and Masséna, his hair gone grey during the siege, marched out his half-dead remnant and surrendered.

All day long on June 14th, 1800, Soult lay in the Austrian hospital in Alessandria and listened to the sound of the guns at Marengo. He knew very well that the fortune of France was at stake, and that the First Consul, by coming over the St. Bernard instead of making a frontal attack along the coast route, was staking everything on a single battle. For hours there was no news at Alessandria, but Soult's expert ear told him all that he needed to know. The bombardment was getting fainter and fainter, and that could only mean that the First Consul was being driven back. A French victory meant that Melas was fatally cut off from Vienna. But the coin had two sides, and an Austrian victory meant that Bonaparte was fatally cut off from France. In the afternoon of that thundery summer's day the first Austrian wounded began to come in to Soult's hospital with their stories of victory all along the line, and at 4 p.m. there was a terrible silence in the east. But an hour later the noise of the guns flared up again and became louder and louder, and at eight o'clock at night the Austrian surgeons came rushing to their distinguished guest with the news of the utter rout of their men.

The story is one of the most famous and most frequently described of all the Napoleonic epic; how Bonaparte underestimated the Austrians and strung out his divisions on too wide an arc; how Melas attacked and rolled the French back; how Lannes and Victor and Marmont fought desperately against the tide; how Bonaparte sent his message to Desaix, about which a man who claimed to have seen the scrawl, reported that it said, 'For God's sake come back'; and how Desaix came back. The French counter-attack was, by chance, one of the most perfectly timed tactical operations by combined infantry, artillery, and cavalry in the whole history of warfare. Marmont, commanding the guns, had fought furiously all day until he had only five pieces left. Five more were brought up from reserve and Desaix had eight. For twenty minutes Marmont's battery of eighteen kept up the bombardment which Soult heard in his hospital between five and six o'clock that afternoon, and then Desaix went forward. Marmont managed to limber up four of his guns and went up in support. Suddenly, through the dense smoke he saw, not fifty yards in front, a battalion of Austrian grenadiers advancing in perfect formation to counter the counter-attack, and some of Desaix's men were tumbling back in confusion. Marmont, whatever his faults might be, was a quick thinker, and he unlimbered his four guns and fired four rounds of canister at point-blank range into the compact battalion, and at that precise moment, while the Austrians were staggering under the blow, and an Austrian ammunition-wagon was exploding with a monstrous detonation,

Desaix went forward with a shout, and young Kellermann, son of old Valmy Kellermann, came thundering
down on the flank, through the mulberry-trees and the
tall luxuriant vines, with a handful of heavy cavalry. A
minute earlier, or three minutes later, and the thing
could not have succeeded, but the timing was perfect,
and North Italy was recovered in that moment for the
French Republic.

'It is some consolation to you,' spluttered Berthier to an
Austrian officer the day after Marengo, 'that you have
been defeated by the greatest general in the world.'

'The battle of Marengo,' replied the Austrian, 'was not
won here; it was won under the walls of Genoa.'

* * *

On June 14th, 1800, Bonaparte was thirty-one, Desaix
thirty-two, young Kellermann thirty, Marmont twenty-
six, Lannes thirty-one, and Melas seventy.

CHAPTER VII

MAKING THE *GRANDE ARMÉE*

THE Treaty of Amiens was signed in May, 1802, and the First Consul was free to devote his unique orderliness of mind to the creation of a new, united France, and the Generals, flocking from their various commands to Paris, were free to devote their time to intrigue against 'Sultan' Bonaparte. For the little man was getting on too fast. While all the world was discussing and arguing, he was putting in his steady eighteen hours a day at his desk, and the results that flowed incessantly out of his office were setting the devil of a pace. The Republicans wanted to use the Peace for consolidating the Republic, and they did not yet understand that the First Consul was already using it at a furious speed for consolidating France, for merging parties, for fusing loyalties, for reconciling old enmities, so that there should no longer be Jacobins and Royalists, Catholics and Atheists, pre-Revolution and post-Revolution but only Frenchmen and France. There was a howl of dismay when France was officially reconciled, by means of the Concordat, with the Religion which the Revolution had dethroned with so much labour and blood. And the howl was not diminished in intensity when it was seen that the First Consul's prestige, immense already, was actually increased among the common people to whom a thousand years of rooted Catholicism meant more than a dozen years of compulsory Atheism.

It was all very well for Augereau to say furiously, 'The only thing lacking at this ceremony are the million dead men who died to get rid of this nonsense,' and for him and Lannes to talk loudly to each other throughout the Te Deum which was sung in Notre Dame in Thanksgiving for the Concordat. The common people preferred the new regime, even though it was almost dictatorial, of ordered government and amnesties for the past and revival of trade and guaranteed land-titles, to the old regime of corruption and inefficiency in the sacred name of the Republic.

But a *coup d'état,* properly engineered, can often override the Will of the People, and Siéyès, the disgruntled Abbé, was out again on the hunt for a sword. This time there was a much larger selection of distinguished officers to choose from. The Rhine Army men were all in Paris, and their jealousy of Bonaparte made them feel more disinterestedly Republican than ever. Moreau, of course, was their leader, and with him were Oudinot, Lecourbe, and Gouvion St. Cyr.

Then there were the Jacobins, Augereau, Jourdan, and Brune, and also Macdonald, who had helped Bonaparte at Brumaire, and now changed sides again. Of the men of the armies of Italy and Egypt all were faithful to the First Consul except two. Lannes, for some inexplicable reason, joined the Rhine men (and his defection was at least balanced if not outweighed by the fact that Ney, of the Rhine, was now a strong adherent of Bonaparte) and Masséna. Masséna had a very good reason for discontent. He had some right to think that he had deserved well of the State at Rivoli, Zürich, and Genoa, and when the Army of Italy was completely reorganized with 60,000 infantry, 10,000 cavalry, and no fewer than a hundred and sixty of Marmont's new standardized field-guns and a hundred and twenty of his new siege-guns, he naturally was justified in expecting the command. But the subtle cabin-boy, smuggler, dried-fruit seller, was building up a military glory that was getting a little too close to that of the First Consul himself, and Masséna was recalled and the command given to General Brune. Masséna, in a fury, went straight to Paris and joined the ranks of the intriguers and the discontented.

Brune was thirty-four years of age at this time. He was the son of a lawyer in Brives-la-Gaillarde in the department of Corrèze, and himself had been designed for his father's profession. But he had hankerings after a literary career, and in 1788, while still a law student, he published a book of travel in eastern France. After the Revolution he found it more difficult to get his immortal works published, and so he set up a printing establishment to print and publish his writings, and to print his own newspaper, *Le Magazin Historique ou Journal Général*. He was especially addicted to the art of writing poetry. But in 1790 he made an excursion into another branch and wrote a pamphlet for his intimate friend Danton on military matters. Brune was very proud of this pamphlet, and was much mortified when Mademoiselle Gerfault, a celebrated actress of the Palais Royal, glanced at it and remarked, 'You will be a General when people fight with quills.' Brune, in a great rage at the taunt, proved her wrong by obtaining a major's commission from Danton and, within a year, the rank of General. His first mission was to escort the Terrorists who were being sent down to do their work in Bordeaux, and for many years the citizens of that city held Brune in kindly remembrance for his labours in diminishing the horrors of the Terror. It is almost certainly untrue that Brune was present at, and therefore partially responsible for, the atrocious murder of the Princesse de Lamballe in 1792. But the rumour cost him his life twenty-three years later.

The early part of Brune's military career was spent mainly in Switzerland and Italy, but in the beginning of 1799 he had a remarkable piece of luck. For he was despatched to command the Republican Army in Holland against the English, and there he found in the Duke of York probably the only commander in the world whom he could have defeated. And defeat him he did at the battles of Berghen and Kastricum.

Brune was an exceptionally tall man with long arms, and Napoleon greatly admired his figure. He was a great reader, but only retained a vague jumble of memories from his reading. Marmont described him as having a head like a badly arranged library, and as being endowed with neither courage nor character. According to Marmont he was an honest nonentity.

The new commander of the Army of Italy was delighted at his new command. But his ingenious habit of trying to march three divisions simultaneously along the same road led to confusion in the army. The troops had to hang about all day waiting for a chance to move, and it was usually dark before a start could be made. *Marcher à la brune* became the proverbial expression for the perpetual night-marching and muddling of the new Army of Italy. The First Consul stood it for a few months, and then despatched the poetically minded gentleman to represent the Republic at Constantinople.

In all the intriguing against the Consulate it was the attitude of Bernadotte, as in 1799, that was the key to the situation. When the necessity for hiding in the forests, after his lamentable series of indecisions at Brumaire, was over, and Désirée was able to resume a more feminine costume, Bernadotte had been, half contemptuously, half politically, pardoned by the First Consul, and despatched to the command of the Vendée, and he was spending many wearisome months, either at his headquarters at Rennes in the west, or on leave in his house in Paris, intriguing rather vaguely with Madame de Staël. Madame was immensely impressed with him and thought him 'the true hero of the age'. Bernadotte was also respectfully adoring, without disloyalty to his Désirée, the famous Madame de Récamier. It was at Madame de Récamier's country house that he and Moreau met Lord and Lady Holland and Charles James Fox, and it was from there that the rumours began to reach Whitehall that the two famous Republican generals were putting their heads together on the subject of a rising against the all-powerful First Consul.

During these intrigues an incident took place which led to a lifelong hatred between two of the Marshals, and which more than once had a direct influence on Napoleonic strategy. Davout was back in Paris after the vicissitudes of his desperate escape from Egypt with Desaix, when they were captured off Sicily by Admiral Keith, released by diplomatic pressure after a month in Livorno Prison, captured again off Fréjus by Barbary corsairs, and released again by the providential arrival of war-ships. His devotion to Bonaparte, which had begun after the battle of Aboukir, had already grown to such an extent that he was appointed Commander of the Military Police, and in this capacity he hired a room overlooking Bernadotte's house and garden in Paris, and used it for a continuous service of espionage. Bernadotte never forgave him for this.

But the Abbé Siéyès was even less fortunate in his second attempt at a *coup d'état*, for a batch of seditionary placards was discovered to have been composed by Bernadotte's retired chief-of-staff and brought to Paris by a soldier servant of Bernadotte's headquarters, and the whole conspiracy fizzled out. The First Consul talked so furiously about having Bernadotte shot out of hand, that the latter hastily retired to take the waters at Plombières. The shooting did not materialize, and Bonaparte allowed his sense of humour to have a chance for once, when he shortly afterwards offered Bernadotte the Governorship of Louisiana, and then the Washington Embassy.

Moreau was exiled to America, and Macdonald retired in disgrace to his country house where he busied himself with gardening and the raising of beet for sugar. His gardener was not much use at beet-growing, but he was one of Fouché's most reliable police spies.

* * *

On May 18th, 1803, the British Government declared war on France, and the First Consul had to turn to the business of making an army. But this time it was to be no brilliant improvisation like the Reserve Army at Dijon of 1800 which had startled Europe at Marengo. It was to be a real, full-dress, organized, trained fighting-machine. Its training-ground was to be the north-east coast of France, and its objective was England. The years of peace had brought home a great mass of human material from which to choose, and much of it was quite useless for the new fast-moving warfare. The ancient warriors, whom thirty and forty years of service had turned into badly oiled clock-work toys, were no use as sergeants, and there were so many brilliant young generals available that the old-fashioned type could be ruthlessly discarded. The First Consul's purge was strong and drastic, and the camps at Boulogne, Wimereux, and Ostend, began to buzz with manœuvres, inspections, parades, artillery target-practice where old hulks took the place of Nelson's cruisers, and courses of technical instruction for officers. Time schedules were carefully drawn up – so many days a week for battalion-drill, so many days for combined brigade-manoeuvre, so many hours at cartridge-manufacture, or trench-digging, or bullet-founding, or bayonet-sharpening.

The Army of the Coasts of the Ocean consisted of seven army corps, six divisions of heavy cavalry and a division of the Imperial Guard, and it numbered altogether about 190,000 men. It was strung out in a long line along the coast with the right wing at Hanover, and the left wing seven hundred miles away at Brest.

Bernadotte commanded the First Corps at Hanover. There had been a sort of reconciliation between him and the First Consul, and the two men had had a long private interview.'I did not promise him affection,' Bernadotte told Madame de Récamier, 'I promised him loyal cooperation, and I shall keep my word.' Bernadotte was not particularly interested in the routine of commanding a corps in peace time, and he spent more time being agreeable to his men and his junior officers than in teaching them how to drill. He was especially friendly to the Hanoverian civilians on whom his Corps was quartered.

Marmont, the hero of the last five guns at Marengo, had the Second Corps at Utrecht. It was his first big command, and he drilled his three divisions every Sunday with all the zeal of a new broom. He took his work very seriously, studied the psychology of his men, built dykes and entrenchments and fortifications, and organized concert-parties to make the evenings pass more pleasantly. He also amused himself by setting his men to build a pyramid seventy-five feet high, to be called the Marmontberg. Marmont was quite at home in Holland, for during the peace he had been sent there by the First Consul to employ his charming personality and keen intelligence in wheedling a loan out of the thrifty Dutch on the security of the great Regent Diamond. His resilient personality was in no way cast down by the failure of his mission.

Next came Davout with the Third Corps, which lay between Flushing and Dunkirk, with Headquarters at Bruges. Davout divided his time between a meticulous execution of the First Consul's schedule of drill instruction, and the hanging and shooting of spies, clouds of whom came over into his district from England.

Soult was at Boulogne with the Fourth Corps. He also was full of professional enthusiasm and personally directed corps-manoeuvres, sometimes for twelve hours on end, three times a week, so that even the First Consul expressed alarm at the severity of the training. The Fourth Corps became a sort of training-school for young officers. A very large number of what would nowadays be called 'Soult's young men' won high rank in other corps during the next twelve years. Soult greatly enjoyed himself at Boulogne in building a grand monument. To make an impressive job of it, he borrowed a large amount of bronze from the Emperor for the bas-reliefs, giving him an assurance that the Army would recover an equivalent quantity of cannon from the enemy at the first opportunity. His personal popularity was somewhat dimmed with both officers and rank-and-file later on, when they discovered that their pay was to be docked by one day's pay per month, to settle up for that infernal monument which they had so greatly admired when they thought the Government was paying for it. 'If glory was picked up like money,' said one of his indignant colonels, 'our Marshal would be the greatest man in the world'.

Soult, like Marmont, was a believer in concert-parties, but he insisted on censoring the 'turns'. On one occasion he refused to let a 'vaudeville', which an N.C.O. had written, be acted because it contained the part of a cowardly French soldier. 'There are no cowards in the French Army,' said the Marshal, but the N.C.O. had the soul of an artist and refused to alter his manuscript, and the vaudeville was never acted.

Lannes had the Fifth Corps, near Boulogne. After the failure of Siéyès' last intrigue, Lannes had hastily returned to the Consular fold, and was fresh from an excursion into diplomacy. For although he was more at home on a scaling ladder than a ballroom floor and 'stormed a fortress more easily than a woman',[1] he had been shrewdly selected by Bonaparte as the man to negotiate a treaty of neutrality between France and Portugal. His ambassadorial methods, which consisted mainly of clanking an enormous sabre upon the palace tiles, struck terror into the Portuguese heart of the Regent, the Prince of Brazil, and were a complete success. His expedition to Lisbon was a complete success also from his own private point of view, for Lannes had been in serious financial straits, having over-spent by three hundred thousand francs his allowance for the equipment of the Consular Guard which he was then commanding. Bessières, hearing of this in a round-about way, ran off with the news to his hero Murat, and Murat, delighted to have a thrust at Lannes, reported the matter to the First Consul. If there was anything that infuriated Bonaparte it was unnecessary wastage of money by anyone except Joséphine, and he ordered Lannes to make good the deficit or be cashiered. Murat and Bessières were delighted at their success, and furious when the openhanded, roystering Augereau lent Lannes the whole of the money free of interest. It has been darkly suggested that Lannes bullied a handful of diamonds out of the terrified Portuguese Prince. However that may be, the fact remains that on his return from Lisbon Lannes was able to repay the whole sum to Augereau.

Lannes had divorced the charming but inconstant lady who had given birth to the son fourteen months after Lannes went to Egypt, and had married a second time. His wife, according to Madame Junot, was one of the most beautiful ladies of the Court, and her kindliness and beauty went a long way in Lisbon to counteract her husband's remarkable methods of diplomacy, especially

[1] *Madame Junot.*

after the occasion on which he tipped the English ambassador's coach, ambassador and all, into a ditch.

The Sixth Corps was under Ney at Montreuil. Ney had been brought over from the Rhine Army group of officers to the Bonapartist group through the charms and graces of Joséphine, who had been told by Bonaparte to lure the dashing young Hussar, recently appointed Inspector-general of Cavalry, to her drawing-room. Once Joséphine had got her tapering fingers upon Ney, she provided him with a wife, Aglaé, daughter of a lady who was a niece of the celebrated Madame Campan, and had been a lady-in-waiting to Marie Antoinette. Bonaparte chose his man well, and Madame Bonaparte chose the wife well, for they were a devoted couple during their thirteen years of married life. Madame Ney seems to have been a charming person. She was simple and very intelligent and very beautiful, and everyone loved her.

Ney, like Lannes, came to his command from a diplomatic mission.

It has often been debated why this plain, blunt soldier was selected for the task in the year, 1803, of conducting the extremely tricky negotiations, quasimilitary, quasi-diplomatic, partly under the instructions of Bonaparte, and partly of Talleyrand, by which the Act of Mediation was pushed, blarneyed, and thrust, upon the free Swiss Cantons. The answer, invariably overlooked, is simple. The mission had to be conducted by a man of war who was also a man of sense, and it was a mission to a nation that did not speak only French. There were, at this time, five senior officers at Bonaparte's command who were bilingual in French and German: old Kellermann, who was a man of sense but no soldier, in spite of Valmy; General Lefèbvre, who was neither man of war nor of sense; General Augereau, who was more an urchin than a diplomat; Colonel Rapp, who was a man of sense but had not a sufficiently distinguished reputation as a soldier;

and Ney. It is significant that Rapp was sent at the same time to Switzerland upon a subsidiary mission, and that a large measure of Ney's successes in tact and diplomacy was due to the speeches which he delivered at Berne in the two languages while he was negotiating with the Helvetian Senate.

At Montreuil Ney threw himself earnestly into the study of infantry tactics. Hitherto he had specialized mainly in light cavalry work. But with the expert assistance of Jomini, a Swiss mercenary soldier of great reputation who attached himself to the Sixth Corps, Ney soon began to pick up the details of infantry work. He even wrote manuals of instruction for his Corps. The two main precepts which he insisted on over and over again, were 'fast marching and straight shooting'. In the subsequent campaigns the Sixth Corps certainly marched fast, but it is doubtful if any French infantry of those days ever shot very straight. Apparently a soldier of the Boulogne Army had to fire only one musketry course, and that consisted of three shots at a target at point-blank range. If he hit the target he was passed as a marksman; if he missed, well there was always the bayonet.

In the technical instructions which the enthusiastic Corps-Commander drew up for his men there are two singular paragraphs. One shows Ney's passionate belief in the essential goodness of the French character.

'Our soldiers ought to be instructed about the cause of each war. It is only when aggression is legitimate that one can expect prodigies of valour. An unjust war is utterly repugnant to the French character.'

The second paragraph illuminates Ney's whole theory of life. It gives an outline of how the evening of a victory ought to be spent. The victorious regiments should be paraded on the battlefield in the soft quietness after the tempest, each near the scene of its glory, with the regimental bands playing, and the generals inspecting and congratulating; then there would be a *feu de joie*, five cartridges per man and five rounds per gun, before the glorious victors retired to bivouac. This queer notion of a sort of militarized Te Deum, a sacramental worship of Victory and Glory is the key to Ney's character. He had no use for money or ambition or politics or anything except military glory. His only passionate conviction was that every soldier ought to die in battle, and that those who died in their beds were not true soldiers. Rank and medals did not mean glory to Ney. He twice refused promotion on the ground of inexperience, at a time when his contemporaries were racing gaily up the ladder. But when, later on, at the siege of Michelsburg, Napoleon sent an order that he was to wait for Lannes' Corps, Ney replied: 'Tell His Majesty that here we don't share glory with anyone.'

For Ney there was only one God, the God of Battles, and if his Deity gave him Victory, the one divine and perfect gift in the religion, it was only right to thank Him with rolls of musketry and cannon salvoes.

This paragraph in the Marshal's text-book illustrates two other things. The first is that he never imagined that a battlefield on the evening of a victory could be anything but a beautiful place. For him it was a great, quiet cathedral. He never thought for a moment of the groans and cries of the wounded or the bodies of the dead. He probably never heard them or saw them. He was not afraid of wounds himself. As for the dead, they had fulfilled the only true function of a soldier and had died in battle.

And the second is that even then, in 1804, when he was a Marshal and a Corps-Commander, he had not the faintest idea of the way in which his Commander-in-Chief was in the habit of waging war. Having missed the miraculous Italian campaign of '96, and Egypt, and Marengo, Ney was still living in the days of Frederick, Condé, Villars, and Luxembourg. A battle was a battle. At the end of the day the vanquished retired, the victors bivouacked on the field, and there was a gentlemanly pause. Ney did not know that all that had been changed, and that in the new warfare a battle was the breaking of the crest of a wave, and that the flood which swept irresistibly after it was the real victory. He was soon to learn.

It throws an interesting sidelight on the characters of the seven Corps-Commanders, that when an ingenious civilian gentleman arrived in the Pas-de-Calais with an observation balloon of his own invention to sell, it was to Ney that he took it. That civilian was a student of character as well as a salesman. Bernadotte would have listened attentively, given the man a drink, and charmingly bowed him out. Marmont would have gone into the mechanics of the contrivance, analyzed the materials, and proved its fallaciousness. Davout would have arrested the man out of hand as an impostor, and tried to hang him as a spy. Soult would have resolutely declined to part with a franc. Lannes would have laughed uproariously, and professed his complete inability to understand what it was all about, and Augereau would have kicked him downstairs. But Ney was by now an earnest student of his profession, and neglected nothing to improve the fighting efficiency of his Corps. He was also the only one of the seven who had fought at Fleurus in '94 and seen the ascents of Colonel Coutelle and two staff-officers in the captive balloon on the day before that battle. So the civilian gentleman returned happily to Paris, and Marshal Ney was left to rely still upon light cavalry for information, and to mourn the loss of thirty thousand francs of his savings. It was an especially unfortunate moment for such a loss, for the Marshals had just given the Empress a ball in the newly redecorated Opéra, and although the ball was declared a grand success, and Joséphine and her sister-in-law wore for the first time the Bourbon jewels, so that the scene was described as a *feu de diamants*, nevertheless it cost each of the eighteen Marshals a cool twenty thousand francs apiece.

The Seventh Corps was at Brest under Augereau, who, as usual, had blandly ignored his own last outbreak of intrigue. Bessières commanded the Imperial Guard, and he contributed greatly to the gaiety of the coast by trying to teach his veterans to swim.

Jean Baptiste Bessières, formerly a barber in Languedoc, joined the Guard of Louis XVI as a private in 1792, and on the 10th of August of that year fought hard in defence of his master and helped to save some of the Queen's household. Luckily for him, he was too obscure to be prescribed for this loyalty, and, after hiding for a month or two, he re-emerged in the Republican Army of the Pyrenees. Subsequently he was transferred as a cavalry captain to the Army of Italy.

***

The Reserve Cavalry was under Murat. Murat had done well for himself when he fetched up the guns in 1795 and linked his fortunes with those of Bonaparte. But later on he had done even better. For he had married Caroline, the great man's sister, and so became a member of the Family. It had been touch and go whether he got her or not, for Napoleon gave long and earnest thought to the matrimonial affairs of his brothers and sisters. The brothers were to marry princesses and establish their royal dynasties in Spain, in Holland, in Westphalia – poor silly little midshipman Jerome almost threw away his Westphalian crown before he ever got it by marrying a Baltimore bourgeoise called Patterson – but the sisters must also play their part in welding the great structure of Bonapartism in Europe together. Caroline was an important card. It is thought that Napoleon offered her to Moreau, but that Moreau declined to come up to scratch. It would have been a wonderful coup if the brilliant Republican general had been lured into the Dynasty. Lannes would have been a candidate, but his divorce had not yet gone through, and Murat was pressing his suit. There was an awkward moment, however,

when the rumours began to circulate in the drawing-
rooms that the dashing light cavalryman was overdoing
the sentimental ties which connected him with the
Bonaparte family. To pursue the great man's sister was
one thing; but surely it was another matter to toy with
his wife. There was the unfortunate episode of the breakfast party which Murat gave to some of his cavalry
friends at which, after much champagne, the host offered
to mix a famous rum punch made with special Jamaica
rum. The emphasis he put on the word Jamaica, and
his description of the charming Creole, 'the finest and
prettiest woman in Paris, who had taught him the
recipe and many other things as well,' aroused hilarious
congratulations from the young men. And their enthusiasm was unbounded when they discovered the Bonaparte
stamp upon the silver lemon-squeezer. The story reached
Bonaparte, and Murat hastily abolished the squeezer and
denied everything. For a while, Bonaparte is said to have
contemplated giving Caroline to Augereau, so profound
were his suspicions of Murat. But the project could
never have been really serious, and Murat got the lady
in the end, and they retired to their grand new apart-
ments in the Hôtel de Brionne, in the northern part of
the Tuileries, and kept high state, and intrigued with
Bernadotte against the First Consul. But in spite of
all the sudden brilliance of the innkeeper's son from
Cahors, two stories prove that he retained much of his
native simplicity. He had never learned to dance, and at
the innumerable glittering balls of the Consulate and
the Empire, he always stood meekly behind Caroline,
holding her gloves and fan. And after the grandest meal
in the Brionne, he always brought out a large stone jar
of preserved raisins, quinces, and pears. 'It is the treat of
my native country; my mother makes it and sends it to me
always.'

***

No other army has ever contained such a number of brilliant cavalry leaders as this Army of the Coasts of the Ocean. The wild exaltation that was a legacy both of the new spirit of the Revolution and of the Army of the Sambre-et-Meuse, the opening of the higher ranks to young men, the passionate enthusiasm for the Emperor, and the natural individualism and *élan* of the French national character, all combined to give an irresistible dash to the cavalry arm of the first Imperial Army. But although there were many famous leaders of horse, nevertheless there were four who seem in some curious way to be almost symbols in themselves of the whole Napoleonic saga with its mixture of fantasy, high adventure, and tragedy. None of these four were yet thirty years of age, and all were handsome, brilliant, and reckless, and all were generals. The greatest was Lasalle, the adored of the Light Cavalry. The other three were Colbert of the hussars, Sainte-Croix of the dragoons, and the big, black-bearded Montbrun of the Light Chasseurs.

***

On December 2nd, 1804, the First Consul crowned himself Emperor of the French in Notre Dame. The Imperial Sword of State was carried by staunch old Republican Lefèbvre, and the cushion on which lay the Imperial Crown was carried by staunch old Republican Kellermann. No special places had been reserved for the sixty senior generals and they were jammed together, standing, in the nave. There was an unseemly commotion when Masséna jerked a smug little priest off his seat, and the fifty-nine other veterans followed his example and ejected the minor clergy.

***

It was on May 19th, 1804, that the eighteen generals had been created Marshals of the Empire. Six—Moncey, Jourdan, Kellermann, Lefèbvre, Pérignon, and Sérurier—represented the great days of the Republican armies. They were the men who had stood like an iron wall against Europe when the Old Ideas were driving in upon the Republic to extirpate the New. To the people of France they represented the spirit of '93. They had been soldiers when the Sansculottes stood calm under the plunging fire of Valmy, and had captured and recaptured Wattignies, and had won at Fleurus and Jemappes, and now they were Symbols. That is why they were made Marshals of the Empire. Six came from the miraculous Army of Italy – Berthier, Murat, Masséna, Augereau, Lannes, and Bessières; three from the Army of the Rhine – Soult, Mortier, and Ney; Brune, because he had defeated the English; and lastly, Davout, whose baton was the least obvious of all, and Bernadotte, whose baton was the most obvious.

CHAPTER VIII

AUSTERLITZ

WHEN the list of the Marshals was published there was instantly a vast ripple of heartburning throughout the senior ranks of the Army. The list was scrutinized and discussed and criticized in a thousand messes.

'Allow me to congratulate you,' said a friend to Masséna.

'One of fourteen,' said Masséna drily.

'That's a fine coat,' remarked someone to Lefèbvre on the day on which he appeared for the first time in his Marshal's uniform.

'So it ought to be,' replied the old warrior, 'I have been thirty-five years at the stitching of it.'

Bitter were the feelings of Marmont, the Emperor's oldest friend, the comrade of Italy and Egypt, the Commander of the Artillery at the passage of the St. Bernard, and the hero of the last five guns at Marengo. He alone of the Corps-Commanders of the *Grande Armée* was not to be a Marshal. The promotion of the great soldiers of Italy and Switzerland and the Rhine he could understand, and the sentiment which had given the baton to the Old Republicans, but why Davout, who had never done anything? Brune, though an incompetent ass, had at least won battles against the ridiculous Duke of York, but what had Mortier ever done? And why, why in Heaven's name Bessières? 'It is true I had not commanded an army in the field,' Marmont wrote bitterly, 'but the choice of Bessières justified the promotion of the whole world.' (The obvious reason for the passing over of Marmont was his youth. Napoleon believed in promoting young men, but Marmont was only just thirty and had shown himself to be young for his age.) Suchet was passed over, and Macdonald, both of whom had commanded in the field, and Oudinot, a solid fighter, and the brilliant St. Cyr, who had made the fatal and characteristic mistake of refusing to sign either the petition to the First Consul to become Emperor or the address of thanksgiving at his escape from the Pichegru-Cadoudal conspiracy. He had also refused to attend the coronation. Lecourbe, the great mountain-fighter, was left out, and Molitor, who had put the finishing touches on the harrying of Suvorov into the Grisons in 1799, the ferocious Vandamme and Loison and Gudin and Friant and many another tough soldier, and yet the gentle Bessières was made a Marshal, and the ridiculous Brune and the dull Moncey.

But there was not time for heartburning. For the Austrians were moving up the Danube valley, and the Prussians were stirring restlessly, and the stubborn armies of Russia were trudging westwards, and already a mysterious Colonel Beaumont, who bore a remarkable resemblance to Marshal Murat, was unobtrusively reconnoitring the approaches of the Black Forest, and noting down the cavalry roads.

At the end of August, 1805, the great camps along the coast of the Pas-de-Calais were struck, and the most superb army in equipment, training, experience, morale, men, officers, and Commander-in-Chief, that the world has ever seen, turned its back on the white sails of England's fleet and the white silhouette of England's cliffs, and went swinging across France and Holland and Germany, sixteen miles a day, to its first concentration line.

The army marched according to mathematical schedule; after each hour of marching there was a halt for five minutes for a smoke, and it became almost a custom for the senior officers to stand drinks to the juniors; at midday there was an hour's rest. In dusty weather each man had to carry a straw in his mouth to keep his lips shut.

Thirty days after the issuing of the first Imperial orders, and within three or four days of each other – so mathematically precise had the orders been, and so steady the marching – the seven Corps, the Imperial Guard, and the glittering Reserve Cavalry had reached their first line of concentration. This line was a vast semicircle, the northern tip of which was Bernadotte at Würzburg, the centre span was the line of the Rhine, and the southern tip was Augereau at Bâle.

So far it had been easy work for Berthier, poring over his maps at Headquarters. The weather had not been too bad, the routes lay through the home country, the men were keen and, with one exception, the discipline, especially in the Corps of Davout and Soult, was first class. The former reported no stragglers, Soult about thirty. Marmont was the exception, and he could not be blamed for the wholesale desertions of his Dutch auxiliaries. Marmont was also much handicapped by the optimism which had led to his artillery horses being cooped up for weeks in ships, waiting to be transported to England. But even the trouble with his deserters and his horses could not damp that young man's resilience. 'What a country to make war in,' he wrote. 'There is no trouble about requisitioning. The Germans are reasonable folk, and know that soldiers must eat. What one takes from them goes to a useful destination, and that consoles them. Disorder alone annoys them.'

But now things were to be difficult. Austrian General Mack had been located at Ulm, covering the valley of the Danube, with his communications running either south on to Russian and Austrian supports, or east to

Vienna. Somewhere in the distant obscurity of the Hapsburg Empire lay another Austrian army, and beyond that again, far in the misty east, the main forces of Muscovy.

Napoleon's next move is usually dismissed as an exceptional *tour de force* of strategy. It was far more. It was an exquisite work of art, and the beauty of it is the beauty of anything that is symmetrical. He pulled Bernadotte and Marmont, the northern wing of the great arc, southwards and sent the centre, the Rhineland Corps, northwards to meet it. The gap thus left in the centre and right was covered by a colossal fan-shaped screen of the Reserve Cavalry, and the extreme right was held still by Augereau. Thus, within forty-five days of the quiet tents of Boulogne, Bruges, and Montreuil (distant, as the crow flies, four hundred miles from Ulm), Napoleon had laid more than 150,000 men, concentrated and co-ordinated, on the northern flank of General Mack, while Murat's cloud of horsemen in front prevented the Austrians from knowing what storm was about to burst.

Not that Mack would have believed it, even if he had flown over the *Grande Armée* in an aeroplane. He knew exactly when the *Grande Armée* left its tents, four hundred miles away in the north-west, and at the normal, old-fashioned, Austrian rate of marching, it should by now be having a certain amount of trouble with its rations and its boots in the neighbourhood of Nancy, Metz, and Luxembourg. So the cavalry screen worried him not at all, and he remained at Ulm with his 30,000 men, perfectly calm and confident. It was not till Bernadotte, with the extreme left tip of the iron arc, crossed the Danube at Ingolstadt, behind Mack, between him and Vienna, that he began to think that something was up. It was becoming quite a normal experience with Austrian commanders, that their first intimation of Napoleon's whereabouts was his arrival astride their communications.

The rest is history, how the *Grande Armée* marched clean round Mack and captured the whole 30,000 of his army with only a single brisk skirmish, at Elchingen. This skirmish at Elchingen brought Ney into prominence both as a strong fighter and a strong quarreller. His Corps, the Sixth, was suddenly joined to the Fifth, Lannes' Corps, and both were put under the orders of Murat, because he was husband of Caroline Bonaparte and brother-in-law of the Emperor and therefore one of the Family. Lannes hated Murat, and both he and Ney were furious at being put under the swaggering cavalryman, whose knowledge of infantry work was, they considered, nil.

Ney soon started to make trouble over what he thought was Murat's faulty disposition of the Sixth Corps upon the two banks of the Danube, and at last Murat impatiently told him to stop bothering him. 'I only make my plans in the presence of the enemy,' he declared. But Ney was right, and Murat was wrong, as he very soon discovered when his Imperial brother-in-law arrived and had a glance at the situation. The Sixth Corps was in a mess, and the only way out was the immediate storming of the bridge over the Danube at Elchingen and the capture of the high ground beyond it. Ney took charge of the assault. Just as he had received his final orders from Napoleon and was leaving the glittering Head-quarter Staff, he gripped Murat by the arm and exclaimed loudly, 'Come with me, Prince, and make some plans in the presence of the enemy!' It is not recorded whether Marshal Lannes laughed out loud or only internally. Murat's reply was characteristic. A few days later he wrote to Napoleon accusing Ney of requisitioning 50,000 crowns illegally. Napoleon's reply was also characteristic. Knowing Murat and knowing Ney, he paid no attention.

The attack on the bridge and the high ground was a complete success, and the red-headed Marshal (his men called him *le rougeaud*) led it in person, in his full-dress marshal's uniform with the Star of the Legion of Honour blazing on his breast.

During all this scuffling and skirmishing and manoeuvring Napoleon rode with his staff and his Chasseurs of the Guard into the field of fire of an Austrian field-gun battery, and refused to retire. Lannes, who was never afraid of the Emperor, seized the bridle of his charger and bundled him by force out of range.

So ended the first stage of the triple campaign. The first Austrian army had been eliminated to a man; there remained the second, the mixed Austro-Russian army which was presumably somewhere near Vienna; and the third, the reserves of Russia, somewhere in the east.

The 400-mile march from the camps on the coast to the capture of Ulm was a mathematical and administrative triumph for Napoleon and Berthier. On only two occasions did a corps cross the line of march of another corps, and one of these occasions was unavoidable the moment the vital decision was taken to turn north-east from the Rhine. For the only way in which the turn could be masked was by throwing out the cavalry screen, and that could only be done by sending Murat across the lines of Ney and Lannes. The second crossing is harder to understand, and certainly seems unnecessary from a tactical point of view. In the great wheel round behind Mack, Marmont was brought across the lines of Davout, and Davout was sent south-eastwards and outwards (that is to say, he was taken off the encircling movement), whereas it would have been much simpler to have made Davout continue the wheel and sent Marmont, being outside him, off to the south-east. The only reasonable explanation is that Napoleon trusted Davout on a semi-independent command rather than Marmont with his mixed and somewhat unreliable Corps.

Whether this is the case or not, the whole manoeuvre was a triumph of those two men with their maps and their compasses and their logarithms and their hours and hours of incessant toil in bivouac, billet, carriage, and office. It was a stupendous feat to arrange those daily marches for seven corps of 30,000 or 40,000 men apiece, plus the Guard, plus the Reserve Cavalry, so that no units clashed, or took the wrong road, or crossed each other, or got fatally separated, or arrived at the wrong place, especially as the weather had broken at about the time of the arrival on the Rhine. Intense cold at night was accompanied by wind and driving sleet, and the roads were already getting muddy. No wonder Mack was bewildered. The New Warfare was reaching its height of efficiency already, and Mack did not even know that it existed.

The instant that the first Austrian army had been engulfed and abolished as completely as if it had never existed, the second task was tackled. Not an instant was lost. There was no hour to waste on congratulations or reviews or holidays. The huge, concentrated army was uncoiled, hurried back on to the road, and spread out again in a colossal arc for the drive on Vienna.

The weather was vile and went on being vile, the men were tired after the incessant marching of seven weeks, during which almost five hundred miles had been covered, the roads were heavy and rations scarce. Only the Imperial Guard had commissariat wagons, and the rest of the army fed itself on the country as best it could and, after Murat's cavalry-men had gone on ahead, there was not much left in the barns and byres for the weary line regiments. It was an exceptionally severe October with sleet, snow, and often high winds. On the 16th, for instance, the night was so bad that sentries were not posted, and even the artillery was left unguarded. There was an incessant struggling for billets, and blood was often shed in the hunt for rations. On one occasion Oudinot's grenadiers organized a ration hunt, sword in hand, and about fifty men were killed that night. But there was little to collect, even sword in hand, when the Inspector-General of Artillery, with plenty of horses and carts at his disposal, had to live for six days on potatoes and a hunk of pork. There were incessant temporary desertions and a great deal of looting. But at the first sound of fighting the men rallied to the nearest unit, and the advance went on furiously.

Berthier crouched over his maps, and now his task was becoming almost incredibly difficult. For the corps had to be spread out over a huge frontage in order to protect the flanks of the advance, and yet they had to be sufficiently under the hand of the Chief-of-Staff to concentrate, almost at a moment's notice, whenever the enemy made a stand. Ney, the bilingual speaker of German and French, was despatched to Innsbruck and the Tyrol to keep in check the Austrian Archduke John. Bernadotte entered Munich (greatly to the indignation of Davout, who complained to Napoleon that the capture of Munich should have fallen to him), and then pushed on to Salzburg. Marmont was detached altogether from the main army and sent off in a south-westerly direction towards Graz to cover the main army against attacks from South Hungary, and to establish contact with Masséna, who was marching up with 50,000 men from North Italy. On the extreme left a new corps was formed, given to Mortier, and pushed across the Danube, where it was caught isolated by the Russian Kutusov and roughly handled. Then followed another inexplicable cross-over of the lines of march, for Bernadotte was brought from the right wing across the lines of Marmont, Davout, Soult, and Lannes, to the extreme left of the army. The remainder with the Guard and the Cavalry pounced on Vienna, leaving behind them a devastated, burnt, and pillaged countryside. The rate of march from Boulogne was beginning to tell, and the Danube valley was a mass of stragglers and looters. Only the Guard maintained its splendid appearance, but then the Guard had supply-wagons, and six-horse teams for even the smallest limber. Already the Guard was detested throughout the rest of the army, which complained that it was always given the best billets, the best food, and the least fighting.

There was no resistance at Vienna, for the enemy had gone, and once more the corps began to spread out. Davout went east to Pressburg, Bernadotte north-north-west to Iglau, and only Soult, Lannes, the Guard, and the Cavalry were available to push northwards into the dismal country of Moravia to catch the second combined Austro-Russian army before the third, the reserve Russian and the Austrian Archduke Charles, could join it.

But before any army can push northwards out of Vienna, the Danube has to be crossed, and the only route for Napoleon was by a great wooden bridge at Spitz, and the bridge was mined by the Austrians, and the northern end held by Austrian infantry, artillery, and engineers. At the first sign of an attack the bridge would be blown skyhigh, and invaluable weeks wasted, and the third Austro-Russian army would have time to come up. The vital problem was how to capture the bridge intact. The problem was solved by two of the Gascon Marshals. Murat and Lannes, combining for once, put on their best uniforms with their ostrich feathers, and their blazing stars, and their red morocco boots, their diamond-hilted swords, and their gold-embroidered tunics, and rode out together, alone, without an escort, to the bridge. The Austrian garrison was not unnaturally astonished at this amazing sight, and not a shot was fired as the two horsemen rode coolly across the bridge. Soon the garrison realized that two of the already famous Marshals were approaching, and they pressed forward to have a look at these redoubtable young men, who had made history in Italy and Egypt and Syria. The Austrian commander was old Prince Auersperg, and he came forward to ask the meaning of this brilliant arrival. The Gascons pretended to be surprised.

'Haven't you heard of the armistice?' they inquired, 'it has just been signed, and by the terms of it the bridge has been handed over to us.

Prince Auersperg was astonished and suspicious, and a lot of arguing took place. Meanwhile a party of French grenadiers, commanded by Oudinot, was creeping up under cover towards the French end of the bridge and, behind a small screen of men, sappers hastily uncoupled the fuses at that end, and threw them into the river. But there were still the explosives and the batteries at the Austrian end to be dealt with. Luckily Prince Auersperg was very old and very, very foolish. He had just agreed to retire from the bridgehead when an Austrian sergeant spotted Oudinot's grenadiers. The sergeant, with a great deal more sense than his commander, ordered his men to fire on the Marshals. Murat brilliantly remarked, 'Is this your famous Austrian discipline, where sergeants countermand the orders of generals?' The Prince, greatly hurt at this suggestion, put the sergeant under arrest. Then an Austrian gunner, also of an independent turn of mind, started to lay his gun at the Marshals. Lannes promptly countered this by sitting down on the gun-barrel. Oudinot's grenadiers then started to advance across the bridge, and even Prince Auersperg's suspicions began to be aroused. But once again the Marshals had their answer ready. 'They are not advancing at all,' they said, 'but the weather is so cold that they are marking time to keep their feet warm.' While the Prince was digesting this one, Oudinot came over at the double and the trick was won, and the two flamboyant Marshals rode back to Vienna for dinner.

But although the trick had been won, Napoleon's position was exceedingly dangerous. The *Grande Armée* was now scattered in a colossal horse-shoe from Iglau in the north, east fifty miles to Brünn, south eighty miles to Pressburg, south-west a hundred miles to the passes of Styria where Marmont was on guard, west again eighty miles to Ney in Carinthia, and two hundred more to Augereau in distant Swabia. Masséna, coming up from Italy, ought to have been by this time in touch either

with Ney or Marmont, but was still dallying, far away
to the south of the Carnic Alps. Masséna was finding the
territory of Venice so profitable a land to loot, that he was
reluctant to exchange it for the poor and sterile uplands
that lay between him and Vienna. The centre of the impending maelstrom was at Brünn, and there lay the
Emperor himself, but he had only 40,000 men under his
hand and north-east of him were the Emperors of
Austria and Russia with 90,000 men, and Bennigsen was
coming up from the east to join them, and the Archduke
Charles was on his way with another army, and at any
moment English diplomacy and cash might bring the
famous Prussians into the field across the five hundred
miles which lay between Brünn and the Rhine. Murat
and Soult began to lose their nerve, and were strongly in
favour of a retreat, but neither of them fancied the task
of putting the case to the Emperor, so they persuaded
Lannes, because he notoriously feared Napoleon least, to
put the case for them. Lannes did so, but with great
reluctance. Napoleon was more puzzled than angry, and
re-marked shrewdly, 'This is the first time that Lannes has
ever advised retreat.' Soult obsequiously agreed that it was
both unusual and inexplicable. Whereupon Lannes, with
some justification, instantly lost his temper and challenged
Soult to a duel, a challenge which Soult ignored.

The two Emperors of Austria and Russia, with their
professional soldier Kutusov, had only to wait for
Bennigsen and young Charles and the game was in their
hands. But prestige is a terrible malady, and the prestige of
two dynasties, Romanov and Hapsburg, had to be maintained against the pretensions of the dirty little Corsican
usurper, and the Allied Emperors decided that they, and
Kutusov, should stand and fight near the squalid Moravian
village of Austerlitz. But the Divine Right of Emperors
is a poor substitute on the day of battle for a knowledge
of distances, and Bernadotte came in from Iglau, and
Davout's iron discipline and training raced his Corps

seventy miles in forty-four hours from Pressburg to hold the right of the line. The hereditary Emperors saved their prestige on that day, December 2nd, 1805, for they stood and fought. But their prestige cost them 30,000 men and almost all their artillery and all their baggage and it lost the war and it destroyed the Third Coalition and it killed young Pitt, who rolled up the map of Europe in the far-off watering-town of Bath, and turned his face to the wall.

In this thunderclap of a battle, Lannes, who had chosen the very morning of the battle to repeat his challenge to Soult, held the left; Davout, after all his marching, stubbornly held the right and retreated very slowly before the main Austro-Russian attack, until the moment came when Napoleon turned to Soult in the centre and said, 'How long will it take you to get up that hill over there?'

'Twenty minutes, Sire,' replied Soult.

'Ah! Then we can give them another quarter of an hour,' said Napoleon looking at his watch. For another fifteen minutes Davout held on while the great masses in the French centre stood, masked from the enemy, motionless, waiting. Then the Emperor waved his arm, the lock-gates were opened, and Soult and Oudinot and Bernadotte, with Bessières and the Guard in reserve, went forward. In twenty minutes the hill was captured and the second greatest tactical masterpiece in history (Hannibal's Cannae being the first) was well on the way to completion, so closely to the minute-hand of the watch did Napoleon design, Berthier transmit, and the Marshals execute.

But even after this triumphant day the Marshals found occasion for quarrelling and bad temper. Davout went about suggesting that Bernadotte had lacked energy in pursuit, while Bernadotte complained bitterly that Berthier had deliberately kept him short of cavalry, and Soult officiously reported Davout for arriving late, and Murat had some complaints to lodge about Lannes. The Emperor was kept busy smoothing over difficulties between them, but he

himself was unintentionally responsible for the worst outbreak of all. For in the bulletin of victory, Napoleon's only
mention of Lannes' Corps was that it had advanced as if
on parade. That fiery commander, who had expected at
least a paragraph on the subject of his stout holding of the
left while the great stroke was maturing in the centre,
immediately departed full-tilt for Paris without a word
or a by-your-leave. Murat, the fellow-Gascon and cham-
pion horseman, was despatched in pursuit, but failed to
catch him up, and there is no record of Lannes being
reprimanded for this amazing conduct. Lannes hardly
drew rein between the field of Austerlitz and his native
village of Lectoure in Gascony, where he remained for
some time, spending his money royally on the simple
friends of his youth.

Soult, who was extremely anxious that his part in the
battle should not be overlooked, melted down captured
cannons and sent 49,000 pounds of bronze to Napoleon
in repayment of the capital and interest of the bronze borrowed for the column of the *Grande Armée* at Boulogne.
Soult, indeed, was inclined to regard the battle as his own
personal triumph, and hinted that if, at any time, there
were to be any titles, he would have no particular objec-
tion to being called the Count, or Marquis, or Duke, of
Austerlitz.

The second stage in the campaign was over, finished
with the same spectacular abruptness as the first, and the
third and last of the three armies began to think better of
the situation. Muscovy's unknown reserves, which the
proud Emperors should have waited for, might have
turned the scale. Now it was too late, so they went home
instead. Napoleon rode back to Vienna, and the sons of the
innkeepers and barrel-coopers and flower-sellers swaggered and clinked in the corridors of the Imperial
Schönbrunn.

* * *

At the date of the battle of Austerlitz Napoleon was thirty-six, Berthier fifty-two, Bernadotte forty-two, Davout thirty-five, Soult thirty-six, Lannes thirty-six, Bessières thirty-seven, Murat thirty-eight, and Mortier thirty-seven, the average age being thirty-nine.

Kutusov was sixty.

CHAPTER IX

JENA AND AUERSTÄDT

THE Marshals had made themselves at home in Schönbrunn, and had mingled with the brilliancies of the Imperial Court. But their only titles to match against the Peers of Austria were a hundred exploits upon battlefields, and the new Emperor began to toy with the idea of making a new aristocracy. Hapsburg and Romanov could not do much in the way of fighting, but at least they were surrounded with princes and dukes and barons. The victory at Austerlitz, which had rolled up Pitt's map of Europe, had unrolled Napoleon's, and there were plenty of duchies and princedoms to play with. And there were also eighteen quarrelsome Marshals to keep in order. They would appreciate titles, and their wives would appreciate titles, and what duke in his senses would contemplate a return to Bourbonism if it entailed the instant loss of his dukedom? A new aristocracy would consolidate the throne and the new regime, and might keep the Marshals in order for a year or two. Besides, Austerlitz was bringing numbers of the old aristocracy back to France clamouring for places, not in the Imperial Army but at the Imperial Court, and the fighting men would look askance at the titled *embusqués*.

'I opened my armies to them,' said Napoleon bitterly, 'and not one came forward. I opened my ante-chambers and they crowded in.'

But the change to a new social hierarchy would have to be done carefully, and no one knew this better than the Emperor.

Murat, of course, had to come first. Brother Joseph had got the Crown of Naples, and Sister Caroline was screaming with jealousy, so Murat was made Grand Duke of Berg and Cleves, a small Rhineland state, and Caroline became a Grand-Duchess. It was not so good as a throne, but at least it was a spoke in Sister Pauline's wheel, for Pauline was only a mere duchess, and that was nothing compared with a Grand-Duchess.

Murat was enchanted, not so much with Berg, which was a tiny little principality, but rather with the opportunity of designing some new uniforms. Murat loved designing uniforms. The livery colours of the Duchy were gold and white and amaranth, a range which afforded good scope for inventiveness. It was two years since Murat had become a Marshal, and a year since he had been appointed Senator, Prince, and Grand Admiral of France. All these had given him fine scope for uniform-designing (although he had allowed the famous painter, Jacques Louis David, to design him an Admiral's uniform consisting of doublet and hose, a sweeping mantle, a plumed cap, and a sword with a gold sheath), but a year was a long time, and the Grand-Duchy came at the right moment.

After Murat came Berthier, with the Princedom of Neufchâtel. So far so good. The Chief-of-Staff was a man apart. He was the senior Marshal by rank and by age and he was admitted by all to be the Emperor's right-hand man when it came to campaigning. But the Corps-Commanders watched each other like hawks until, on June 5th, 1806, they were stunned into apoplectic fury by the news that two new princes had been created,

Talleyrand and Bernadotte. Nobody minded Talleyrand. He was only a lame ex-parson, of whom Lannes said that if he was sharply kicked behind while talking to you, his face would never betray the indignity. Besides he was a civilian. But Bernadotte! The man who lurked at home while Murat was throwing the deputies out of the Orangerie, and Lannes was holding the Tuileries; the man who was intriguing with the de Staël woman while Masséna was standing immovable in the gates of Genoa; the man whose name was linked with five separate plots against Napoleon while the six Corps-Commanders were welding into an army, with unceasing toil, the seven great corps which marched from the dull mists of the English Channel to the splendid sun of Austerlitz. It was utterly intolerable, and to those simple, unpolitical souls it was inexplicable. They knew nothing of politics, and Bernadotte's Prince-dom was a political one. For even now the most bigoted Republicans might not be completely reconciled to the Empire. Marshal Bernadotte might still be a Jacobin at heart, dreaming of '93 and the Sambre-et-Meuse, and longing for the return from America of his old friend Moreau. But His Highness the Marshal-Prince and Duke of Ponte-Corvo, Our Cousin, could not turn back. He must irrevocably be an Imperialist. There could be no more Jacobinism for him. It was for more than a hand-ful of silver that Bernadotte left his old principles – the revenues of Ponte-Corvo were about a million francs – and more than a riband to stick in his coat, but the idea was the same. And so on June 5th, 1806, the last of the Revolutionary generals was gently gathered into the Im-perial fold. The Emperor was rid of them all. Hoche and Marceau and Joubert and Desaix and Kléber were dead. Kellermann of Valmy and Jourdan of Fleurus were Imperial Marshals, Moreau and Dumouriez were in exile, Pichegru had strangled himself in a prison-cell, and Bernadotte was His Highness the Marshal-Prince and Duke of Ponte-Corvo.

Of all the Marshals who now had to give precedence to the Prince of Ponte-Corvo, none was so furious as Davout. Davout had married a sister-in-law of the exquisite Pauline Bonaparte, and thus considered himself just as closely related to the Emperor as the man who had married the sister-in-law of the wretched Joseph. And Davout was by now making a great parade of his devotion to Napoleon; whereas the other had for years paraded his indifference, if not his active opposition. There was also that business of the overlooking window from which Policeman Davout, now only a Marshal, had tried to get evidence to convict Traitor Bernadotte, now Prince of Ponte-Corvo. And Davout was of the old gentry, and Bernadotte was a potty little attorney's son. After June 5th, 1806, Davout usually referred to his colleague as 'Le misérable Ponte-Corvo,' and the hatred between them was more bitter than ever.

But there was heavier work afoot than bickering over titles. Prussia, the Prussia of Frederick the Great, of the Seven Years' War, of Rossbach, Leuthen, and Silesia, was turning over in its sleep at last. These French were getting a bit above themselves, simply because they had beaten once or twice the Austrians, whom everybody, except the Italians, of course, had always beaten. It was high time that they learnt a lesson from soldiers who really were soldiers. And in all Europe there was no military machine to compare with the iron Infantry of Prussia, the legacy of Frederick, led by the veteran generals who had actually served with that great man himself. It was true that Ulm and Austerlitz had been a bit of a shock, but then what are effeminate Austrians and barbarian Russians? So in September, 1806, Prussia declared war on France, and orders were sent throughout the country from Berlin to race the great machine into position. Actually, the racing did not materialize. There was rather more creaking and groaning than had been anticipated, and rather less oil in the cogs, but nevertheless 150,000 invincibles were eventually hoisted and tugged into line near Weimar, north of the wooded hills of Thuringia, by the beginning of October, 1806.

The French were lying in cantonments in South Germany, recuperating after the terrific exertions of 1805, when war was declared. Six of the seven Ulm Corps were there – Marmont with the Second was busy governing Dalmatia – mustering 170,000 men, and the 20,000 men of the Guard were being scampered down from Paris in relays of four-horse wagons. Lannes was still sulking in Gascony and old Lefèbvre was leading the Fifth Corps in his absence.

In the first days of October Davout had to give up his waltzing, an art to which he was passionately devoted, for the Army began to move, and a new phase in the art of warfare began. For this was the first occasion on which Napoleon used what is sometimes called the *'bataillon carré,* and sometimes the 'lozenge formation'. It is easiest explained by a diagram (see overleaf).

A huge fan of light horsemen rode in front, picking up information about the enemy, and preventing the enemy from doing the same, while the lozenge marched behind, on a front of sixty or seventy miles, and as far as possible on different roads. The beauty of the formation was that it was able to turn at a moment's notice at any angle. Thus, if the cavalry reported that the bulk of the enemy was on the left, each unit turned left, and the left-wing corps became the leader, what had been the leader became the right-wing, what had been the right-wing became the reserve, and what had been the reserve became the left. And, of course, *vice versa.*

On September 28th, 1806, the Emperor arrived from Paris at Mainz to take command of the Army. It was high time that he arrived, for even the greatest may make mistakes, and Napoleon had given the temporary supreme command of the Army to Berthier, had forgotten that he had done so, had then given it to Murat, and forgotten

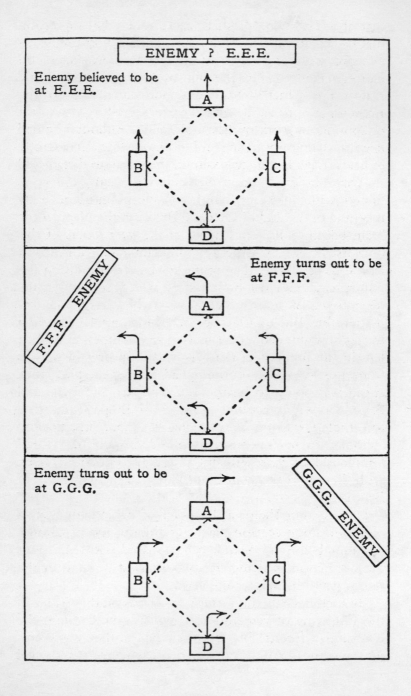

ENEMY ? E.E.E.

Enemy believed to be at E.E.E.

A

B   C

D

F.F.F. ENEMY

Enemy turns out to be at F.F.F.

A

B   C

D

Enemy turns out to be at G.G.G.

G.G.G. ENEMY

A

B   C

D

that also. The two Marshals, each under the impression that he was in supreme command, had been issuing separate orders for some little time. Furthermore, Napoleon had expected to find Berthier at Mainz, but for some reason the Chief-of-Staff was not there, and so the Emperor at once sat down and performed the greatest feat of continuous work of his whole career. Although he had been travelling from Paris and working almost incessantly in his carriage for thirty-six hours, he began to dictate and to write orders at noon on September 29th, and continued with an occasional hour's sleep until the early morning of the 2nd of October. But even the Napoleonic brain began to flag, and many of the later letters of this outburst of energy were almost incoherent. Thus, for at least four days at the beginning of the Jena campaign the unfortunate Corps-Commanders were receiving three separate sets of orders, all contradictory and many incomprehensible. But by October 5th things were beginning to get straightened out. On that day Lannes arrived at last, in the sunniest of tempers, and took over his Corps from Lefèbvre as if nothing had happened. The work ahead was going to be too strenuous for Lefèbvre, and Napoleon wrote tactfully to him, 'The Emperor, desiring to employ you more particularly about his person, appoints you to the command of a division of his Guard.' Simple old Lefèbvre was just as delighted as he had been with the gift of the sword on the day of the *coup d'état* of Brumaire.

Lannes chose Victor as his chief-of-staff. Victor was an old companion of Bonaparte's at Toulon, and of Lannes' at Montebello and Marengo. He shared with Marmont the distinction of being the two angriest generals in the Army at not being created Marshals.

By October 8th, the *Grande Armeé* was on the road, and the vast army of veterans went pouring up through the Thuringian forests. That autumn the weather was glorious, and the terrific rain-storm of September 30th had made little impression on the summer-hardened country-side except that it had laid the dust. The guns rattled along over the firm surface of the sun-baked roads. The country was rich in provisions and forage, and 190,000 men, cheerful, confident, with implicit belief that their leader could overthrow even the far-famed infantry of Prussia, averaged eighteen or twenty miles a day with easy regularity. Lannes averaged seventeen miles a day for five days and fought three engagements while doing so, and Davout marched fifty-four miles in forty-eight hours. By October 13th, 1806, the first trick had been won, for the Emperor had laid this great army across the left flank of the Prussians, just as silently and swiftly as he had laid it across the flank of Mack the year before. All that remained now was to defeat them.

The great marching had, as at Ulm, won the campaign before a shot was fired, and not even bad blundering by the French could have saved the Prussians. That this is clear is proved by the blunders which actually were committed on the day of the battle. Napoleon himself had no idea of the real position or strength of the enemy. All he knew was that there were Prussians in front of him, and he determined to attack on the following morning, October 14th. Throughout the night of the 13th the Corps of Lannes and the Imperial Guard marched up on to the little plateau of the Landgrafenberg outside Jena, and were there massed all night so closely that the men stood shoulder to shoulder and breast to knapsack. By all the rules of war this great concentration should have been blasted away before it could move by the Prussian artillery at the first light of dawn. But it so chanced that the morning of the 14th broke foggy, and the French were able to deploy unmolested. It was an incredibly lucky chance. The next to blunder was Ney. Ney had orders to bring the Sixth Corps into line between Lannes in the centre and Soult on the right, but it is obvious that he did not read his orders. The main body of the Sixth Corps, struggling through the night of darkness and fog, only reached Jena at dawn, and its advance-guard, under the dashing young Colbert, was on the road behind Lannes. Ney himself, who had spent the night reconnoitring with Napoleon, Lannes, and Berthier, waited near the Land-grafenberg for his men in an agony of impatience. For the hours were passing and Lannes seemed to be doing all the fighting himself, and would gain all the glory. At nine o'clock in the morning Ney could stand it no longer, and chancing to find Colbert in the mist, he rushed him into the line. But the red-headed Marshal was so wildly impatient that, instead of glancing at his orders, he went like a bull at the part of the line that was nearest to him. This was Lannes' left, between Lannes and Augereau, and not as it should have been, in the gap between Lannes and Soult. Worse was to follow. Ney's handful not only charged into the wrong place, but it charged too far. The mist suddenly rose, and there, within musket-range, were the serried ranks of the Prussian infantry. 'The wine is drawn,' said Ney to Colbert with a shrug, 'and we must drink it.' And the two cavalrymen led a desperate charge and managed to extricate themselves. In the meanwhile Ney's main body came pounding up from Jena, and its Corps-Commander could not be found. It was some hours before one of the A.D.C.'s had the common sense to do what he ought to have done at first and looked for Ney in the front line.

By one o'clock Soult, on the right, had worked his way round the Prussian left, Ney's infantry was in line, Murat was massed with all his squadrons behind the Guard, and Augereau was easily holding the Saxons on the left. In Napoleon's words 'the battle was ripe'. The whole line went forward, and two hours later, at about three o'clock, there were no more Prussian battalions standing on the battlefield, and Murat took up the running.

But the direct frontal attack on the narrow front of Jena was not the whole of Napoleon's plan for the discomfiture of the Prussians. They were to be not merely defeated. They were to be destroyed in a single day. And so while the main action was being fought on the plateau above Jena, the design was that Bernadotte's Corps was to swing far round the Prussians' left by way of Dornburg, and, beyond him again, Davout was to swing even further still by way of Naumburg, so that by the time the Prussians had been hammered on the Landgrafenberg plateau they would find two fresh corps, in all nearly 50,000 men, sweeping in upon their flank and rear. Napoleon's last instructions to Davout were, 'Go by Naumburg. If Bernadotte is with you, you might march together, but the Emperor hopes that he will be in position at Dornburg.' It so happened that Bernadotte was with Davout, and saw this letter, but decided to keep to his original order and push on to Dornburg.

But there was one miscalculation in the Emperor's plans and when, like a good husband, he sat down after the battle and wrote to Joséphine that he had done some fine manoeuvring against the Prussians, he did not know that the main forces of the enemy had not been in front of him on the plateau at all. Before the battle of Jena began, the main strength of Prussia and the King and the aged Commander, the Duke of Brunswick, had slipped away and headed north-east, so that when Davout came down from the north to turn defeat into annihilation, he found instead that his 27,000 were face to face with 60,000 Prussians. There was nothing for it but to stand and fight. All that day Davout, with his three famous Divisional-Commanders, already known as the Three Immortals, Gudin, Friant, and Morand, held out near the little village of Auerstädt, clinging desperately to his line, galloping from square to square of his battered infantry, with his face powder-blackened, his uniform covered with blood, his hat shot off, and hoping against hope throughout that interminable day that at any moment he might hear the thunder of Bernadotte's artillery, and see the skirmishers of Bernadotte's battalions come crowding through the pine-woods. But Bernadotte did not come.

Strategists say that the Prince of Ponte-Corvo was right to make for Dornburg. Apologists maintain that he got no message from Davout asking for help. Disciplinarians say that he was right to obey the letter of his orders. But the essential point of the whole controversy is, Did Bernadotte on October 14th hear the sound of the guns of Auerstädt? If he spent the whole of that day without the faintest idea that 80,000 men were tearing each other to pieces not more than seven miles away, then, of course, he was entirely justified in pushing on. But if he knew that there was a desperate battle in progress to the north, it was inexcusable not to tear up his written orders and march to the sound of the guns. At 4 p.m. he had reached Apolda, after drifting lazily along at the rate of eight miles in six hours. Apolda is six and a half miles from Auerstädt. There is no doubt that the sound of artillery fire travels extraordinary distances in certain conditions, and very short distances in other conditions. It is impossible to say that if a gun fired in Derbyshire is audible ten miles away, it is therefore audible ten miles away if fired in Scotland. The sound of the heavy artillery bombardment in the weeks preceding the third battle of Ypres in July, 1917, were clearly audible at St. Albans, a hundred and thirty miles away, but not audible at all at certain places in Sussex, eighty miles nearer.[1] October 14th, 1806, was undoubtedly foggy in the early morning, and this would have helped to deaden the sound. But it is difficult to believe that Bernadotte could have spent that entire day halfway between two battles and yet heard the sound of neither. But whether Bernadotte, during his leisurely march on that day, was in a freakish zone of silence, or

---

[1] *I have myself seen, on a windless night in spring, the sky blazing with the flashes of the French artillery in the great battle for the Chemin des Dames in 1917 only thirty miles away, and yet not the faintest sound was audible.*

the little room from which Davout had spied upon him in 1801 was still rankling in the Gascon's mind, the fact remains that Bernadotte took no part in the actions either of Jena or Auerstädt. One of Davout's A.D.C.'s says that he found Bernadotte at half-past four on that afternoon seated on his horse, surrounded by his staff and a cavalry escort, on some high ground on the left bank of the Saale. It was about four miles and a half from Auerstädt. The A.D.C.'s message was to implore him to take up the pursuit of the retreating enemy. Davout's Corps was exhausted, and a third of his horses were out of action.

'Tell your Marshal not to be afraid,' replied Bernadotte, 'I shall be there.'

Considering all the circumstances, it was not a tactful message and it only made Davout's hatred of *'Le misérable Ponte-Corvo'* more profound, more tenacious, more bitter.

Napoleon was aghast at the discovery of what had happened. A blunder of his own had been redeemed by one of the Marshals. It was so much better for his prestige when it was the other way round, and he at once decided to treat Auerstädt as if it had been simply the right wing of the Jena battle. He described in his bulletin how well Davout had held the right and reprimanded Bernadotte for failing to come into action in the right centre. Auerstädt is the only one of the great Napoleonic battles which is not upon the Arc de Triomphe.

But if Davout received few laurels from Napoleon, he was henceforward a different man in the eyes of the Army. The Marshal who had got his baton by the backstairs route, had proved himself on the field of battle to be as brilliant a tactician as Ney, as dogged as Masséna, and as brave as Murat or Lannes. From October 14th, 1806, Davout was still hated by most, but he was respected by all.

***

If Napoleon had miscalculated about the whereabouts of the Prussians at Jena, he made no mistake about the subsequent proceedings. His original intention, to pin down the enemy's front while Davout and Bernadotte curled round on to his flank and rear, had failed. The routed columns had escaped. But not for long. For now Europe, appalled, was to watch the War Napoleonic at its most stupendous. Marengo in 1800 could not be followed up because the French troops were too exhausted; Austerlitz could not be followed up because the French troops were five hundred miles from the Rhine, and Prussian thunder-clouds were rolling up behind them and might explode into a storm at any moment. But after Jena the army was still fresh, the communications secure, and the Rhine within reach. On the very evening of the two battles of Jena and Auerstädt, Napoleon hurled his army north-wards in the greatest sustained pursuit in history. The pursuit is sometimes called the Pursuit of the Three Marshals, because Murat, Bernadotte, and Soult were in at the death. But it started with all of them. Ney, whose Boulogne ideas of a Te Deum upon the field on the evening of a bat-tle were being rudely shattered, rushed off with his fresh infantry to Weimar, and found to his annoyance that Murat had got there before him and had installed himself in the Grand Ducal Palace. After finding the time for a brief but brisk quarrel, Ney spent the night in an inn, and next morning dashed on to Erfurt. Again Murat was there first, and his horsemen were sitting in a cir-cle round the town waiting for Ney's infantry and guns to make Marshal Mollendorf, who was inside with 14,000 men, surrender. As soon as Mollendorf did so, Murat claimed all the credit. There was another quick quarrel and once more Murat disappeared into the north. Ney pushed on to Magdeburg, the great fortress, and to his infinite fury found that the intolerable cavalryman was there too, riding round and round the town and pretend-ing that he could capture it with light hussars. Fortunately there was other work for the cavalry and the two colleagues parted, not a moment too soon for either of them. Ney, without siege-guns, bluffed Magdeburg and its garrison of 22,000 men into surrender in eighteen days. He spent part of this time in the composition of a long letter to the Emperor in which he tried hard to explain away his peculiar conduct at Jena.

Lannes made for Berlin and terrified the Governor of the fortress of Spandau into surrender by the violence of his language. Bernadotte, his Corps as fresh as daisies after its quiet, pastoral day on October 14th, stormed Halle, crossed the Elbe and, picking up Lannes on the way, followed Murat north-east towards Stettin. Every day Lannes and Murat wrote to the Emperor to lodge complaints against each other, and the Emperor sent back a ceaseless flow of tactful, smoothing, complimentary despatches. But though Lannes and Murat quarrelled with each other on paper, they did not for one moment slacken off the furious pursuit. Von Hohenlohe, toiling away with his remnant, was caught by the light cavalry at Prenzlau and surrendered with 10,000 men, and the brilliant young Lasalle impertinently galloped up to the fortress of Stettin, planted an empty wagon upon a hill to represent his siege-train, and summoned the eighty-year-old Governor to surrender. This he did with 5,000 men.

The pursuit then turned west, picked up Soult, who had been doing a steady sixteen miles a day for weeks, and chased Blücher and the Duke of Weimar towards Lübeck, their last refuge, on the frontier of Denmark.

Meanwhile Mortier was coming up hot-foot from Frankfurt in the west; Davout, allotted the place of honour in the entry into Berlin on account of Auerstädt, led his Corps down the Unter Den Linden to the *Ça Ira* and the *Marseillaise* (Bessières' Guard, more refined, entered to the music of Gluck's *Iphigénie*), and then went north and captured Küstrin, and then wheeled east to Posen and thence towards

Warsaw; Lannes turned east to Thorn, and was followed by Augereau.

On November 6th Blücher surrendered in Lübeck, and the mighty machine of Frederick the Great had vanished. There was not a single man, horse, or gun left. Twenty-three days had done the entire trick, and Murat wrote to the Emperor that the fighting was over for lack of opponents.

A pleasant incident of these wild days was the capture by Augereau, lock, stock, and barrel, of the entire battalion of Prussian Guards from which he had deserted a score of years before in order to become a Dresden dancing-master. The colonel, the second-in-command, and the regimental sergeant-major were still the same, and they found it a little difficult to recognize their old trooper in the blazing, bemedalled Marshal of France. Augereau characteristically gave the sergeant-major twenty-five louis, and distributed a couple of louis apiece to every man who had served in the regiment with him.

A less picturesque incident, but a much more important one, took place at Lübeck when Bernadotte captured a number of Swedes and behaved to them with the habitual courtesy and kindness that he showed to all prisoners. The Swedes were sent to their homes and carried with them a vivid and grateful recollection of the big handsome Gascon with his glittering eyes and his hair floating in the wind. Bernadotte never did a better stroke for himself than when he befriended these men.

***

So fell the Prussian Army, and Napoleon symbolically removed the sword of Frederick from the tomb in Potsdam.

***

At Jena, the Emperor was thirty-seven, Berthier fifty-three, Bernadotte forty-three, Davout thirty-six, Soult and Lannes and Ney thirty-seven, Bessières and Mortier thirty-eight, and Murat thirty-nine.

The Duke of Brunswick was seventy-one, Hohenlohe was sixty-one, Blücher sixty-four, and Mollendorf eighty-four.

***

During 1806 Marshal Masséna received the greatest defeat of his life. After sweeping into Naples at the head of a strong army to place King Joseph Bonaparte upon his new throne, the old smuggler settled down to a life of ease, luxury, and profit. For the blockade against England and English goods, though not in full force until the Berlin Decrees towards the end of the year, was sufficiently strong to make the sale of trading licences a very profitable business. Masséna threw himself into the trade with zest, and the money came pouring in. But the all-seeing eye was watching, and a despatch arrived from the Imperial Headquarters ordering King Joseph of Naples to inform the Marshal that three million francs, which he had secretly hidden in a bank in Livorno, had been confiscated. The King had not the nerve to face the cold, hard eye of Masséna, and he sent a general instead. The general received his orders at midnight, and, trembling in his shoes, he repaired to the vast, gloomy pile of the Acton Palace and knocked nervously at the Marshal's door. The Marshal came out after a long delay, wearing a cotton night-cap and a huge dressing-gown of green taffeta, and the perspiring general broke the news. With iron self-control Masséna restrained his temper, and said coldly, 'The Emperor thinks, then, that we are fighting to give a throne to this puppy of a king. I do not want the money for myself. I have been a private on five sous a day. But the Emperor has given us a position and the title of Marshal, and we must maintain them.'

Up to the end of his life Masséna mourned the loss of his Livorno millions.

CHAPTER X

HAPSBURG and Romanov had gone down at Austerlitz and Hohenzollern had gone down at Jena. But Romanov was up again, and Alexander's men were slowly coming west out of their steppes and marshes, and preparing for a campaign in the spring and summer of 1807. But Napoleon was the first commander who paid no attention to seasons, and he plunged into Poland in the early winter of 1806 to meet them, and by the end of November the outposts of the French and the Russian Armies were in touch with each other, thirty miles west of Warsaw. The main body of the Army, under Lannes, Davout, Soult, Augereau, Bernadotte, and Ney, had a fairly good march through the sand of Brandenburg and Pomerania as far as Posen, although Lannes complained to the Emperor that the sand was worse than Syria. But east of Posen conditions changed abruptly for the worse. The glowing splendour of the Polish autumn, with the dark golden chestnut-leaves and the wild pear's vermilion *mèche* against the deep holm-oaks and the scarlet apples and the last amber butterflies, had been at its height when the guns of Jena and Auerstädt were firing, and by the time that Murat, Grand-Duke of Berg, was curveting and prancing towards Warsaw, the rains were coming down in sheets.

119

Right up to the end of November the weather had been extraordinarily mild and there had been neither snow nor ice. Snow and ice would have been vastly preferable to the rains. For not even the main road from Posen to Warsaw was paved or ditched at the sides, and when it crossed the innumerable marshes it degenerated into a jumble of un-shaped tree-trunks lying side by side among the reeds.[1] East of Posen the rations grew scarcer, and the capture of a great drove of sucking pigs only gave the men dysentery, and the peasants escaped into the dark forests, driving their cattle before them. But on November 28th Murat rode into Warsaw and was received with raptures by the population.

Immediately the Marshals began to eye each other un-easily once again. The title-habit had not yet completely gripped them, but there was no doubt that titles were in the air. Any pre-Revolution sergeant had found it easy in '92 to spring into the command of a brigade or a division; but only those of transcendent merit had reached the Marshal's baton. And if their merits were so transcendent why should they not go higher still? Bernadotte and Berthier were Princes already, Murat a reigning Grand-Duke with a real, if somewhat small, Grand-Duchy. And what had Joseph Bonaparte ever done that he should be the King of Naples? And here was Poland, a fine, historic kingdom, longing for independence and for a real martial king to wield the sword of Jagellon and Sobieski. Murat was frankly entranced with the idea, and the population of Warsaw was frankly entranced with Murat, as he rode into the city at the head of his brilliant squadrons, with his nodding plumes and his gold lace. Prince Poniatowski presented him with the sword of Stephen Báthory, and Murat took it as an omen. Davout and Bernadotte scowled at each other, and Bernadotte began to study the customs,

---

[1] *These crossings must have been exactly the same as the great tree-trunk road which the German engineers drove across the heart of the Pripet in 1916.*

traditions, and habits of the country. Ney examined the interminable plains with a view to winning more glory, and Augereau, utterly disgusted with the remote chances of loot, and sighing for the diamonds of Italy, went to bed with rheumatism. Rheumatism has been the refuge of the old soldier throughout the ages. Soult kept his own counsel and said nothing. Lannes, blunt and disinterested, warned Napoleon that the Poles were untrustworthy soldiers, and Davout hanged some deserters, and the rank and file cursed the detestable beer and the billets that had to be shared with cows and pigs.

There was only time for a very little dalliance in the pleasant town of Warsaw, and the Army pushed on north-eastwards through the mud. It was a strange new country that the *Grande Armée* was entering now. The olive-groves and vineyards of Italy, and the wooded valley of the Danube, and the rich, pleasant lands of South Germany, seemed very far away. The towns were few and far between, the villages were small and incredibly dirty, the houses were little more than four walls of logs and a huge clay stove, and everywhere there were Jews. Jews owned the shops, Jews sold the vodka, Jews sold the dried fish, and Jews spoke the only language that was remotely like any language that any of them had heard before. The only words of Polish that the whole Army very quickly learnt were the word for 'bread' and the word for 'there isn't any'. The rations were mostly potatoes and water, and the light cavalry devoured most of what little there was. The infantry had to tie their boots on with ropes so as not to lose them in the mud, and muskets were carried on the back so that both arms were free to haul each leg in turn out of the mire.

The glittering Marshals sighed and envied Mortier snug in Hanover, and still more old Masséna basking in Italy, doing a nice business by selling licences to trade with England on the sly, and making love to every woman he met. The new Decrees of Berlin, tightening up the

Continental blockade against England, would be a great help to Masséna. The more stringent the regulations, the more money merchants would be ready to offer in bribes to the crafty old smuggler. As for the women of Poland, the ladies of Warsaw had been for a brief hour delicious – none could testify to that more gratefully than the Emperor – but out here in the mud and the slush and the vermin, young Lasalle thought of his adored boulevards, and Berthier longed for Madame de Visconti. It was a horrible country and a horrible winter and a horrible campaign. Nerves grew frayed. Ney lost his temper with Bessières and sent him an insulting letter via Bernadotte, who was commanding a Group of Corps, but Bernadotte tactfully suppressed it. Bernadotte himself complained bitterly that over and over again Berthier was antedating his orders so as to get him into a row with Napoleon by making him always appear to be late. And Soult was convinced that Berthier was deliberately blocking the promotion of his 'young men'.

Murat alone was happy, for to him these dreary stretches of mud were a potential kingdom, and he added a little Polish riding-cloak to his wardrobe, and white fur boots, and a huge fur pelisse, and several Polish hats to his already enormous collection of hats, and sent to Paris for twenty-seven thousand francs worth of ostrich-feathers. Another of his notions, designed to emphasize to the Poles that he was of a different class altogether from his colleagues, was to make his aides-de-camp discard their French uniforms and dress up in the livery of the Grand-Duchy of Berg. This livery was a very handsome affair, gold and white and amaranth, but the hot-headed young men of his staff strongly objected. They were soldiers of an Emperor, they said, not flunkeys of an innkeeper's son, and handsome young M. de Flahault led a mutiny of staff-officers against it. Young M. de Flahault, Talleyrand's illegitimate son, a pretty youth who sang like an angel, was not going to be dressed and undressed at the whim of

the Grand-Duke. Had it been the Grand-Duchess, all
Paris and all Berg knew that it would have been a different story. (Young de Flahault was afterwards the lover of
queen Hortense of Holland, and later still the grand-
father of the fifth Lord Lansdowne.)

But even Murat became a little depressed by the conditions, and one day remarked gaily to Soult, 'What a
climate, and what a ghastly country! Did those donkeys in
Warsaw really think that the Emperor was going to give
me their kingdom? A fine present that would have been.
I wouldn't have touched it at any price.'

In December frost and thaw alternated bewilderingly,
and Berthier practically lived with his thermometer in his
hand. Murat, leading the advance-guard, which consisted
of his own cavalry and the infantry of Soult's Corps,
watched his horses growing thinner and more miserable
every day, and he hit upon the device of using the infantry
to screen and save the cavalry. Soult was not unnaturally
furious. For ten consecutive days Murat had the infantry
on their feet from before dawn until they bivouacked after
10 p.m. But Soult had his revenge at the engagement of
Heilsberg, when Lasalle's hussars were routed and Lasalle,
Murat, and Soult had to take refuge in a square of half a
battalion of the 105th of the line. The square retired in
perfect order, Murat shouting gaily all the time in his
Gascon accent, *'Tenez bon mes amis, c'est le cas.'*[1] But when
Soult pointed to the plain that was covered with flying
cavalry and said to Murat, 'What about the merits of
cavalry and infantry now, my boy?' the Grand-Duke
abruptly stopped shouting and made no reply. It is, however, to his credit that, greatly though he disliked Soult
at all times, nevertheless, after this incident, he sent him
one of his famous gold-hilted swords as a present. The
struggling Army was surrounded day and night with a vast
cloud of half-starved, marauding soldiers. Even the iron

[1] *'Hold on, boys. That's the ticket.'*

discipline of Davout could not prevent his division from joining in the desperate search for food and vodka. The different corps never hesitated to steal the convoys of each other, and the Marshals winked at the thefts of their own men. A general, for example, of Soult's Corps captured by threats and violence a convoy of bread and wine destined for Ney, and thus reduced still further the fighting power of that Marshal's Corps, which had lost most of its horses, and was suffering from the incessant desertion of the new drafts of conscripts from the Lower Rhine.

The winter in Paris, on the other hand, was exceptionally brilliant. All the ministers gave receptions, and Caroline, Grand-Duchess of Berg, was queen of the day, and Madame la Maréchale Ney revealed an admirable talent for amateur theatricals.

***

The semi-starvation, the cold, the wet, and the mud, all could have been cheerfully endured by the Imperial soldier of the line, if his Emperor had been using his devotion to win great and glorious victories. But for the first time the Imperial Machine was slowing down. First there was the check at Heilsberg, then another at Pultusk. They were not first-class battles, but they showed that the Russians were more obstinate than the Austrians or the Prussians had been, and the Emperor, genius though he was, seemed to be finding the mud a little difficult. But at last he brought the Russian Army to bay near the village of Eylau on February 7th, 1807.

The country round Eylau is open and there are no hills. There are many lakes, but in that winter they were frozen so hard that cavalry could ride across them. The Russians mustered 75,000 men, and on the morning of the 8th Napoleon had only Augereau, Soult, Murat, and the Guard, in all 50,000 men. Davout was marching up on the right, and Ney had been called in from the north, but the orders to Bernadotte had gone astray and he was two days' march behind. In order to distract the Russians from Davout's flanking movement, the Emperor sent Augereau forward, and the Marshal, with a huge white scarf round his head to protect him from the cold, led his Corps to the attack. But a blinding snowstorm was driving from the east into the faces of the French, and Augereau lost direction. Instead of attacking straight ahead he went forward at a slant, and the Russian artillery caught him on the flank at point-blank range, and blew his Corps to pieces in a moment. Augereau himself was wounded. Never since Marengo had an army commanded by Napoleon been in such desperate straits, and it needed a desperate stroke to save it. Fortunately the man for such a stroke was at hand, and 100,000 men of the two armies watched one of the most famous spectacles in the whole history of warfare, when ninety squadrons of the Reserve Cavalry galloped across the snow to attack unbroken infantry and artillery, with Murat himself at their head, wearing his gold-embroidered uniform, his ostrich-feathers in his hat, with his saddle over a great leopard-skin, and carrying a gold-headed cane in his hand. The *Grande Armée* was saved from complete destruction. But on that day in the snow at Eylau it had lost 15,000 men, and it had met an enemy in open battle and failed to win. Even the iron-nerved Ney, who arrived on the evening of the battle and walked over the field next day, was shaken by the spectacle, and when the troops shouted *'Vive l'Empereur'*, as was their wont when Napoleon rode past, for the first time since the whirlwind days of 1796 there were voices in the ranks which cried also *'Vive la Paix'*, *'Vive la France et la Paix'*, and *'Du Pain et la Paix'*.

On the night of the battle Soult rode through the heavy snow to the Emperor's headquarters, and the two men went to the warehouse which was serving as the operating-theatre for Surgeon-General Larrey. The surgeons were working away furiously, in spite of the intense cold which made it difficult for them to hold their instruments, and every corner of the warehouse was heaped up with amputated arms and legs. The operating-table was given a hasty rub down, and the great maps laid upon it, and candles brought. Then Berthier and Murat came in, and the four men stooped over the table and talked in whispers. At last they decided to hold their ground for the next day at least, but as Soult was leaving the warehouse to go back to his Corps, the Emperor said to him, 'Marshal, the Russians have done us great harm.' Soult made the spirited reply, 'And we them. Our bullets are not made of cotton.' But as he rode back through the darkness, the words of the Emperor kept ringing in his ears, 'The Russians have done us great harm.'

It was at Eylau that, for the first time in the history of warfare, the artillery arm gained an ascendancy over the cavalry and infantry, an ascendancy that it has maintained ever since.

On that evening the Minister of Marine gave a superb ball in Paris to which fourteen hundred of the brightest and most brilliant were invited.

According to Madame Junot, another desperate struggle took place immediately after the battle between Murat on one side, and Augereau and Lannes on the other. That witty lady records that Augereau's language was positively terrific, that Lannes described the Grand-Duke of Berg to his Imperial brother-in-law as a scoundrel in pantomime dress with plumes like a dancing dog, as a mountebank, as a tight-rope dancer, and as a plumed cock, and that when the Emperor protested, Lannes, white with rage, transferred his attack and taunted Napoleon with having failed to defeat the Russians. But Lannes was not at Eylau at all. He was lying sick with fever in Warsaw. The story may, however, be true of Augereau. The language rings true.

For a week the Army remained near the fatal field of Eylau, and then slowly went back to cantonments in East

Prussia. Here Augereau's Corps was broken up, and the survivors of the snowstorm were distributed among the other corps. It was the first break-up of a corps of the Boulogne Army, and the men shook their heads, and thought that it was a disastrous omen. But their Emperor only paid attention to omens when they were favourable, like his Star, or the Sun of Austerlitz, and, while the men of the *Grande Armée* were wandering in their thousands among the dreary lakes of Masuria and the hideous desolation of East Prussia in search of scraps of food, Napoleon was calling up reinforcements from the south and west. Mortier went to Stralsund to watch Sweden; Masséna arrived, re-luctantly, from Italy, silently cursing Poland and the change from his beloved south; conscripts came marching across the Rhine and the Elbe; and Marshal Lefèbvre was given 25,000 men, a motley crew, mostly Germans and Poles, and ordered to capture the ancient city of Danzig.

There were three reasons for this last arrangement. Firstly, Danzig, even more than Stralsund, threatened Napoleon's long and difficult line of communications across North Germany. Secondly, its vast Hanseatic ware-houses were full of corn and oil and brandy and forage. And thirdly, the Emperor wanted to take his next cautious step in the making of a new aristocracy. Again it was the Republicans that he was thinking of, and he decided that if Lefèbvre could be induced to swallow a dukedom, then nobody else would have the faintest right to com-plain. It would cut the ground clean away from under the Republicans. But the trouble was that Lefèbvre had never performed any military exploit that would deserve a dukedom, nor was there the slightest prospect of the dear old man ever performing one, unless it was specially manufactured for him and, so to speak, handed to him on a plate. Danzig was a heaven-sent opportunity. All Lefèbvre had to do was to do nothing at all, and his men and guns would do the rest. But just in case the old man succeeded in achieving a hundred to one chance and failing to capture the town, Lannes and Oudinot were told off with their 'diabolical columns' of gre-nadiers to stand by. They were strictly forbidden to give advice, or to take part in the siege-operations, unless called upon by Lefèbvre. They accordingly acted as spectators. But even as a spectator Oudinot succeeded in getting wounded. Oudinot was wounded during the Napoleonic wars thirty-four times.

On March 11th, 1807, the town was invested. The first shot was fired by the French batteries on April 24th – Lefèbvre was no hustler – and by the end of May the town had fallen, and not so long afterwards Madame la Maréchale-Duchesse de Danzig, the buxom, kindhearted, jolly old washerwoman, was visiting the Tuileries to thank the Empress on behalf of herself and her husband the Duke. They were simple souls, the new Duke and Duchess. She used to begin half her sentences with the words 'When I used to do the washing', and he was naïvely proud of his new grandeur. But at the same time he was very conscious of the years of hard work that had raised him so high. On an occasion when an old friend of his youth was admiring enviously the splendours of his house in Paris: 'So you're jealous of me,' exclaimed the veteran, 'very well; come out into the courtyard and I'll have twenty shots at you at thirty paces. If I don't hit you, the whole house and everything in it is yours.' The friend hastily declined to take the chance, whereupon Lefèbvre remarked drily, 'I had a thousand bullets fired at me from much closer range before I got all this.' It is possible that even before Lefèbvre accepted his dukedom he had moved a certain distance from his old Republican principles, for in a short speech to the magistrates of a small town in Franconia, he had remarked, 'We have come to bring you Liberty and Equality, but don't lose your heads about it; for the first one of you that moves without my leave will be shot.'

***

The fall of Danzig and the coming of spring made a profound difference to the material and moral condition of the *Grande Armée*, and the clouds of summer dust and the flies were better than the mud and the gangrene and the starvation, and once more Napoleon's Star came to take a hand in affairs. First of all the Russians pounced upon Ney's isolated Corps, and were much emboldened by their success in driving it back, although Ney, quite unsupported, brought off the first of his consummate rear-guard actions. He lost all his kit, however, and had to borrow a pair of breeches from Soult, saying with a cheerful laugh that the nankeen pair he was wearing were the only ones he had in the world. Then the Russian Bennigsen caught Lannes between a river and a wood, and crossed the river to pounce upon him. But Lannes was not so isolated as he appeared, and the other Marshals came racing up to the rescue, and at last the Emperor had got what he wanted, a pitched battle in favourable conditions.

The result was the destruction of the Russian Army at the battle of Friedland on June 14th, 1807, the anniversary of Marengo. Ney led the main attack on the right wing, and Berthier wrote home to Paris, 'You can form no idea of the brilliant courage of Marshal Ney. It is to him chiefly that we owe the success of this memorable day.'

It was at Friedland that Napoleon, the gunner Emperor, for the first time made use of a giant battery of massed artillery.

So the campaign ended with a smashing victory, but even at the peace negotiations at Tilsit, where the Imperial Guard shone as if it was in Paris, and entertained the Guard of the Tsar Alexander at dinner with powdered and white-aproned cooks, even in all that splendour there were few who did not remember the snowstorm and the slaughter at Eylau.

* * *

Napoleon was almost thirty-eight. Bennigsen was sixty-two.

***

Bernadotte had been slightly wounded in one of the skirmishes before Friedland, and his Corps was led into action by General Victor. Victor had been a drummer-boy in the days before the Revolution, and had been one of the most turbulent sergeants in the regiment of which Davout was a subaltern. He had been one of the storming-party at the siege of Toulon in 1794, and was, therefore, one of the Emperor's oldest friends. He had commanded a division in Holland during the Consulate, and had been designated for the command of the Army of Louisiana, an expedition which did not materialize owing to the sale of Louisiana to the United States.

He was a small fat man with a round, rosy, jolly face, and he was a stupid and reckless soldier. On account of his appearance, his joviality, and his good connoisseurship in red wine, he was nicknamed '*Beau Soleil*'. His real name was Perrin. He assumed the name of Victor. It was the nearest he ever got to a victory.

He was made a Marshal after Friedland.

***

Peace was signed at Tilsit on July 9th, 1807, and the Army was free to amuse itself for a bit. Davout's Corps went down to Warsaw, and Davout could not only return to his waltzing but had his first real opportunity of showing his extraordinary capacity for administration. His task was very difficult, for the Poles had been sadly disillusioned by the affair at Tilsit, and the Austrians in the south were secretly hostile and full of intrigue, and Polish officialdom was honeycombed with corruption and fraud. But Davout was a resolute man, and in a short time had effected a wonderful improvement.

The main body of the Army marched westwards in the blazing heat of the summer into cantonments in North Germany. In spite of the summer growth of grass and corn and leaf, the country was still appallingly devastated, and the field of Eylau was a ghastly reminder of that day in February. After the miseries of the campaign, discipline relaxed to an alarming extent, and all the efforts of the Marshals could not prevent indiscriminate hunting and poaching, and looting from the peasants. Great crowds of camp followers, who had not ventured into the mud of Poland, came streaming back to the billets, and the in- habitants soon established the principle that four French privates were preferable as compulsory guests to one private of the Confederation of the Rhine, and ten French privates were preferable to one officer's wife. There were, of course, the usual grumblings and quarrellings about bil- leting areas, but the Army had one bond in common, a hatred of the staff-officers, who always billeted themselves in the towns, and never went out under canvas. For by this time, in 1807, the staffs of the *Grande Armée* were beginning to show the influence of drawing-room in- trigue. The Republican armies had been full of young colonels and generals who had forced their way up by sheer merit, but the Imperial Staffs were getting cluttered up with young men who had only influential con- nections. A nephew of Talleyrand, for instance, was a staff-colonel at twenty-five, Grouchy's son a staff-captain at twenty, and young Oudinot a staff-major at twenty- three. It was particularly noticeable that the dashing young men of the light cavalry, with their brilliant uniforms, were more likely to creep into staff jobs than their col- leagues of the infantry, and both the Staff and the light cavalry went down in quality very quickly. But no con- siderable body of men leapt up the military ladder with anything like the speed of the lovers of the dainty Princess Pauline.

It was during this period that Murat invented another new uniform for himself. It apparently combined the more brilliant features of a French general's uniform and a Polish general's uniform, and the Grand-Duke was greatly cast down when his Imperial brother-in-law took one glance at the new confection and told him abruptly to go and put on his uniform, adding rather unkindly that he looked like Franconi the circus-rider.

The Treaty of Tilsit was the real beginning of the splendours of the Imperial Court in Paris. Madame Junot has described it:

> The numerous Memoirs which detail the magnificence of Marly and Versailles convey no idea of the splendour which surrounded Napoleon's court during the winter of 1808. One of its greatest attractions, and that which no other court in Europe could equal, was the collection of beautiful women by whom it was graced. This may easily be accounted for when it is recollected that almost all the French generals and the superior officers of the Imperial Guard had married for love, either in France or in other countries, during their campaigns. I have already spoken of the elegance which embellished the Consular Court; but we have now arrived at the period of the Empire when that elegance was doubled, nay tripled, in refinement and magnificence. The Emperor's desire was that his court should be brilliant; and this wish, being agreeable to everyone's taste, was implicitly fulfilled. The revolutionary law which prohibited embroidered coats was now forgotten, and the gentlemen rivalled the ladies in the richness of their dress and the splendour of their jewels. I well recollect the truly fantastic appearance of the *salle des Maréchaux* on the night of a grand concert, when it was lined on either side by three rows of ladies, radiant in youth and beauty, and all covered with flowers, jewels, and waving plumes. Behind the ladies were ranged the officers of the imperial household, and lastly the generals, the senators, the counsellors of the State, and the foreign ministers, all clothed in rich costumes and wearing on their breasts the decorations and orders which Europe offered to us on bended knee. At the top of the hall sat the Emperor with the Empress, his brothers, sisters, and sisters-in-law. From that point he, with his eagle glance, surveyed the plumed and glittering circle.

There was a St. Martin's summer that year, and the weather throughout October and up to the end of November was superb. Almost every day picnic-parties and hunting-parties went out from the Court into the forests round Paris.

> 'The ladies wore a uniform,' says Madame Junot, 'of chamois cashmere, with collars and trimmings of green cloth embroidered with silver, and a hat of black velvet, with a large plume of white feathers. Nothing could be more exhilarating than the sight of seven or eight open carriages whirling rapidly through the alleys of that magnificent forest, filled with ladies in this elegant costume, their waving plumes blending harmoniously with the autumnal foliage; the Emperor and his numerous suite darting like a flight of arrows past them in pursuit of a stag, which exhibiting at one moment its proud antlers from the summit of a mossy rock, in the next was flying with the fleetness of the wind to escape from its persecutors.'

The ordinary hunting uniform for the gentlemen of the Court was green cloth, turned up with amaranth velvet, and laced *à la* Brandenbourg on the breast and pockets with gold and silver. The resilient Murat, having entirely dismissed from his mind the unfortunate reference to Franconi, again rose to the occasion and designed himself a special hunting kit, consisting of a short green coat trimmed with gold braid, green breeches, a three-cornered hat, also braided, and a hunting-knife with jewelled hilt hanging from a broad belt.

Berthier, the great organizer of the marches of the Army-Corps, tried his hand at organizing a shoot in order to please Napoleon. Every detail for the day's sport was worked out with the same meticulous accuracy with which the *Grande Armée* had been swept from Boulogne to Austerlitz. The carriages arrived on the stroke at the Tuileries, the beaters were ready, the keepers in their best clothes, a beautiful lunch waiting to be eaten, and a thousand rabbits, brought the night before and dumped in the park, waiting to be shot. But poor, ugly little Berthier made one trivial mistake. Instead of buying wild rabbits, he bought tame ones and did not know that they were accustomed to be fed twice a day. When the Emperor took his gun in hand and advanced into the park, the rabbits, all thousand of them, mistook him for the man who provided their daily lettuce, and leapt to their feet and charged towards him. Berthier and his staff beat them off with horse-whips, but the rabbits, who were more expert in the Napoleonic warfare than some of the Marshals, wheeled round on both flanks and actually reached the Emperor's carriage before the Emperor could mount and drive off back to Paris.

Another curious incident of the shooting-parties of these splendid days was when Napoleon, who was a better hand with a field-gun than he was with a fowling-piece, accidentally shot Masséna in the eye. With characteristic readiness, the Emperor put the blame of the accident on Berthier, who with characteristic subservience accepted the blame, while Masséna, who lost his eye, with characteristic tact accepted the transference of blame. He could forgive the loss of an eye more readily than the loss of the three million francs from the bank in Livorno.

* * *

At about this time Brune, Governor of Hamburg, fell into disgrace and was dismissed from his post, the nominal excuse being that he had described himself in a report as a Marshal of France instead of as a Marshal of the Empire.

* * *

At last, in early 1808, the long-expected dukedoms were gazetted, and once again there was a wave of bitterness throughout the Marshalate. For it was seen at once that the Marshalate had been divided, so far as the dukedoms were concerned, into three categories. There were, firstly, the titles that were derived from provinces or territories that had formerly been part of the Venetian State. Soult became Duke of Dalmatia, and Bessières Duke of Istria, though neither of them had ever had the slightest connection with these two provinces. Marmont got Ragusa, but he at least had been governing there for two years. In this category also were Moncey, Duke of Conegliano; Victor, Duke of Belluno, and Mortier, Duke of Treviso.

In the second category, the titles were taken not from haphazard and disconnected patches of foreign soil, but from the battlefields on which each recipient had performed his greatest feat of arms. Masséna got Rivoli to commemorate the great stand outside Mantua in 1796. Ney got Elchingen, the fight which sealed up Mack irretrievably in Ulm. Davout became Duke of Auerstädt, and Lannes Duke of Montebello, the village below the Alps from which he had swept the Austrians on the march to Marengo, and old Kellermann's dukedom was a memory of that day in 1792 when he stood immovable beneath the mill at Valmy; and Augereau was made Duke of Castiglione, in memory of the day in 1796 when he stoutly advised General Bonaparte not to retreat. In the third category were the Marshals who got no titles at all, and these were Brune, Jourdan, Pérignon, and Sérurier.

The Marshals who received the battle-titles were delighted, because henceforward, wherever they went or were spoken about, their great feats of arms would be remembered. The Marshals who received the province-titles were furious, because all the world would infer that they had performed no feats of arms worth remembering. Soult in particular had longed to be Duke of Austerlitz, for it was he who had directed the crucial blow in the centre of the battle, and Victor had been hoping for

Marengo. But there were four battles which the Emperor would share with no one, Marengo, Austerlitz, Jena, and Friedland, and, to the Emperor, the greatest of these were Marengo and Austerlitz.

But not one of the Marshals who received a province-title was half so angry as the rosy little Victor. For not only had he not been given Marengo, but Pretty Paulette, the Emperor's mischievous sister, had suggested that he should receive the beautiful title of Belluno, and the Emperor had agreed. It was not until the dukedom had been gazetted that Pretty Paulette pointed out to her brother, with a great deal of silvery laughter, that 'Belle Lune' was an admirable match for 'Beau Soleil'. Napoleon at first was furious at the idea of anyone having a joke at the expense of his famous dukedoms, but when he saw the apoplectic rage on the ruddy countenance of little Victor, the Emperor joined heartily in Paulette's laughter. Victor never forgave him.

The ladies of the Marshals agreed that Madame la Maréchale Lannes had got the prettiest title, from her husband's exploit at Montebello.

CHAPTER XI

THE FIRST TRIUMPHS IN SPAIN

WHEN Napoleon was standing on the Landgrafenberg outside Jena, on October 14th, 1806, watching the once invincible Prussian infantry as it melted away into the gathering twilight, a despatch arrived from the distant south. It contained a copy of a proclamation of Godoy, Minister of Spain, appealing for a levy *en masse* against 'the enemy. Spain, Bourbon Spain, was an ally of Napoleon. Who then was the enemy? Napoleon was thrown into a paroxysm of anger by this document, and from that moment he never forgot that, although on the north-east and east and south-east the frontiers of France marched with vassal kingdoms, dependent grand-duchies, or feudatory confederations, on the south lay a kingdom of the hated Bourbon.

Godoy, thunderstruck at the collapse of Prussia, hastened to explain that the 'enemy' of his proclamation was the English. Unfortunately, in his manifesto, he had stressed the appeal for horses, and made no appeal for ships, so that, unless he envisaged a cavalry attack across a frozen Biscay and Channel, his explanation was somewhat lame, and Napoleon was left to wonder what would have happened to France if an army of Spain had marched on Bordeaux while he was engaged with Prussia or, worse

still, while the *Grande Armée* was strung out the year
before in its vast horseshoe round Vienna. But the result
of his wondering did not make him declare war on Spain.
Instead, he used Spain as an ally to coerce Portugal,
England's oldest and most tenacious friend, and it was as
a brother-in-arms of the Spaniards that General Junot
crossed the Spanish frontier on October 18th, 1807, at
the head of the Corps of Observation of the Gironde
and marched on Lisbon in search of Glory and his
Marshal's Baton, the second of which had been promised to him by Napoleon if he acquired the first for
himself. Up to this time, Junot's only military exploit
on which a dukedom might have been based was the
affair at Nazareth in the Syrian campaign of 1799.
Napoleon several times told him that he might have
been Duke of Nazareth if his name had been anything
else but Junot.

The Corps of Observation of the Gironde! It was a
strangely gentle, quiet name for the advance-guard of all
those hundreds of thousands of fighting men who poured
into Spain during the next six years, bringing with them
that infinity of bloodshed and groans and miseries and
horrors and cruelties that tortured the unhappy Peninsula
from the moment Junot crossed the Bidassoa, going
south, till the moment on October 7th, 1813, when
Wellington crossed it, going north.

Junot entered Spain with 24,000 men. On November
29th, 1807, with 1,500 starved, ragged, footsore, cold survivors, with neither gun nor horse nor dry cartridge,
he arrived in front of Lisbon. The Portuguese Army
could not be found; the Lisbon mob had lost their
nerve, and next day the leader of a defenceless rabble
of Frenchmen entered Lisbon with some trepidation,
and appointed himself Governor of Portugal. The echoes
of the cannon-fire of Austerlitz, of Jena, and of Friedland
had reached the coasts of the ocean, and Junot was
protected by their reverberations. When the veterans of

THE FIRST TRIUMPHS IN SPAIN

the *Grande Armée* shouted *'Vive l'Empereur'*, the sound carried a long way in those days.

In the meanwhile a second Corps of Observation of the Gironde, 24,000 conscripts under General Dupont, came stealing across the Bidassoa, and in the first weeks of 1808 the first of the Marshals to serve in Spain came over the border. True, it was only slowcoach old Moncey, the stickler for drill and prudence, but he brought with him yet a third army, entitled magnificently the Corps of Observation of the Ocean Coast. It numbered 30,000 men, and its cavalry was commanded by Grouchy. These imposing reinforcements for Junot halted in northern Spain, and made no effort to move on Lisbon. Spain was appalled at this sudden massing of silent, mysterious armies. And yet another, half French, half Italian, was creeping down the other coast towards Barcelona. No one in their senses would reinforce Lisbon by way of Barcelona, and in the middle of February 1808 the cards were laid on the table with devastating abruptness when the French armies seized the frontier fortresses of their Spanish ally. Pampeluna and San Sebastian at one end of the Pyrenees, and Barcelona and Figueras at the other, were captured by a mixture of force and fraud, and with that seizing of the fortresses the first drops of poison, that grew and grew into the destroying ulcer, were injected into the Imperial system.

War was not declared at once, however. One side was not ready enough, the other side was much too ready, especially as the Emperor began to reinforce the High Commands of the armies of occupation. On March 23rd, 1808, the gay and flamboyant figure of Murat, Commander of the Reserve Cavalry, Grand-Duke of Berg, and Grand Admiral of France, came riding into Madrid with 20,000 infantry, a large force of cavalry, the new title of Lieutenant of the Emperor, and a staff that was described by a contemporary as a *boutique de charlatan*. Murat was in his best form, ready for anything from a kiss to a charge, from an intrigue to a massacre. The sunny land of Spain was, to the child of Gascony, as vast an improvement over the dismal marshes of Poland, as the mantillaed *señoritas* over the verminous peasants, and besides, here was another kingdom in the air. There was only a degenerate old Bourbon to get rid of and a stupid young prince, and presto! there was a fine throne standing empty.

On the frontier yet another new army, the Corps of Observation of the Pyrenees, was beginning to roll down into Castile under the command of Marshal Bessières. This was Bessières' first independent command since he had led his squadron as a simple captain in Italy in '96. His chief-of-staff was also a cavalryman, Lefèbvre-Desnouettes, who was later captured by the English 10th Hussars at the skirmish at Benavente, and broke his parole from Cheltenham in 1811 and got back to France; while the leader of Bessières' cavalry was young Lasalle, who had just ridden across Europe from Warsaw, where he had been commanding Davout's cavalry and making love to the ladies of Poland.

For a month Napoleon's intrigues went on, but there was no war. The senile old King Charles of Spain and the young Prince Ferdinand were lured to Bayonne, on French soil, and seized and vehemently ordered to abdicate their ancient throne. Napoleon stormed. Old Charles would abdicate; young Ferdinand would not. There was a deadlock. But in Madrid the people were restless. Their King and Prince had vanished; the armed strangers, supposed to be on their way to Lisbon, had not vanished; Murat had stolen out of the royal armoury the great sword of Francis I of France, which had been taken at the battle of Pavia in 1525; and on April 29th, 1808, a certain Navarrese, who had escaped over the high mountains in disguise, arrived in the city with the news of the happenings of Bayonne, and on May 2nd the explosion burst and the Madrileñan mob sprang to their daggers and their brickbats.

But Murat had learned what to do with a mob as far back as '95, when he had fetched the guns which blew the Revolution away, and in four hours he had Madrid in hand. He then shot a hundred men, pardoned the rest, and sat down to dinner in high good-humour, satisfied that Spain was conquered.

The news appalled Bayonne. Napoleon, furious, offered Ferdinand the choice of abdication or death, and Ferdinand, remembering perhaps his cousin of Enghien, preferred abdication. The last throne of the Bourbons was empty. Murat was thrilled with anticipation. Even after drinking rather too much Spanish wine and getting an attack of Madrid colic, an illness that was new to the French army doctors and had to be treated with an experimental compound of camphor, opium, musk, and quinine, his native jauntiness was not diminished. But Joseph Bonaparte got the throne of Spain, and Napoleon offered the indignant Murat the choice of Portugal or Naples. Murat wisely chose Naples, recovered his temper and rode gaily out of Spain, which he thought he had so completely conquered, about the middle of June, 1808. He never returned to the Peninsula, and he was well quit of it.

On August 1st, 1808, King Joachim I ascended his new throne.

***

On May 25th, 1808, the principality of Asturias, a mountainous, bleak, barren country in the north-west of Spain, declared war against the invader. Galicia followed and then Estremadura, the cradle of the tough fighting-men of mediaeval Spain, and Old Castile, and Valencia, and Andalusia, and Murcia, and Aragon, until every town and village and hamlet and isolated farmhouse was a focus of the uprising of a nation. Moncey and Bessières, alone of the Marshals, were on the spot, and their troops were mainly conscripts, while the seas from the Bidassoa in the north, round by Vigo, down the long coast of Portugal, in the narrow seas, and north again to Barcelona, were dotted with the white sails of England, and already there was talk of a British Expeditionary Force.

But what use were peasants, and the ridiculous Spanish Army, and the still more ridiculous Portuguese, and the English whom even Marshal Brune had defeated in Flanders, against the invincible Frenchmen? The 110,000 men in Spain might be mainly conscripts, and the two Marshals not of the most celebrated, but Junot, Delaborde, Loison, young Kellermann of Marengo fame, Dupont, Grouchy, Merle, Harispe, Reille, and Duhesme, and the one and only Lasalle, were more than a match for any opposition they were likely to meet. Within two months 8,000 men under Marshal Moncey had marched through the mountains from Madrid to Valencia, been heavily repulsed, and, enjoying almost fantastic luck, had marched dismally back to Madrid; the amateur levies of Saragossa had repulsed a series of desperate attacks; the third-rate fortress of Gerona, with the help of an Irish regiment, had successfully driven off two assaults, and General Dupont had surrendered his entire army of 17,000 men at Baylen to a pack of wretched Spaniards.

It was true that Bessières was victorious in his one and only independent pitched battle at Medina del Rio Seco, where Lasalle was in his most brilliant form, hut nobody paid any attention to that. It was the surrender of Baylen that mattered, the capitulation of Frenchmen, the humbling of the Eagles in the dust, the destruction of the legend of Invincibility. And at the hands of wretched Spaniards.

The news whirled through Spain to the remotest hamlets in forgotten valleys, and in a moment the Spanish people awoke from its long trance. All Europe buzzed with excitement and the Emperor almost had apoplexy. More was to follow, and quickly. On August 1st, 1808, the

British Expeditionary Force landed in Mondego Bay, Portugal, and on the 21st of August Junot and his Corps, which ought to have been peacefully engaged in observing the Gironde, met for the first time the full blast of organized musketry-fire at Vimiero, and on that day the English volleys blew away in smoke Junot's chance of winning Glory and his Marshal's Baton. By the Convention of Cintra, which was signed after the battle, Junot's army, 25,000 strong, evacuated Portugal and was sent by sea back to France.

Here was a fine start to an Imperial campaign. Portugal lost, one army lost, and another ignominiously shipped home like cattle, and the miserable Spaniards not only daring to defend themselves in antiquated fortresses, but defending themselves successfully. And then Brother Joseph, poor Brother Joseph, King of All the Spains, had to make matters even worse by losing his nerve and bolting out of Madrid across the passes into Old Castile, and all his Court bolted with him. Moncey escorted them in as dignified a way as the courtiers' hurry permitted.

Europe gasped. The Eagle's feathers were really beginning to look positively dilapidated. But Napoleon, watching at Bordeaux, found one consolation amid his gusts of fury. The English had made their fatal mistake. They had come ashore after all these years from their floating fortresses, and the leopards at last were within range. Couriers were sent furiously galloping to the Rhine and the Elbe, and in a twinkling three whole corps of the veteran army, and two shining divisions of heavy cuirassiers, and two of dragoons, and the whole of the Imperial Guard from Paris, broke cantonments and set out for Spain. A hundred and thirty thousand real soldiers were on the march, and the Emperor was calling for Berthier and his compasses and his maps. The sending of Marshal Jourdan, the old commander of the Sambre-et-Meuse, from Naples to Spain meant nothing. He was merely a stop-gap. Heavier metal than Jourdan was on the

143

way, and on August 30th, 1808, there arrived at Irun, on the Spanish frontier, Marshal Ney, 'the toughest and most resolute of all the Emperor's fighting-men, who brought with him a spirit of enterprise and confidence which had long been wanting in the Army of Spain.'[1]

Against this overwhelming mass the Spaniards could only range a fanatical patriotism and a handful of Englishmen. But Baylen had put heart into them, and the strange and romantic arrival of the Marquis De La Romana with 9,000 of the flower of the Spanish regular army added to the desperate confidence of the nation. It is a curious story, this appearance of De La Romana at Santander.

When Spain was nominally an ally of France in 1807, Napoleon insisted on removing the pick of its army and sending it to do garrison duty, first in the neighbourhood of Mecklenberg and then in Denmark. Marshal Brune had been for two years in command of the Hanseatic Cities, and had recently been removed in disgrace, and his place had been taken by Bernadotte. In the beginning of 1808 Bernadotte was moved from Hamburg north to Copenhagen. He was a great believer in astrology, and before setting out to Copenhagen he told General Bourrienne that a fortune-teller had predicted that he would become a king, but that in order to reach his throne he would have to cross the sea.

De La Romana, on duty in Denmark, was under Bernadotte's command, and his men were carefully scattered throughout the Danish islands in order to prevent organized disaffection. But in 1808 the news from Spain, and particularly the news from Bayonne and Baylen filtered through to the north, and the Spanish commander, De La Romana, found himself surrounded, not by allies, but by the oppressors of his country. The Spaniards longed to get back to Spain, but escape by

[1] *Sir C.W.C. Oman.*

land was impossible. The sea was far more promising, for the Baltic was crowded with English war-ships, and when an enterprising Scottish priest, who had lived most of his life in a monastery at Ratisbon, arrived at De La Romana's headquarters in the disguise of a commercial traveller in cigars and chocolate, and with a scheme for an escape by sea, he was welcomed eagerly by the Spanish commander. From that moment De La Romana began the incomprehensible habit of falling asleep evening after evening over the whist-table. No one could understand his extraordinary drowsiness. But it was his only chance of sleep, for now he was working secretly all through the night organizing the escape, and during the daytime he had to appear on parades and in his office in order to avoid suspicion. He was so successful that by the time Bernadotte got the notion that something was afoot, it was too late, and on August 21st, 1808, Admiral Keates arrived with troop-ships and an escorting squadron, and the Spanish Army was safely embarked. On October 11th it landed at Santander in the north of Spain.

* * *

The arrival of these regular troops, the consecutive victories over inferior French Generals and half-trained troops, and the stubborn resistance of the semi-fortified towns, filled the Spaniards with the wildest confidence, which was not even diminished by the news that the veteran Army of Germany, with closed-up ranks, carefully oiled muskets, great masses of new artillery, and well-fed horses, was rolling towards the Pyrenees like a river of steel.

The march from the Elbe across South Germany and France was a triumphal progress for the 'old moustaches'. By the end of October the veterans of the Rhine and the Elbe had crossed France and had been fêted and wined and cheered and kissed at every town and village all through those golden months of autumn and grape-harvesting. It was their first homecoming since the great sweep upon Ulm in 1805, and the exchange of the dreary mud of Poland for the country of Vougeot and Chablis and Montrachet was very pleasant, and it was not until the desolate country of the Landes was reached that the weather broke and the rains came down.

Lefèbvre was already across the Bidassoa, and so was Victor. Mortier was close behind. Ney's reinforcements had closed up. The Imperial Guard was pouring in from Paris, and Junot's army, somewhat recovered from sea-sickness after a painful voyage in the English troop-ships from Lisbon to Rochefort, was heading for the Peninsula again. A quarter of a million men were ready, and they were not going to be led by second-raters.

The Marshals were arriving in force. The latest creation, Marshal Victor, commanded the First Corps; Bessières handed over, rather crossly, the Second Corps to Soult, who had ridden so hard to his new headquarters that he left even his A.D.C.'s behind and arrived alone on a tired packhorse, and Bessières went to command the Reserve Cavalry. He had always been Murat's understudy, both on and off the field. Moncey (of whom Lannes wrote later, 'he is a long way from understanding your Majesty's kind of war') temporarily had the Third, Lefèbvre the Fourth, Mortier the Fifth, Ney the Sixth (Ney had had the Sixth from the day when it was formed, at Montreuil, when the *Grande Armée* was the Army of the Coasts of the Ocean), and Gouvion St. Cyr, not yet a Marshal but as brilliant as any of them, had the Seventh, and Junot (his baton lost for ever at Vimiero) the Eighth. And before the actual blow was struck at the Spanish centre, Moncey was superseded in the command of the two 'storm-corps' by the redoubt-able Lannes. Lannes had fallen, with his horse, over a pre-cipice near Vittoria and his injuries were so severe that his life was despaired of. He was saved by being sewn up in the skin of a newly flayed sheep and was leading his Corps into action at Tudela within a fortnight. They needed to be tough men in those days. (Lannes was getting very tired of war, and he had written to the Duchess of Montebello that his departure for Spain was the greatest proof of devotion that he had yet given to the Emperor. His only consolation was the prospective shortness of the campaign. 'There will be no fighting,' he wrote, 'for the Spaniards are everywhere in flight, and we shall be back by the spring-time.')

By the time that the men and the Marshals were ready, the Plan of Campaign had been evolved in Paris. Like all Napoleon's plans, it was brilliant and yet simple. The two Spanish armies on the right and left were on no account to be frightened into retreat. They were to be left alone, while a sledge-hammer was to hit the Spanish centre one single smashing blow. Then the sledge-hammer was to split into three. One part was to curl round behind each of the Spanish wings, while the third hurried on for Madrid. The Plan very nearly succeeded to perfection. The centre was smashed, and Madrid was entered. But the capture of the wings was not wholly successful.

The reason why the Spanish left wing army escaped was a curious one. In order not to frighten it into premature retreat, Napoleon, always the subtle psychologist, despatched poor old Lefèbvre, the least enterprising of all the Marshals, slower even than Moncey, stupider even than Brune, to take command opposite the Spanish left. But for once his psychology broke down. He forgot to reckon with Vanity, the least offensive and most universal of human foibles. Poor Lefèbvre had never commanded in a victory, and in his solemn, honest old heart he longed secretly and passionately to stand on a hill, surrounded by a glittering staff, and direct the pursuit of a flying enemy. When he looked at the amateurish rabble in front of him, and then at his own army of invincibles behind him, the temptation was too strong. Vast strategic combinations meant nothing to him. A victory was in his grasp after all these years, and he launched his infantry through a dense Pyrenean fog in beautiful rows and columns, each in perfect alignment and dressing, and on the evening of that day Marshal Lefèbvre was a victorious general at last, exactly the same as Masséna and the rest of them. But the Spanish left-wing army fled and escaped the curl of the pincers.

Of the right-wing army, several thousand escaped into Saragossa, because Napoleon did not allow Ney, the other arm of the pincers, enough time to cross the fearful mountain roads. Napoleon, riding down the main metalled road from Bayonne to Madrid by way of Vittoria and Burgos, had the idea already fixed in his mind that Spain was traversed everywhere by main metalled roads. It was an idea that strongly contributed to his ultimate downfall.

Though the Spanish wings were not annihilated, the essence of the Plan succeeded, and the Emperor pushed Brother Joseph back into his palace within eleven days of the first attack.

Berthier's uniform made a great sensation as he rode at the head of the general staff into Madrid. For he was outrivalling Murat himself with a black Hungarian pelisse, a black dolman trimmed with gold braid and astrakhan fur, a black-and-gold sash, a small gold-embroidered cartridge-box, and a scarlet shako with a white aigrette of heron's plumes. The whole staff was mounted on grey Arab horses with long manes, and the saddle-cloths were panther skins with gold-and-scarlet fringes. Murat's uniforms were probably too unorthodox and startling for the junior officers to imitate, and it was Berthier who set the fashion throughout the army. The despair of the younger officers is recorded by a contemporary when the Chief-of-Staff appeared one morning with his dolman trimmed with grey astrakhan, instead of the black which they had all just bought.

But the war in Spain was not to be won by gold embroidery, and the army had realized this almost as soon as it crossed the Pyrenees. The queer, primitive villages of the Basque country with their narrow and tortuous streets, their heavily barred windows, their massive doors, which always seemed to be shut, and the grim hostility of the peasants, had been a painful change from the easy-going life of South Germany. Almost at once the ration supply broke down, and at once the marauding and looting began which led to the terrible reprisals and counter-reprisals that only ceased when the last Frenchman left Spain six years later. The Marshals very soon gave up the attempt to preserve discipline, and town after town and village after village was sacked and burnt. When Jomini, Ney's methodical and precise Swiss chief-of-staff, was shocked by the atrocities, Ney replied that the Emperor himself did not wish the soldiers to be deprived of the chance of making up for their arrears of pay. In these early days of the Spanish war the peasants had not learnt by bitter experience to drive their cattle into the forests and hills at the first approach of a Frenchman, and even the infantry officers found horses to steal, and many of the stragglers of Ney's Corps followed the line of march on donkeys.

But in these early days the Spaniards had already learnt one thing, and that was the military value of incessant assassination, and the French Army was appalled at the ruthlessness with which isolated men, looters, despatch-riders, pickets, or stragglers were stabbed in the back, shot at from behind walls, poisoned in taverns, or strangled in their sleep. It was a new style of warfare, and the French hated it. They could think of only one way to combat the murdering, the oldest and stupidest and least suc-cessful of all ways, the method of Reprisal, which is, and always has been, a failure against people of spirit. For every soldier that was murdered, the French burnt a village or disembowelled a priest or sacked a nunnery, and every such act of Reprisal inflamed the sullen and fanatical Spaniards to new and more terrible murders. So the wheel of horror turned faster and faster through the years.

The first part of Napoleon's programme, the smashing of the Spanish Army and the recapture of Madrid, was complete. The second part was to invade Portugal, destroy the English and capture Lisbon, and then the whole trivial episode of the Peninsular campaign would be neatly and finally polished off. Again a plan was made; the corps were strung out to cover the several routes to the west, and Lasalle's light horsemen had almost reached the frontiers of Portugal, when the news came into Madrid that Sir John Moore, with thousands of English redcoats, was stalking Soult in Old Castile, and that the leopards were within reach at last. The Emperor sprang to action like a thunderclap.

> Napoleon acted with a sudden and spasmodic energy which was never surpassed in any of his earlier campaigns. He hurled on to Moore's track not only the central reserve at Madrid, but troops gathered in from all directions, till he had set at least 80,000 men on the march, to encompass the British corps which had so hardily thrown itself upon his communications. Moore had been perfectly right when he stated his belief that the sight of the redcoats within reach would stir the Emperor up to such wrath, that he would abandon every other enterprise and rush upon them with every available man.[1]

Ney's cavalry went in front, and then the Guard cavalry, and behind them the infantry. But for the second time in the campaign the Emperor imagined that a road in Spain was the same as a road in France. Ney got safely over the Sierra Guadarrama, but a raging blizzard blocked the passes in front of the Guard, and the wind was so strong that horsemen were flung over precipices, and huge drifts were piled up in a few minutes. It was so cold that

[1] Sir C.W.C. Oman.

the snow froze hard and the horses slipped at every step and at least half of the cavalry and all the flying artillery had to halt on the slopes of the Sierra. In spite of Napoleon's personal efforts – he himself dismounted and directed the pioneers in their work of clearing the track, and walked on foot through the night in the midst of the Guard, just as he had done in the old days when the Army of Reserve was going up the Great St. Bernard on its way to Marengo – in spite of all that he could do, sixteen valuable hours were lost and Sir John Moore had been warned of the storm that was about to burst upon him and had turned and bolted for the sea. Whether the French would have caught him or not before he reached the sea, if Napoleon himself had commanded the pursuit, will never be known, for on January 1st, 1809, a courier arrived from Paris with the news that intrigues were on foot in the capital, and that Talleyrand and Fouché were putting their heads together with the new King Joachim of Naples and his Queen Caroline. The Emperor in a fury handed the pursuit of the English over to Soult, and galloped off to the north.

CHAPTER XII

NAPOLEON never visited Spain again. It was a minor affair, a side-show, and could safely be left to the Marshals. He himself had weightier matters to attend to.

In these first days of 1809, while Napoleon was galloping to Paris, Sir John Moore's army was running for its life, and Soult went after it, with Ney's cavalry to help, and Ney himself in support. Young General Colbert led the pursuit, the handsomest hussar in all the French Army. Colbert might have been a rival of Lasalle himself if he had had the brains of the other, and the sense of humour, as well as the dash and the courage. 'I shall soon be decorating you,' said the Emperor to him a few weeks before. 'Make haste, Sire,' replied the young general boldly, 'for though I am not yet thirty I feel that I am already growing old.' But the Emperor did not make haste enough, for the pursuit had hardly begun when Colbert was dead, shot through the head at long range by Rifleman Tom Plunket of the 95th Foot. The first of the four gay young men was down.

Over the wild, mountainous desolation of northern Spain swept the pursued and the pursuers, through icy rains and sleet, until at last the sea was reached and the leopards had to turn and fight. Soult's clumsiness at the

battle of Corunna saved the desperate survivors of the
retreat from annihilation, but the moral effect of the campaign made a powerful impression. The English had
ventured ashore and had been flung out to their sea again
in double-quick time, and Europe fancied that they would
not come back in a hurry.

Soult, having gratified his passion for monument-
building by erecting a handsome column to the memory
of Sir John Moore, dropped down into Oporto, and halted there for a time on his way to recapture Lisbon. It was
a pleasanter place than the horrible rocks of Galicia. There
were stores of provisions, churches to loot, and houses to
shelter in from the wintry blizzards. Week after week Soult
lingered in Oporto. In front of him only the Portuguese
and a handful of stray Englishmen blocked his line of
advance – even the women and young girls had to be
enlisted to defend the villages against the advance-guards
– and behind him the Galician *guerilleros* were swarming
like hornets between him and Ney, and yet Soult made
no move on Lisbon.

There was a reason for the Duke of Dalmatia's lethar-
gy. The same old vision which Junot had seen before
Vimiero, which Davout had seen in Poland, which
Bernadotte saw always, was shining in the clouds, and the
Duke of Dalmatia could not take his eyes off it. It was the
vision of a golden throne, with a sceptre on one side and
an orb on the other and a crown above it, and below were
the words, inscribed in great, blazing letters of fire: 'Murat
is a King.' Day and night as Nicolas Jean-de-Dieu Soult
lay at Oporto, ghostly voices whispered in his ears 'Murat
is a King, Murat is a King,' and other ghostly voices whispered, 'Why not King Nicolas of Northern Lusitania?'
King Nicolas the First! Even the lost Dukedom of
Austerlitz paled before it, and Soult, cursing himself for his
short-sightedness, hastily began to replace the gold and silver vessels, and the rich vestments, and the sacred pictures,
which he and his men had looted from the churches and

the mansions and the monasteries in the first intaking of the city. At the same time he opened among the citizens of Oporto, a personal campaign of conciliation, flattery, and orderly government. It was too late to do anything about the thousands of Portuguese civilians, women and children, who had been so unfortunately drowned at the pontoon bridge on March 29th, 1809, when the French burst through the entrenchments and the people panicked. But at least he was open to receive signatures to a petition begging him to assume the throne, and small squads of partisans were organized to shout *'Viva o Rei Nicolao'* in the streets. It was a very lucky circumstance that Alcantara, which one of Soult's generals had just sacked with a thoroughness and a brutality that was exceptional even in the Peninsula, where the standard of efficiency in such things was already extremely high, was on the other side of the Spanish frontier. The Army was puzzled by all this intriguing that was going on at Headquarters, and two of the divisional commanders made tentative plans together for arresting their Marshal if he tried on any of his nonsense, and there was a general feeling that it was hardly worth while to risk death by mutilation, by bayonet, by shell-fire, by torture, starvation, and disease, in a loathsome country of brutes and fanatics, simply to make Nicolas Jean-de-Dieu Soult into a king. But the grumbling of the troops, and the intriguing of the Marshal, came to an abrupt and simultaneous end when Wellesley crept up to Oporto in broad daylight, and in a handful of hours flung the visionary, day-dreaming king out of his Lusitanian mirage. The last scene of Soult's invasion of Portugal was his feverish retreat over the tops of four mountain-chains back into Spain, by tracks and obscure paths, in nine days of torrential rain, and all he brought back with him to show for his trouble was neither loot nor treasure, for he had given it all back, nor gun nor wagon nor any single wheeled vehicle, but only a new nickname. For his men now called him *'Le Roi Nicolas'*. It was with profound and undisguised relief that the unfortunate Duke of Dalmatia found himself at last within the protective reach of the strong arm of Ney, up in Galicia, although Soult disliked Galicia intensely, and disliked Ney even more.

The two Marshals remained together for some time, quarrelling incessantly, until at last red-headed Ney, whose temper was never of the most serene, drew his sword on Soult, and at once the officers and men of the two corps took their cue from their chiefs, and fought and duelled and brawled in the streets. Things got so bad that even the angry Marshals realized that something must be done, and they drew up a scheme for a combined advance towards the ocean.

As soon as Soult's Corps had been refitted by Ney, they started off. Ney carried out his part with his invariable tactical perfection, but Soult vanished into thin air. The moment Ney heard of his colleague's disappearance, he blew up in one of his wildest fits of temper, and marched back not merely to Lugo, their starting-place, but clean out of the entire province, right back to Astorga, sacking and destroying every village and hamlet out of sheer rage as he went. This was the only occasion in Ney's career in which he behaved with brutality towards civilians.

***

It was not only the English who were giving trouble in Spain. The province of Catalonia was being very tiresome. Strategically, this province was unimportant; the lines of communication from Galicia and from Portugal and from Seville, northwards to Paris, run through Madrid and Burgos and Vittoria by Irun and Bayonne. The other end of the Pyrenees, the Catalonian end, was nothing in comparison. But any set-back to the Eagles in any region, however unimportant, was intolerable, and the stubborn resistance of the ridiculous walled city of Gerona, which du Guesclin or Cœur-de-Lion would have captured with catapults and arquebuses and arbalests, was infuriating. The Catalan is a stubborn man, and in 1809 he had not even the sense to know that resistance was useless, and so Gerona held out, grotesquely, month after month through the torrid Spanish summer. At first the polite and frigid General Gouvion St. Cyr was in command of the besiegers, but in May, 1809, he was superseded in disgrace, and the Emperor discarded politeness and frigidity for a new method. St. Cyr's successor was our old friend, the former dancing-master and gutter-boy, Marshal Augereau, Duke of Castiglione. Augereau, who had recovered from his Eylau wound, was torn between two desires. On one hand he longed for a quiet life in which to enjoy his title and his wealth, and his diamonds and his new aristocratic wife, and on the other there was the re-awakening call of military ambition. He had served in Catalonia in the old Republican days and knew the country well, and it was years since he had held an independent command, and, besides, there were capital rumours filtering north about the treasures in the Spanish churches. There seemed to be loot going a-begging in Spain, and Augereau felt that it would be a downright flying in the face of Providence to let Soult have it all. Ney and Mortier could be trusted to leave the churches alone, and Masséna was safe in Germany, but Soult would bag the lot if Augereau did not hurry. So he tore himself away from his country-house and his fashionable duchess (part of her household duties was to grease the Marshal-Duke's leather riding-breeches), and set out for the south. But at Perpignan he was seized with an attack of gout, and repaired to the baths at Molitg for a cure. In a short time he was almost congratulating himself on the attack, for at Molitg the news of Gerona reached him. To conduct a second Saragossa either from the scorched and bare hillside above Gerona, where sunstroke and dysentery were frequent, or from below in the valley of the Ter, famous for its malaria, was not Augereau's idea of a campaign, now that his youthful enthusiasms had been succeeded by middle-aged notions of comfort. The wily old soldier, therefore, thanked his stars for the gout and coolly stayed on at his watering-place until St. Cyr should have finished off the siege. But St. Cyr, of whom more later, was a cool card too, and on October 1st he wrote to congratulate the Marshal on his convalescence, resigned the command, and went off home, for which exploit he was duly put under arrest by the enraged Emperor.

There was nothing for Augereau to do but to leave his pleasant watering-place, and go off to a command that now seemed perfectly beastly. The weather had turned cold, and it rained incessantly in October, and the town did not surrender till December 11th, 1809, after a siege of eight months. The Marshal behaved with the utmost severity to the miserable and heroic garrison.

The siege of Gerona provided Augereau with an opportunity of showing what he could do with a pen as well as with a sword, and the following proclamation to the Geronese is a fair sample of his prose style:

> Unhappy inhabitants – wretched victims immolated to the caprice and madness of ambitious men greedy for your blood – return to your senses, open your eyes, consider the ills which surround you! With what tranquillity do your leaders look upon the graves crammed with your corpses! Are you not horror-struck at these cannibals, whose mirth bursts out in the midst of the human hecatomb, and who yet dare lift their gory hands in prayer towards the throne of a God of Peace? They call themselves the apostles of Jesus Christ! Tremble, cruel and infamous men! The God who judges the actions of mortals is slow to condemn, but his vengeance is terrible. . . . I warn you for the last time, inhabitants of Gerona, reflect while you still may! If you force me to throw aside my usual mildness, your ruin is inevitable. I shall be the first to groan at it, but the laws of war impose on me the dire necessity. . . . I am severe but just.

Unhappy Gerona! If thy defenders persist in their obstinacy, thou shalt perish in blood and flame.

(Signed) AUGEREAU.[1]

Augereau was not the only Marshal to experience the unpleasantness of the siege of a Spanish town. When Napoleon made his great attack on the Spanish armies, smashed their centre to pieces, and marched into Madrid, the remnants of the Spanish right wing fled in confusion to Saragossa. Thither they were followed in a leisurely fashion by Moncey. But although Saragossa was practically unfortified, and although its garrison consisted of fugitives, priests, and civilians, and although Moncey had 15,000 men, nevertheless that cautious old gentleman did not assault at once, but drew back and waited for Mortier, who was on his way to help. By the time that the siege was begun in earnest, the inhabitants had put the existing fortifications into repair, had added new ones, and above all had loopholed and barricaded the houses for street-fighting. 'The shell may break,' they said, 'but the kernel will be harder than the shell.'

A summons to surrender was proudly refused by Palafox, the Spanish leader, and the siege began in earnest at the end of the year. For three weeks the garrison repulsed every attack, and the Spanish enthusiasm mounted as French enthusiasm fell. The whole of Aragon was swarming with patriots, and as many soldiers were required to defend the besiegers as to besiege the city. Every attack was driven back with heavy losses and French morale fell lower and lower.

But on January 22nd, 1809, Marshal Lannes arrived to take command, and from that moment the French Army began to recover its spirits. For one thing, Lannes called in all the outlying troops, and let Aragon look after itself. For another, instead of living in a handsome château outside

[1] *Sir C.W.C. Oman*

the camp like the other commanders, Lannes established his headquarters in a small inn in the middle of the troops. And for another, it was known wherever men of the French Army met together, that Marshal Lannes led his troops from in front and not from behind.

Lannes made one general attack on Saragossa, and it was a complete failure. At every point, except the Convent of St. Monica, it was driven back with heavy losses, and Lannes realized that, without an immense siege artillery, the place could not be taken by storm. He settled down, therefore, to a siege of mines and saps and bombs. Each house was treated as a separate fort, was undermined, blown up, and its ruins occupied and then consolidated. It was a slow business, for the Spaniards defended desperately, not only house by house, but floor by floor, and every man and woman had a pocketful of grenades. But if progress was slow, at least it was economical of human life, and after the first assault the French casualties were small. Lannes himself was on view all day and often far into the night, directing, encouraging, and reconnoitring, and, like Ney and Murat, he was a source of perpetual inconvenience to his staff, for he always insisted on wearing, even within musket range of the enemy posts, his full-dress Marshal's uniform and all his orders and stars.

Week after week the struggle went on and the air became foul with the plague and the dead bodies and the smell of powder and the burning houses. House by house, and wall by wall, Lannes sapped his way into the town, detesting every moment of this style of warfare. 'I would sooner have ten battles a day,' he wrote to Madame la Maréchale, 'than this war against houses. I am so tired that I can hardly keep awake as I write.'

On the 18th of February the sapping had got sufficiently far forward for another assault and some progress was made against a fanatical resistance, and on the following day Saragossa surrendered, and Lannes set to work to clean up the appalling conditions in the city.

The state in which Saragossa was found by the French hardly bears description. It was a focus of corruption, one mass of putrefying corpses. According to a report which Lannes elicited from the municipal officers, nearly 54,000 persons had died in the place since the siege began. Of these about 20,000 were fighting-men, regular or irregular, the rest were non-combatants. Only 6,000 had fallen by fire and sword: the remainder were victims of the far more deadly pestilence.... It was weeks indeed before the dead were all buried: months before the contagion of the siege-fever died out from the miserable city.[1]

Poor old Lefèbvre, Duke of Danzig, came to grief at the beginning of 1809. For he was dismissed from his command by the Emperor and sent back to France. There appears to have been some considerable justification for this drastic action. Lefèbvre had been forgiven for ruining part of the Grand Plan in his pathetic eagerness to win a victory, and had been despatched on Christmas Eve, 1808, to cross the river Tagus, scatter the Estremaduran levies, and return to Talavera. But as the mental equipment of Lefèbvre was well known at Headquarters, the Emperor's despatch was repeated five times by Jourdan. Lefèbvre crossed the Tagus, scattered the Estremaduran levies, turned northwards, marched across the high mountains between Old and New Castile, and re-emerged, to the profound astonishment of everybody, at Avila. This was too much, even for the old hero of the Republic, and Napoleon wrote:

This Marshal does nothing but make blunders: he cannot seize the meaning of the orders sent to him. It is impossible to leave him in command of a corps, which is a pity, for he is a brave enough fellow on the battlefield.

[1] *Sir C.W.C. Oman*

* * *

161

Napoleon reached Paris from Spain in early January, 1809, and he found not merely intrigues against him in the capital, but a stirring of great forces against him in Central Europe. The ripples of Baylen had reached even the minds of Austrian politicians, and they had no further to go, and the Austrian common soldiers were beginning to use strange new words such as Fatherland, and Patriotism, and Freedom.

For several months Davout had been reporting from Warsaw and Breslau that Austria was arming. 'They are levying transport horses,' he was writing as early as September, 1808, 'in Old Galicia,' and a few days later the levy was extended into New Galicia. In the same month Davout reported that Austrian units were sending to Cracow to draw their mobilization equipment of guns. By the end of February, 1809, the Austrian mobilization was complete and, without any formal declaration of war, they pushed bravely up the valley of the Danube and into Bavaria to overwhelm the various isolated French corps before the Emperor could arrive.

Davout came hurrying down and understood the situation at once. The only possible strategy was to concentrate every available man at Donauworth and hold on against the Archduke Charles until the Emperor should arrive with reinforcements. With great rapidity and energy Davout proceeded to concentrate on Donauworth. But unfortunately, instead of the Emperor, it was Berthier who arrived first and, being senior to Davout on the list of Marshals of May 19th, 1804, he assumed command of the Army. It was now thirteen years since Berthier had begun to work at the side of the greatest military genius in the world, and he had played an intimate part in every single one of the sensational and wonderful victories of those thirteen years. But during all that time he had not grasped the vaguest elements of Napoleonic strategy. He had not even grasped the ordinary common-sense principle that it is better for an army to do the wrong thing decisively and with energy than to wobble about uncertainly between one policy and another.

The first thing Berthier did on superseding Davout was to cancel the orders for the concentration on Donauwörth, and order a concentration on Ratisbon. Davout stormed and raged and begged and threatened. The staff wizard was adamant, and in a twinkling the French Army was thrown into desperate confusion. Four days later, on April 17th, the Emperor arrived, and it required all his genius and all Davout's amazing tactical skill and all Lefèbvre's professional bulldog obstinacy to restore the situation. The battle of Eckmühl, which clinched the matter, was a simple affair in comparison with the work of Napoleon and Davout that made the battle possible. It was to Eckmühl that Masséna was summoned by the immortal message, 'Activité, activité, vitesse, je me recommande à vous,' and the old smuggler bravely responded to the galvanic scribble. Five days were enough, and on the fifth the fighting was brought to an end by the capture of Ratisbon by Lannes.

The assault on Ratisbon was Lannes' most spectacular feat of arms. The walls were high and strongly manned, and there was a deep ditch outside, so that the place looked impregnable to a sudden storm. But to sit down in front of the walls and open siege-works, and dig trenches and emplacements and mines and batteries, would fatally delay the campaign. Under cover of a siege of Ratisbon, the Archduke Charles would quickly reorganize his defeated army.

Lannes went forward to reconnoitre, and noticed a small house outside the wall on the edge of the ditch. Not far away was a large group of buildings which might shelter a battery and a storming party. He fetched up a battery, and in a short time demolished the house so that the debris fell into the ditch and made an improvised causeway. Lannes then brought up his grenadiers, and sent forward a party of volunteers with ladders. The party was mown down by the fire from the walls. A second party of volunteers took the ladders, and in turn was destroyed. No more volunteers came forward. Even the 'infernal column' was daunted. 'Very well,' said Lannes, 'I was a grenadier before I was a Marshal,' and, tucking a scaling-ladder under his arm, he set out alone for the wall. As usual he was in full-dress uniform with all his orders. Immediately a group of staff-officers ran to help him, and an A.D.C. politely offered to carry the ladder. The Marshal refused, and a good-natured scuffle for the pos-session of the ladder took place in the open ground between the two armies. The spectacle of their beloved Marshal wrangling with his staff for the privilege of car-rying a scaling-ladder up to the walls was more than the grenadiers could stand, and the entire regiment rushed for-ward to the assault. The Marshal led them, and the staff was at his heels, and the grenadiers were close behind the staff, and they all swept irresistibly into the town together.

It was Lannes who spoke sharply once to a colonel whom he overheard accusing a young officer of cow-ardice: 'No one but a swine or a coward ever boasts that he is never afraid.'

Napoleon did not disguise his opinion that in the mat-ter of the concentration Davout had been right and Berthier wrong, and the two men hated each other more warmly than ever.

On May 13th, 1809, Napoleon for the second time rode into captured Vienna, and was faced with the same problem as in 1805. The enemy's capital had been taken, but the enemy's army was on the north bank of the Danube. This time the Archduke Charles was on the north bank with 95,000 men, and if the French were to get at him, they must first cross the river under his nose and then fight with their backs to it. Napoleon, who described himself at St. Helena as probably the boldest general who ever lived, instantly made up his mind to take this great risk, and on May 21st Bessières went across to the north bank and occupied the villages of Aspern and Essling with a single corps of 17,000 men. At once the Archduke came down upon him with a rush. At the first shots, the regimental bands, whose fifes had shrilled above the cannonade on the Landgrafenberg at Jena, turned and bolted. Bessières held on, but he was hard pressed. The French sappers, however, had been working furiously at four pontoon bridges from the Vienna bank to the large island of Lobau, and four more from the island to the north bank, and all day the troops went hurrying across to the rescue. Masséna commanded the left, covering Aspern, and Lannes commanded the right, covering Essling. Officers who had fought beside the famous Gascon for years were painfully struck by the gloom on his face as he rode slowly across the bridges. And the painful impression was heightened when they heard him call out to the chief surgeon of his Corps, Doctor Lannefranque, 'Don't be slow following me. I shall probably need you today. This is going to be my last battle.'

The strength of Essling lay in its huge public granary – a three-storey building made of stone. It could hold four hundred men with ease, and the walls of the ground-floor were strong enough to resist a ball from a field-gun.

Early in the battle Bessières was put under the orders of Lannes, who was delighted at the chance of insulting the friend of Murat, and the man, moreover, who had reported the three hundred thousand franc deficit in Lannes' regimental accounts all those years before. Lannes' device for annoying Bessières was to send him message after message ordering him to charge 'right home'. The implication was, as Lannes intended it to be, that Bessières was attacking in a half-hearted way.

By the evening of that day a deadlock had been reached upon the battlefield. The French could make no headway northwards, nor the Austrians southwards, and when night fell there was a huge semicircle of Frenchmen on the north bank hemmed in by a still larger semicircle of Austrians.

But all the fighting was not yet over. Bessières' pride had been hurt. He had been publicly insulted by the man whom he and his hero Murat detested. That evening he and Lannes met by chance at Masséna's bivouac. Hot words were instantly spoken, accusations and counter-accusations exchanged, and a challenge offered and accepted. Masséna in vain tried to pacify the two Gascons, but when they clapped their hands to their sword-hilts, the older man changed his tone. 'I am the senior Marshal,' he said sternly. 'You are in my area, and I order you in the name of the Emperor not to draw your swords.' Neither of the hot-heads dared to face the dark, flashing eye of Masséna, and bloodshed was averted.

On that night Oudinot's Corps of Grenadiers crossed the river, and also the Imperial Guard (the grenadiers of the Guard threw their shakos into the Danube as they crossed, being convinced that they drew fire). At three o'clock in the morning the carnage began again, and by seven o'clock the French had recaptured both the villages. But at nine o'clock in the morning the French looked over their shoulders and saw that the bridges were on fire. Fire-boats had come swirling down the muddy stream and the pontoons were ablaze.

If the *Grande Armée* had been fighting for a day and a half to defeat the Hapsburg, it now had to fight to save its own skin. Annihilation, utter and absolute, was waiting for it if Aspern and Essling were lost before the sappers could repair the bridges. The battle flared up into a frantic struggle. It is hardly an exaggeration to say that the fortunes of Europe turned upon the race between the endurance of the infantry and the toil of the bridge engineers. If for one moment during that day the nerve of the French Line had failed – and well it might have failed after all those hours of death by bayoneting and bombarding in front and the terrible clouds of smoke behind – there might have been no need for a Waterloo. But the Line held. Aspern was lost at eleven o'clock, but not all the furious efforts of the Archduke Charles could make any impression on the defence of Essling, and when, at midday, the tirailleurs of the Guard went up as a reinforcement, the Austrians drew back, and the battle was over at last. The bridges were rebuilt, and in a grim, sullen silence the *Grande Armée* filed back, with Masséna holding the rear-guard as stubbornly as he had once held Genoa, on to the island of Lobau, leaving the field of a second Eylau behind them. First Russia, and now Austria, had shown that the Invincible could be held. The shadow was beginning to lengthen.

On that day of Aspern-Essling, Whit Tuesday of 1809, the first gap was struck in the glittering ranks of the Marshals, for Jean Lannes had been right. Aspern-Essling was his last battle. On the second day, after one of his divisional commanders had fallen, he himself went up to lead a counter-attack, calling out with a laugh as he went forward, 'I led the retreat from Marengo in just such a fire as this.' Soon afterwards he was mortally wounded. Many years before a fortune-teller had predicted that he would die like the great Turenne, of a cannon-shot, and at Aspern a cannon-shot struck him. Those pliable bones which had diverted so many bullets in the great years, had met more than their match at last, and his knee was broken. He was carried on an improvised stretcher of branches to one of the bridge-heads and Surgeon-General Larrey amputated his leg at once. For four days Lannes lay in hospital in Vienna talking cheerfully of future service, and making an A.D.C. write to a famous Viennese artificer named Master, asking him to come and measure him for a mechanical leg that would enable him to ride. But on the fifth day fever and delirium set in, and the Marshal-Duke of Montebello fought his last battle, shouting for cuirassiers, ordering up flying artillery, steadying the Line, reinforcing imaginary wings, and sending messengers to and fro. Napoleon came and stayed for half an hour, but the dying man was incoherent. At half-past six next morning the

Emperor came again and pushed the doctors aside to have one last look at the dead face of Jean Lannes, once apprentice dyer in Lectoure in Gascony, the old companion of Italy and Egypt, of St. Jean d'Acre, and Brumaire, and the passage of the Great St. Bernard, and Montebello, and the field of Marengo.

The French losses on those two days were 20,000 men, and the wounded suffered terribly in the transit across the bridges. It is characteristic of three of the Corps-Commanders that the egotistical, beauty-loving Masséna had no ambulances in his Corps; honest, incompetent Oudinot had a 50 per cent equipment; while the iron, ruthless Davout had his full 100 per cent of ambulances and his 100 per cent of doctors.

After the battle Surgeon-General Larrey hit upon the ingenious notion of using the cuirasses of dead soldiers of the heavy cavalry as sauce-pans in which to boil horse-flesh soup for the wounded. But the wounded were so numerous that many senior officers came running to the Emperor with the bitter complaint that the Surgeon-General was sacrificing their chargers for the soup. The Emperor instantly made Larrey a Baron.

* * *

All through the last days of May and the whole of June, the Master of Europe and five of his famous Marshals lay cooped up in Lobau, and the Archduke watched them from across the water. Here was a fine change from the rushing pursuit after Jena. Here was a come-down from the meeting with Tsar Alexander on the raft in the Niemen. Cooped up on an island. And by Austrians too. And the news from the other front was not so good either. The letters from the officers and the rank-and-file in Spain were so full of glooms and groans about assassinations, and ambuscades, and reminiscences of the hideous siege of Saragossa, and the revolting taste of

Spanish wine, and the atrocities, and the scarcity of rations, that Davout, temporarily commanding the military police on the island, suppressed all letters from Spain as likely to cause alarm and despondency among the troops. But the army that was pent on this small Danubian island was learning the lesson which the Army of Egypt had learnt ten years earlier, when the French fleet was blown into the sky by Nelson in the Bay of Aboukir, the lesson that its Commander never despaired.

For six weeks Napoleon worked at lightning speed. Secretaries toiled at his diplomatic correspondence, the army commanders at his military orders for the reconstruction of the debris of Aspern and Essling, and, above all, the aides-de-camp galloped far and wide in search of soldiers. Soldiers, soldiers, soldiers. Any reinforcement from a cavalryman to a corps. Any man who wore a uniform or had ever handled a musket. From all directions the streams of help came pouring across Central Europe to the small Danubian island. The most important of all was Marmont with his Corps from Illyria in the southwest, and the roads between Vienna and Ragusa were thick with couriers urging that self-satisfied young man to hurry, hurry, hurry. One despatch began in the usual formal way *'Monsieur le Duc de Raguse,'* and then suddenly the desperate urgency bursts through the etiquette with the cry, 'Marmont, you have the best corps in my army; I want you for a battle that I am going to fight. You are putting me back days by your loitering.' Poor Marmont! He was genuinely trying to make haste in his own way, but he had been three years away from the *Grande Armée*, and had forgotten the Napoleonic idea of hurrying. Besides, he was handicapped by his own fatal passion for building and improving, for his march was held up by the very fortifications of Graz which he had himself insisted on building in 1806.

At last the Army of Dalmatia arrived at the island and, after an independent command of three years, Marmont found himself swallowed up and lost in an army of 165,000 men and, worse still, only a general among Marshals, of whom one was the despised Bessières. 'With 12,000 men,' he reflected bitterly, 'one fights; with 30,000 one commands; but in great armies the commander is only a sort of Providence which can only intervene to ward off great accidents.' His temper was not improved by Davout's spirited attempt to hang his Ragusan servant as a spy.

The men came pouring in, until the Emperor felt strong enough to cross the river again. And now, of an evening, a couple of French infantry sergeants might be seen by the Austrian sentries on the other side, strolling down the bank of Lobau for a bathe in the river. 'Live and let live,' thought the Austrian sentries, and no one fired at the two sergeants, though the sentries might have fired if they had known that it was Napoleon and Masséna reconnoitring for the new bridge that was to be built across the river.

The new bridge was swiftly and suddenly built, and on the night of July 4th, 1809, in a terrific storm of rain, the crossing of the river began. All through the night the lightning sparkled on the bayonets and the guns, and the thunder drowned the roll of the wheels, and the steady tramp of the Line, and the thud of the hooves on the wooden bridges, and by midday on the 5th, 165,000 men were in battle array on that field of Marchfeld where King Rudolf fought in 1278 and founded the power of the House of Hapsburg. Davout held the right, Masséna the left. Masséna, whose horse had put a foot into a rabbit-hole on Lobau a few days before, was too lame to ride, and he took the field in a carriage with four white horses, and drove it, with his doctor sitting beside him, into the thick of the fighting round the gutted ruins of Aspern to direct his Group of Corps.

But the crisis of the battle of Wagram was neither on Masséna's wing nor on Davout's. It was in the centre, and there the Emperor commanded in person. It was in the centre that the fortunes of the battle rose to their fearful climax, and as the hopes of victory swung now to one side, now to the other, the soldier who had for thirteen years been concerned only with the high commanding of great masses of troops of all arms, went back to his first and best-loved weapon. On that day on the Marchfeld, the Emperor became the gunner once again, and blasted the advancing Austrians with his 'grand battery' of 100 guns that Lauriston, descendant of the Laws of Edinburgh, commanded. Then, under cover of this bombardment, Napoleon personally organized the formation of a mighty column of 36,000 men, and sent it under another Scotsman, General Macdonald, against the enemy centre, and the day was won.

The high officers as usual did not spare themselves. Oudinot, wearing not unworthily the shoes of Lannes, was the first man into the village of Wagram. Bessières was hit by a bullet which zigzagged along his thigh, threw him senseless to the ground, and tore his pistol-barrel from its stock.

'Who is it?' called out Napoleon, and someone shouted back, 'It is Bessières.' Another companion of Italy was down and Lannes only a few weeks buried.

'Let us go,' said the Emperor hurriedly. 'I have no time to weep.' But Bessières was only stunned, and the Guard, which loved him, breathed again.

At Wagram died young Lasalle, the handsome, the brilliant, the gay. 'This will be my last battle,' he said gloomily, as he rode at the head of his adoring light cavalry across the Danube bridge in the thunderstorm, and a stray bullet killed him at the very end of it all, when the battle had been won and the Archduke Charles was in full retreat. He was thirty-four years of age, and had been a general for four years. Of the four young *beaux sabreurs* two were dead, Colbert and Lasalle, and only Sainte-Croix and Montbrun were left. The shadows were steadily deepening over the Napoleonic fantasy.

After Jena in '06 the *Grande Armée* thundered across Germany; after Wagram in '09 it lay down and got drunk on the wines of Moravia, and the Archduke Charles retired in good order.

At Wagram for the first and last time, a Marshal was given his baton on the field of battle, when the Emperor rode up to Macdonald and, with the words, 'Let us be friends hereafter,' embraced him and made him Marshal of France. Incidentally, this was the only occasion, except for Brune's indiscretion, on which this phrase was used. All the others were Marshals of the Empire.

***

Étienne Macdonald was the son of a Scots clansman who came from the Island of South Uist. After the '45 the clansman escaped with Prince Charles and enlisted in Ogilvy's Scottish regiment in France, and later settled in Sedan, where the future Marshal was born in 1765. It is recorded of the old exile that he spoke French and English and Gaelic, and that he was a gentle, quiet man, and that he played the violin.

Young Macdonald joined Dillon's regiment as a gentleman–cadet, and spent the last four years before the Revolution in dancing and theatre-going and, like his father, violin-playing. Lieutenant-colonel after Valmy in 1792, a general in '93, he had a command in the famous attack across the ice under the batteries of Nimeguen and Kokerdom when the Dutch fleet was captured by hussars. In 1798 Macdonald was commanding in Naples and Rome, but his command was not a fortunate one. For he was not only seriously hammered at the Trebbia by Suvorov, but he also lost his entire collection of works of art, which he had 'collected' during his occupation of the south. For many years he mourned the loss of his Etruscan vases, his frescoes from Pompeii, his Old Masters, and especially he mourned the loss of a huge piece of statuary, in the shape of a basket of dessert, in which the fruit was made of different-coloured marbles. In 1800 Macdonald saved something of his military reputation by leading his army over the Splügen Pass in the depths of mid-winter, through a three-day hurricane, a feat that some have thought was as splendid as the First Consul's crossing of the Great St. Bernard.

Macdonald was one of those rare characters who are fundamentally straightforward and honest, and yet can reconcile with their own consciences any amount of coat-turning. Throughout Macdonald's long life no one ever impugned his honour or doubted his loyalty, and there is no doubt whatever that he himself was conscious of nothing queer in his various transferences of allegiance. A pre-Revolution Royalist, and an ardent post-Revolution Republican, he helped Bonaparte at Brumaire to overthrow the Constitution. Within two years he was back in the Republican camp, and was strongly suspected of intriguing with Moreau to overthrow the Consulate. After the conspiracies had all collapsed and Moreau had been exiled to America, Macdonald was struck off the active list and spent nearly five years in disgrace at his estate at Courcelles-le-Roi. But in 1809 the supply of recruits for the *Grande Armée* was greatly in excess of the supply of experienced leaders, and Macdonald, recalled to service, was delighted to become a staunch Imperialist. Nor was that the end of his honest and loyal *voltes-face*.

***

A week or two after Wagram, Marmont at last received his baton and became a Marshal. Marmont was Napoleon's oldest friend. He was the son of a rich iron-master in Burgundy who had himself been an officer in the Hainault Regiment, and as a cadet at the Artillery School of Dijon in '92 young Marmont had made the acquaintance of Lieutenant Bonaparte, at that time stationed near by at Auxonne. Marmont went with his friend, by now a major, to the siege of Toulon in 1794, that tiny episode which brought such colossal consequences to the world, and later, in 1796, with him to the Army of Italy. At the battle of Arcola Marmont was one of those who dragged the Commander-in-Chief out of the ditch, when the French assault was being stoutly driven back by the Croatian infantry. In Egypt it was to Marmont, by no means the most senior of his generals, that Bonaparte first confided his plan of escape, and at the *coup d'état* of Brumaire he commanded the artillery. His reward was the command of all the artillery of the Reserve Army at Dijon, and it was owing to his technical skill and inexhaustible ingenuity that the guns were got over the St. Bernard Pass. It is an often-told story how Marmont took the guns off their carriages and put them in hollow tree-trunks, and how he slipped them past the Fort de Bard, with the wheels tied up with straw and the ground covered with manure from local farmhouses to deaden the sound, and with fifty men hauling on each piece. The story of Marengo has already been given, how Marmont with his own last five guns and thirteen others supported the counter-attack of Desaix and the charge of young Kellermann, and how the three of them, under Bonaparte, snatched a victory out of a defeat.

After Marengo the young gunner-general was given the congenial task of reorganizing the entire artillery of the French Army. In standardization of equipment, which was his great passion, Marmont was many years ahead of his time. For example, he found that in the French artillery of the old design of Gribeauval there were twenty-two types of wheel. Marmont reduced them to eight. And it was the same with harness, saddlery, tools, spare parts, and all the rest of the artillery equipment. He took each in turn and insisted upon standardization. He also made the six-inch gun the standard pattern for the field artillery, his reason being that all the Continental armies, except the

Spanish, used this calibre, and by adopting it the French would be able to make use of captured guns and shells. When Marmont seized the great arsenal at Milan in 1800, out of all the vast equipment that he found there, he was only able to mount five Austrian guns for service at Marengo, whereas in 1805 and 1809 the French artillery was almost entirely re-equipped out of the arsenal in Vienna, thanks to Marmont's foresight in adopting the six-inch calibre.

In 1804, after failing to raise a loan for the First Consul from the Dutch on the security of the great Regent Diamond, his energies were employed, first in equipping the Army of the Coasts of the Ocean with artillery, and afterwards with the command of the Second Corps at Utrecht.

Then came the great rush to Ulm and the engulfing of the unfortunate General Mack, and Marmont's Corps was swung out to the south-east to guard the approaches from Hungary, and to join hands with Masséna coming up from Italy. He was not, therefore, present at Austerlitz.

When the war of 1805 came to an end, Marmont was sent to govern the Dalmatian Provinces. It was an ideal opportunity for him and he grasped it brilliantly. His passion for building and road-making and organizing public services was given a free run. He was on his own, he was many hundreds of miles from Paris, and during 1807 and 1808 he thoroughly enjoyed himself. 'There were no roads in Dalmatia,' said the peasants, 'before Marmont came. When Marmont got on his horse, work was begun, and when he got off, the road was finished.' The roadlessness of Dalmatia was due to the fact that the Venetians had held the country from the sea. Marmont's task was to hold it from the land. His activity was prodigious. He set up a new constitution for the ancient city of Ragusa, conducted negotiations with Montenegro and Turkey, created the Dalmatian Legion, appointed new judges, reorganized the finances both of his army and of the country, established large depôts in various towns in order to enable him to march independently of lines of communication, drew up plans for an invasion of Turkey, decentralized the military hospitals, built fortifications, bridges, dykes among the marsh-lands, and cuttings through the rocks, and during his governorship visited every village and hamlet in all Dalmatia, and knew every hill and mountain by its name. 'Certainly the Romans never made anything more beautiful,' says the young commander (who at no time suffered from undue modesty), when writing of his roads, 'or anything more difficult or more admirable.' It was during his governorship that an English squadron forced the Dardanelles, and Marmont commented shrewdly upon this sensational event: 'This feat was regarded as extraordinary, but it is a prodigy that will always be renewed, so long as the straits are only armed with heavy immobile guns, that can only fire one round at a squadron advancing with the wind behind.'

For all this work Marmont was created Duke of Ragusa. After Wagram in 1809, the new Marshal was sent back to govern and reorganize Illyria in the same way. In Illyria his main difficulties were with the Turkish Pashas, and he dealt with them so drastically that for a generation the Turkish mothers used his name to frighten their children.

***

Lannes was dead and, as everyone expected, his understudy, Nicolas Charles Oudinot, stepped into his shoes. Oudinot was the son of a brewer of Bar-le-Duc and had worked for a time in the family business (Ney might have made barrels for his beer), and at the battle of Wagram he was forty-one. He was several times a chief-of-staff, to Masséna at Zürich and Genoa, and to Brune in Italy in 1801, but his natural inclination to slip up to the front line and lead a charge or two when no one was looking was apt to impair the efficiency of his staff-work. As an independent commander Oudinot was so obsessed with the terror of losing his artillery that he seldom allowed it to come into action at all, and his record of success was, in consequence, extremely meagre. But as a leader of the 'infernal column' of grenadiers, he was second only to Lannes. During his career Oudinot was wounded thirty-four times. At Friedland a bullet broke two of his teeth, and he complained, with his loud cheerful laugh, that the Russian dentists were bad at extractions. And the Emperor, seeing him one day recklessly throwing handfuls of money to his companions, observed 'You give away the gold and keep the lead.' He was a simple, hearty man, and he found a congenial and convivial companion in the jolly Marshal Mortier, who shared his love of drinking, singing, and roulette. It is recorded that in the long winter evenings of 1807 in Danzig, the pair of them persuaded even the dignified Soult and the stern Davout to join in their favourite game of shooting out the candles after dinner with their pistols.

Curiously enough there was a long and devoted friendship between the roystering brewer's son and the cold, aristocratic Davout.

Three new titles were created that autumn, and they were the grandest of all the military titles, for Berthier, already Prince of Neufchâtel, was made Prince of Wagram; Masséna, already Duke of Rivoli, was made Prince of Essling; and Davout, already Duke of Auerstädt, was made Prince of Eckmühl. Soult, who had no military title, was angrier than ever that two of his colleagues should have a couple apiece.

***

While these new dignitaries of the Empire were basking in their promotion and their titles (Oudinot became Duke of Reggio and Macdonald Duke of Taranto; neither title was taken from a military exploit), one of their colleagues was in serious trouble.

On the day after the battle of Wagram, Marshal Bernadotte, Prince of Ponte-Corvo, and husband of the delicious little Désirée Clary, supplemented the Emperor's bulletin of victory with a private bulletin of his own, which he published to his Corps of Saxons. In it he thanked them for having won such a notable victory, and implied that practically nobody else on the French side had been there at all. It was the last straw. Bernadotte had foxed years ago at Brumaire, he had intrigued with Moreau, he was under grave suspicion of having let Davout down at Auerstädt in 1806, and be had allowed De La Romana to escape from Denmark with almost an entire Spanish Corps. And now, here he was publicly claiming the credit of the Emperor's victory, the victory which had been won by the Emperor's plans, by the Emperor's grand battery, and by the Emperor's massed column of infantry. Bernadotte was summoned to Headquarters and formally expelled from the *Grande Armée*.

His career seemed to be over. But hardly had he crept back, disgraced, into Paris, when the English handed an army on the Flemish island of Walcheren. Antwerp, Napoleon's naval base, was their objective, and their attack was well timed, for the Emperor was hundreds of miles distant on the Danube, with Davout and Masséna and Bessières and Macdonald and Oudinot and Marmont. And Lannes was dead, and Soult and Ney were in Spain. The cats were all away, and Sir Richard Strachan and the Earl of Chatham landed at Walcheren to play.

But Fouché, the Minister of the Interior and the Minister of Police, cared nothing whatever about what had, or had not, happened at Wagram, and he took upon himself the responsibility of raising an army and putting Bernadotte at the head of it for the defence of Antwerp. The Marshal quickly organized a defence, and then prudently decided to save himself some trouble, and France some thousands of men, by sitting down and allowing the fevers and the agues of the island of Walcheren to do the rest of the work for him. He had no wish to annoy anyone by being too drastic, particularly such people as the English. If crowns were going a-begging, and after all MURAT WAS A KING, the support of the English might be very useful indeed. If he drove them into the sea, they might be cross. But they could not blame him if they caught cold.

So he sat down cunningly and waited. He was a certain winner whatever happened. In a very short time the fevers and agues got to work, and they were effectively helped by the utter incompetence of the English Commanders.

> Lord Chatham with his sword undrawn
> Was waiting for Sir Richard Strachan.
> Sir Richard, longing to be at 'em,
> Was waiting too-for whom? Lord Chatham.

In due course the remnants of the fever-ridden, expensive, tragic expedition went home to England, and Bernadotte returned to Paris.

* * *

After Wagram, the Emperor and the seven Marshals – Berthier, Masséna, Davout, Bessières, Macdonald, Marmont, and Oudinot – went back to Schönbrunn Palace for a rest after their exertions, and couriers arrived with news of their colleagues on the other fronts.

Murat, down at Naples, was enjoying himself and playing with gun-boats, and watching the clumsy manoeuvres of Sir John Stuart, a dawdling, incompetent, evil-minded man. Murat had made his contribution to the victories of Eckmühl and Ratisbon by firing salutes at Reggio and Scilla.

Things were quiet in the north, for Germany had sunk back into hopeless apathy when the huge extinguisher of Wagram damped down the fires which Baylen had lit and Aspern-Essling fanned. Wagram was to Aspern-Essling in 1809 what Friedland had been to Eylau in 1807, a monstrous douche of cold water upon excited heads.

On the other hand, the Napoleonic news from Spain was not so good. Indeed it was worse than that: it was extremely annoying. Marmont, as the junior Marshal, had to read out, at a luncheon in Schönbrunn, the despatch which announced that Jourdan and Victor had attacked prematurely and had let the English slip out of the net at Talavera, when a few more days' delay would have brought Soult and Ney across their lines of communication. It was pure incompetence on the part of Jourdan and Victor, of course, and it was Jourdan's last chance of becoming Duke of Fleurus. Nothing could be simpler than the annihilation of these English, and Napoleon called for his maps of Spain, and stormed against Jourdan and Victor, and dictated floods of orders for vast co-ordinated sweeps of all the various armies in the Peninsula, and the couriers galloped back with the floods of orders from Vienna to Madrid. These orders were masterpieces of the strategical art, with the exceptions that they assumed that the Spanish roads were like German roads, that they ignored the impossibility of gaining military information from the inhabitants of Spain, that they ignored the existence of a ration-supply problem in Spain, and that when they arrived in Madrid they were at least six weeks out of date. Apart from these trifling matters they were brilliant.

Talavera was not the only worrying news from the extreme south-western front. A copy of the manifesto of Soult's chief-of-staff in Oporto, inviting co-operation in the Rei Nicolao movement, reached Vienna, and the Emperor's eyes bulged in their sockets as he read it. His reply was quite free from ambiguity.

'The Emperor is astounded to find the chief of the staff suggesting to the generals that the Marshal should be requested to
take up the reins of government, and assume the attributes of
supreme authority. If he had assumed sovereign power on his
own responsibility, it would have been a crime, clear *lèse-majesté*,
an attack on the imperial authority. How could a man of sense,
like Soult, suppose that his master would permit him to exer-
cise any power that had not been delegated to him? No wonder
that the army grew discontented, and that rumours got about
that the Marshal was working for himself, not for the Emperor
or France. After receiving this circular, it is doubtful whether
any French officer would not have been fully justified in refusing to obey any further orders issued from Oporto.'[1]

It was clear to Napoleon that something would have
to be done about Spain. He would have liked to go
down himself for a few weeks and polish the English off
once and for all, but there was the whole of Continental
Europe to be settled, and, more important still, there
was still the Imperial Dynasty to be founded, and an
heir by Joséphine was now out of the question. Until the
Dynasty was started, the Marshals would have to look
after Spain, and the Emperor would give them all possible help with advice, instructions, lectures, and plenty of
vast co-ordinated plans from Paris, or Erfurt, or Vienna, or
wherever he happened to be.

But changes in the High Command in Spain were
overdue, and the Emperor sat down to consider the matter. Soult was an able strategist, but no tactician; Ney had
not a superior in the handling of a corps, but lacked the
experience to make him a strategist; Victor was a stupid
fool, Mortier a pleasant one; Augereau was an ass; Lannes was
dead. In fact there were only two men who were fit to
take on the job of the Command of the Army of Portugal
and smash the absurd Wellesley, and one of them must go

[1] *Sir C. W. C. Oman.*

to Spain. It had to be either Masséna or Davout. But there were other factors to consider. There was North Germany to be held, for instance. And the neutrality of Sweden was getting wobbly. And Russia was definitely drifting out of the Napoleonic orbit. And Prussia was almost beginning to tap at the walls of its dungeon, and the English cruisers swarmed in the Baltic and at the mouths of the Germanic rivers, running the blockade and evading the Berlin Decrees. An iron hand was wanted in Hamburg, the key to all these locks, and no one could describe Masséna as an iron hand. He was a great soldier on the field of battle, and a passionate worshipper of women and money off it. But he was no administrator and no organizer. And besides, imagine the opportunities for swindling and graft which the old smuggler would have in Hamburg, with all the world clamouring for licences to trade with England. Masséna had done pretty well for himself in Naples in '06, in spite of his lost Livorno millions, and Naples would be nothing to Hamburg. Davout, on the other hand, was as honest as the day, and a superb administrator and a strong man. He was also passionately devoted to the Emperor. It was sometime during this year that someone told Davout that Maret, the Minister of Foreign Affairs, was very devoted to Napoleon. 'Yes,' replied Davout, 'but he is not so devoted as I am. If the Emperor told Maret and me to destroy Paris and everyone in it, Maret would keep the secret, but warn his family. I would not even warn my family for fear the secret might leak out.' So Davout went to Hamburg, and Masséna went to the Army of Portugal.

Jourdan, after many despairing entreaties, was at last allowed to leave Spain, and Soult became Joseph's military adviser.

CHAPTER XIII

THE LINES OF TORRES VEDRAS

IN 1810 the whole of the top-heavy, super-centralized, heterogeneous Empire was at peace, except only in the Spanish corner, and on all the High Seas of the world. Berthier, Prince of Neufchâtel and Wagram, the ugly little map-wizard, found his military occupation gone to such an extent that, instead of regulating the flood of marching columns across Europe, he was at work, armed with a million and a half francs in diamonds, wooing, by proxy for his master, the Princess Marie Louise of Hapsburg.

As usual, the master-psychologist had chosen the right man. Murat would have been too sensational, Bernadotte too handsome, Bessières too polished, Davout too inhuman, and Masséna, of course, would infallibly have seduced the lady. But Berthier was honest and sincere, and crazily in love with the Visconti and, more important, he was so ugly, with his fearful stutter and his frizzy hair, that even the stoutish little Emperor must appear handsome in comparison.

All through 1810 Masséna, Soult, Ney, Mortier, Bessières, Victor, and, each for part of the year, Augereau and Macdonald, struggled on in Spain, hating the country, hating the people, hating the war, and bickering with each other. The war in Spain was the most cruel, the most pitiless, the most desperate of all wars. Not even the Thirty Years' War, not even Alva and his Crusade of Extermination in the Netherlands, was accompanied by such tortures and hangings, such cold assassinations and such wild blazing furies of sack, destruction, and annihilation. Fifty times the Spanish armies were routed. Fifty times their garrisons were starved or stormed. But to the very end the Spanish nation was undefeated. For six years it countered sack with murder, hanging with torture, and the tactical expertness of the French professional soldiers with the horrors of ruthless guerilla warfare. Even the children were taught in their catechism that all men in the world were their neighbours except the French, and that it was a sacred, religious, compulsory duty to kill all Frenchmen.

'In Spain a small army is defeated and a large army starves.' The Marshals had the choice between feeding their men without fighting, or starving their men in preparation for battle. And the Marshals were always fighting in the dark. Each valley, each outpost, each town was entirely cut off from its neighbours by the fanatical peasants with their knives and their ambuscades. To send a despatch by a single courier was infallibly to lose both. It required a couple of hundred cavalrymen, in a poverty-stricken country where forage was scarce, to take a message from one general to another. Masséna in Portugal was three months without receiving a message even from Madrid, let alone Paris. Soult in Andalusia had not the faintest idea what Mortier was doing in Estremadura, or Masséna in Portugal, or Bessières in Old Castile. Augereau in Barcelona might have been in a different continent for all that he knew of Suchet's doings in Aragon, only about a hundred and sixty miles away. Each army was like a ship on the high seas, cutting its way through the water, and leaving no trace behind of how it had come or whence it had come, and giving no indication of whither it was going. Often a Marshal's information about Wellington's manoeuvres was received by courier from Napoleon, who had got it from an English newspaper, which had got it by sea from Lisbon.

And all the time the Emperor was directing gigantic combined operations from France or Germany, just as if he was standing on the hill over against Austerlitz, or on the Landgrafenberg at Jena with his telescope resting on the shoulder of an A.D.C., or in the heat of the fire at Wagram. The orders for the direction and the coordination of the armies in Spain came down unceasingly from Paris, or from the Emperor's travelling carriage, or from Schönbrunn in Vienna, and there were always the two fatal defects about these orders, that they assumed that Spain was a flat, easy country, and that they were invariably one or two months out of date. It has often been said that the Marshals in Spain were bad co-operators. With the two appalling obstacles, the guerrilla warfare and the Imperial orders, it is amazing that any of them achieved anything whatever, and Masséna and Ney and Marmont displayed the highest qualities of talent and resolution. Probably no general in history has ever had such an easy task as Wellington had. Working on interior lines, with a mercenary army, in a country where every peasant and priest was at once an ally, a source of information, and an active assassin, with a constant flow of supplies from England, and with the complete command of the sea, the Duke of Wellington had the game in his hands, and yet it took him nearly six years to advance from Lisbon to the Pyrenees.

***

The redoubtable Prince of Essling arrived at Salamanca in May, 1810, to take command of the Army of Portugal. But he was no longer the man of Zürich. The tenacity with which he clung to Genoa in 1800 was still there, but not the supreme opportunism and

55555

judgement with which he pounced on Korsakov and drove him out of Switzerland and so saved France.

> 'When he first assembled round him at Salamanca' says Sir Charles Oman, 'the staff which was to serve him in the invasion, he astonished and somewhat disheartened his officers by beginning his greetings to them with the remark, "Gentlemen, I am here contrary to my own wish; I begin to feel myself too old and too weary to go on active service. The Emperor says that I must, and replied to the reasons for declining this post which I gave him by saying that my reputation would suffice to end the war. It was very flattering, no doubt, but no man has two lives to live on this earth – the soldier least of all." Those who had served under the Marshal a few years back, and now saw him after an interval, felt that there was truth in what he said. Foy wrote in his diary, "He is no longer the Masséna of the flashing eyes, the mobile face, and the alert figure whom I knew in 1799, and whose head then recalled to me the bust of Marius. He is only fifty-two, but he looks more than sixty; he has got thin, he is beginning to stoop; his look, since the accident when he lost his eye by the Emperor's hand, has lost its vivacity. The tone of his voice alone remains unchanged." '

Ney was appalled at the difference. He too had fought at Zürich and remembered the great days, and he had written to Junot, 'I am delighted with the choice of Masséna. The good of the Service demanded a unified Command.' But disillusionment was quick, and within a fortnight the Duke of Elchingen was writing a letter to Masséna that was simply impertinent. He had sent in to Headquarters a string of reports and letters, none of which had even been acknowledged, and in one of his sudden flaming passions he wrote, 'Tell me either to attack Wellington or to besiege Ciudad Rodrigo, one or the other. If I don't hear from you by return, I shall march my Corps back to their old quarters at Salamanca and wait till you've made up your mind.' The fires of the Sambre-et-Meuse still smouldered beneath the red head of Michel Ney.

But though Masséna's arrival disappointed some of his senior officers, it gravely alarmed Lord Wellington. The game had to be changed, and no more liberties could be taken. There could be no more lighthearted excursions to Talavera to wrestle a fall with Jourdan or Victor; no stealthy pounces upon Oporto to oust the day-dreaming Soult. 'Gentlemen,' said Lord Wellington sternly to some frivolling officers, 'we are in the presence of one of the first soldiers of Europe', and seldom in the history of warfare have two opponents been so closely matched.

'You turned every hair on my body white,' said Masséna to the Duke when they met, years later, at Soult's house.

'We were pretty level,' replied the Duke, but the Prince of Essling insisted that the Duke had had the best of it.

The first encounter reflected little credit on either of them, for Wellington made a stand on the ridge at Bussaco and Masséna attacked him there, without either of them discovering the road that completely turned the English left and should have made the position untenable. Ney, leading the advance-guard, was in favour of attacking the ridge before the English were fully marshalled, but Masséna, ten miles behind was so fully occupied with the charming girl who accompanied him on the campaign, wearing the gay, fetching uniform of a captain of dragoons, that for two hours he refused to listen to Ney's A.D.C., Colonel D'Esmenard, who shouted at him through his bedroom door. Where were the Ghosts of the Sambre-et-Meuse? What were they thinking that Spanish afternoon?

When Masséna finally attacked the ridge – he had not heard an English gun since the days when Admiral Keith's cruisers used to stand in to Genoa and bombard the water-front – he was disastrously driven back by the steady fire of the English Line.

After the battle, Masséna's staff found the flanking road at last. There were eighty-one officers all told on the staff, and as there were no lines of communication and the army was fully concentrated, there was not much for them to do, and they might well have found it before. The moment it was found, Masséna roused a flash of his

ancient, irresistible vigour and bundled Wellington back
into Lisbon in no time, and then sat down in front of
the Lines of Torres Vedras. The greatest compliment to
the strength of the Lines that can be paid is simply to
record that Ney gave them one glance and emphatically
declined to attack them. A place had to be very strong
indeed for Ney to refuse to make even one shot at it. A
few weeks earlier, at the siege of Ciudad Rodrigo, the veteran defen-der, General Herrasti, had appeared in the
breach with a flag of truce and asked to be conducted
through the French troops to meet the French Commander. 'No need for that,' exclaimed Ney, jumping out
of the forward sap where he was preparing to lead the
assault of the breach. But he, like Wellington, drew a line
at Torres Vedras.

In October of this year General Sainte-Croix, commanding Masséna's cavalry, went riding down to
reconnoitre the banks of the Tagus. An English gunboat
tried a pot-shot and cut the general in two. Sainte-Croix,
who was about twenty-eight years old, was the third of
the four brilliant young cavalry generals of the Empire.
He had been Masséna's chief-of-staff on the island of
Lobau, and it was freely rumoured that the Emperor
thought so highly of him that he was actually contem-
plating making him a Marshal. However that may be, it is
certain that only Sainte-Croix was able to force old
Masséna into strong and resolute action, and his loss had
an incalculable effect.

Of the four gay young generals, Lasalle, Colbert, and
Sainte-Croix were dead, and only Montbrun was alive.

The year dragged on in a dreary stalemate of destruction, desolation, barbarity, murder, and disease, and at
last even the stubborn, resolute man who had made
possible the victory of Marengo in 1800 by holding so
grimly on to Genoa, was forced to retreat into Spain. No
man except Masséna would have clung on so resolutely
or so long, and Wellington was amazed at his tenacity.

Wellington himself had said that 100,000 men could turn him out of Portugal, but certainly not fewer. Masséna's army at its full strength was only 65,000.

The retreat was as terrible as the advance had been.

'Every horror that could make war hideous,' says Napier, 'attended this retreat. Distress, conflagrations, death, in all modes from wounds, from fatigue, from water, from the flames, from starvation! On all sides unlimited violence, unlimited vengeance. I myself saw a peasant hounding on his dog to devour the dead and dying, and the spirit of cruelty smote even the brute creation; for the French general, to lessen encumbrances, ordered beasts of burden to be destroyed, and the inhuman fellow charged with the execution hamstringed five hundred asses and left them to starve; they were so found by the British and the mute, sad, deep expression of pain and grief visible in the poor creatures' looks excited a strange fury in the soldiers: no quarter would have been given at that time: humane feelings would have thus led direct to cruelty. But all passions are akin to madness.'

The shortage of horses and mules was so acute that the poor little lady-captain of dragoons had to be carried by grenadiers. Ney held the rear-guard with all his matchless tactical skill (during the retreat he met for the first time, and was greatly astonished by, shrapnel shells), but the friction between him and Masséna increased every day. The gentle dalliance on the eve of Bussaco still rankled, and Ney had publicly 'cut' the little dragoon-lady at a luncheon-party at Headquarters, and, on receiving a present of a telescope from Masséna which had been looted from the University of Coimbra, he had sent it back with the message that he did not receive stolen goods. Masséna, the silent, crafty man, endured all this without a word, as well as a great deal of angry abuse from his fiery junior. Words never hurt Masséna.

***

During this year, 1810, in Catalonia, Marshal Augereau devised the ingenious plan of conciliating the countryside and endearing France to the populace, by hanging everyone in sight. For four months the trees along the Catalonian roads sagged under their load of dangling, dancing, swinging corpses. But somehow the method did not seem to work, and the Emperor tried a new one. Augereau was replaced by Macdonald, whose natural amiability was unruffled even by the gout which attacked him at Figueras, and the policy of indiscriminate hanging was called off. But it was too late. Augereau had made his fatal mark, and Macdonald's clemency and friendliness could not undo what had been done. (For some months the Catalonian campaign presented an unique feature when a Spanish Army commanded by an Irishman, Henry O'Donnell, manoeuvred and fought against a Franco-Italian Army commanded by a Scotsman, Macdonald. Rarely has the ancient Celtic house of Donald been so divided against itself.)

Down in the warm and pleasant south, Soult and Victor and Mortier were having a much better time, each in his different way.

Soult was delighted to escape from Ney, and had marched southwards in the gayest of spirits. On his way from north to south he found some British wounded in Plasencia, and provided them with medical comforts, and muskets with which to defend themselves against bandits.

Andalusia was a paradise after the miseries of the north, and Soult's men began to recover some of their morale as they marched, gazing eagerly around and marvelling, past the orange-groves and the lemon-groves of that enchanting and easy-going land. The Andalusian was not like the fierce, unrelenting, partisan of the north. He forgave and forgot, even the appalling sack of Cordova by Dupont only a year ago, when 'scenes of horror were enacted such as had not been seen since the Christian drove out the Moor in 1236.'[1] Only a year ago the Andalusians had, by way of reprisal, tortured and blinded prisoners, and thrown General Réné into a vat of boiling water. But there was no tenacity of purpose in that lazy land, and Soult found himself in a very pleasant situation.

The visions and the dreams, so rudely dispelled by Wellesley at Oporto, began to flit across the sky once more. 'Murat is a King.' Why not Nicolas, King of Andalusia?

And in the meantime there were plenty of works of art to be collected and churches to be relieved of treasures that they were best without. *'Fais ce que tu dois, advienne que pourra,'* was Soult's favourite motto, and he translated it, freely, 'Take what you can, come what may.' There was a proverb among the French Peninsular armies: 'Spain is the death of the soldier, the ruin of the officer, and the fortune of the general.'

So Soult, who had dallied in Oporto, dallied again in Seville, instead of making the lightning dash on Cadiz that his master would have made. But his master was not in Andalusia. He was in Paris, busy on dynastic affairs. He had proved that he was capable of founding a dynasty, and it was more important to complete the foundation than to bother about a far-off series of skirmishes. Ultimately Marshal Victor sat down in front of Cadiz, when it was much too late to capture it by a sudden onfall.

Victor at Cadiz in 1810 held the western wing of the *Grande Armée,* while Poniatowski the Pole held the eastern wing in Poland, and Murat the southern in Naples, and Davout the northern at the mouths of the Germanic rivers. It was a long front.

The siege of Cadiz was a dull job for a hot-headed ex-drummer-boy, especially as Victor at this time was in a furious rage with Jourdan. For after Victor's grotesquely rash attacks on the English at Talavera had been twice

---

[1] *Foy.*

191

repulsed, Jourdan advised him to give it up. 'If I don't succeed in one more shot,' cried Victor, 'I ought to chuck
soldiering.' He had a third shot, and was heavily repulsed
again, and now old fool Jourdan kept on writing to him
at Cadiz and suggesting that he should chuck soldiering.
But it was impossible in the pleasant land of Andalusia,
even though the wine was bad, to be angry for long, and
Victor soon recovered his spirits, and amused himself with
banging off quite uselessly, at long range, his immense battery of siege artillery which had been captured in, or
founded in, the arsenal at Seville.

It was in Andalusia that Soult discovered a very important principle of looting, namely, that an ardently Catholic
population would much sooner lose pictures by Velazquez
and Murillo than sacred vessels of silver and gold, and he
very quickly put this principle into practice. He must
have smiled many a gentle smile, as every week his Headquarters looked more and more like a great museum, at
the thought of Looter Augereau stuck in that horrible
Catalonia, and Swindler Masséna starving in a devastated
Portugal. There were also some capital quicksilver mines
at Almaden, in which the Duke of Dalmatia drove a roaring export trade, and it is even hinted that he profited
greatly by selling corn, through a chain of secret agents, to
the English armies. Whether this be true or not, Soult was
in clover. From time to time he took the field. For example he captured the fortress of Badajoz, and contrived not
to win the battle of Albuera when by all the rules of war
and common sense he must have won it. For if ever a man
outmanoeuvred another and caught him completely, it
was when Soult laid his entire army athwart the right
wing and even behind the right wing of Beresford, and yet
he managed not to win. The Duke of Wellington made a
shrewd remark when he said that Soult was a good man
at bringing his men on to the field, but he did not seem
to know what to do with them when he had got them
there. French contemporary critics said that the reason

was that he was no hero, and disliked the smell of powder, and thus was out of touch with his tactics. It is certainly true that Soult was never a front-line man like Ney, Lannes, Murat, Augereau, or Oudinot.

The placid Mortier was always content to do what his staff or his wife told him, and he marched about Andalusia and Estremadura in accordance as orders were given or appeals for co-operation made. On one occasion he even proposed to help Masséna against Wellington, thereby causing grave alarm in the latter's camp. But to Soult, now Viceroy of Andalusia, the safety of Seville was far more important than helping Masséna, and Mortier was promptly recalled.

***

Another Marshal who was enjoying himself in the sun was King Joachim of Naples, late Commander of the Reserve Cavalry. He made one pretence of invading Sicily, but that unfortunate strip of water between Reggio and Messina was so much better adapted for English cruisers than for dragoons and cuirassiers, that the attempt was soon abandoned. So Murat confined his main activities to the setting-up of a grand pavilion, with a streaming banner on top, within full view of every English sentry on the Sicilian side, on the heights of Pizzo.

Six years later Murat came back to Pizzo for one brief afternoon.

***

A Marshal of the Empire received a princedom in 1810, but not at the gift of the Emperor. For in the summer the Swedes approached the disgraced Bernadotte, Prince of Ponte-Corvo, and asked him to become Crown Prince of Sweden with a view to his ultimately becoming king. They told him that his government of Hanover and the Hanseatic cities had proved that he was a great administrator, and that his gentlemanly treatment of the Swedes whom he had captured at Lübeck in 1806, had made his name a household word in the north. Bernadotte, though delighted with the offer, was in no way taken in by the reasons for it. 'I have been chosen,' he said frankly to his friends, but not to the Swedes, 'not for my *beaux yeux,* but because I am a general, and with the tacit understanding that I am to reconquer Finland for them.' The Emperor, hearing that the Swedes were on the look-out for a Crown Prince, would have preferred either to transfer brother-in-law Murat from Naples, or to promote one of the three princes, Berthier, Masséna, or Davout.

But the Swedes were firm, and on the 30th of September, 1810, the Prince of Ponte-Corvo departed for Sweden, and on the 20th of October he landed at Helsinborg. On the 21st he was appointed Commander-in-Chief of all the forces of the Swedish Crown on land and sea, and set out on a triumphal progress to Stockholm. It was characteristic of Bernadotte's sense of mass-psychology that on the journey he walked on foot for many miles amid the crowds who came to welcome him. It was equally characteristic that as soon as he was firmly established in his new high position, he set about diverting the eyes of Sweden from Finland to Norway. To conquer Finland would inevitably have aroused the powerful hostility of the Tsar of all the Russias. To conquer Norway would only annoy the potty little kingdom of Denmark.

So Madame la Maréchale Bernadotte, Princess of Ponte-Corvo, became Crown Princess of Sweden. The vivacious little lady of Marseilles had chosen a good husband after all. She might have married Napoleon himself, in the old days before Joséphine appeared, and thus she might have been Empress of the French. Joseph Bonaparte proposed to her. If she had accepted him, she would have been Queen of Naples and Spain. General Junot proposed to her. If she had married him, she would have become Duchesse d'Abrantès. But as it was she married Berna-dotte, the Gascon ex-sergeant-major, and in 1810 she became Crown Princess of Sweden.

* * *

Davout was holding Hamburg when his ancient enemy was landing in Helsinborg. From that moment the Prince of Eckmühl and the Prince of Sweden watched each other like hawks.

CHAPTER XIV

STILL THE PENINSULA

AS in the year before, the story of the Marshals during 1811 is almost entirely the story of the war in Spain.

In Catalonia, in the north, Macdonald found that his gentle methods were no more effective than Augereau's hangings, and his record in the field was one of consistent failure, and towards the end of the year he was recalled to Paris.

Soult's two exploits during 1811 were the capture of Badajoz and the battle of Albuera, but he was getting so much pleasure, and so many masterpieces of painting, and so much money, out of his viceroyalty that he preferred to string out his army of 80,000 men in garrison duty rather than concentrate them for active field operations.

Mortier helped at Badajoz and then went back to Paris.

Victor, as usual, made a mess of every operation that was entrusted to him. He was defeated at Barrosa, failed to storm Tarifa, and failed to capture Cadiz. His entire Corps, from commander downwards, lost their early buoyancy and their first raptures at seeing Andalusia, and grew more and more depressed by their painful record, by the incessant rainfall which flooded the rivers and cut off the ration convoys, by the fevers, by the water-logged trenches in front of Cadiz, and by the impossibility of finding dry wood for cooking and heating. All day and every day Victor's Corps sighed for the pleasures of Seville.

The year opened badly also for the Army of Portugal. It had struggled back from Torres Vedras, and refitted in Spain, and in the spring it was ready to take the field again. But it was a depressed army, and it marched and fought without enthusiasm. The Sixth Corps especially was in a state of gloom, for its beloved Commander had overstepped the mark at last, and had been flagrantly guilty of insubordination, and had been dismissed. Masséna had ordered Ney to march his men in one direction. Ney had flatly refused, and marched them in an-other. This was more than even the long-suffering, silent Prince of Essling could stand, and Ney had to go.

On March 22nd, 1811, the Duke of Elchingen said good-bye to the old Sixth Corps. He had commanded it from the day of its formation, in the Army of the Coasts of the Ocean at Montreuil in 1804. He had marched with it to Ulm, he had led it in all the glory of his medals and stars at the storming of Elchingen, he had taken it into the Tyrol; at Jena he had been side by side with young Colbert in the front line of skirmishers when the mist lifted and the Prussian infantry appeared in front of them; he had rushed it northwards across Prussia in the great pursuit, floundered with it in the Polish mud, stormed at its head into Friedland, and struggled with it through the snows of the Guadarramas in the race to cut off Sir John Moore. He had led it faultlessly on the field of battle whether in advance or retreat, and off the field of battle he had cared for his men as only Davout and Augereau cared for their men. He not only knew every officer in it by name and by sight, but also hundreds and hundreds of the non-commissioned officers and men. On that day outside Carapichina in 1811, when the Sixth Corps was paraded to say goodbye to its Commander, there was not a face of all those tough veterans down which a tear was not running, and not a man among them who did not feel that something of the old glory of the Revolution and the Consulate and the early days of the Empire was departing.

Masséna and Wellington met once more in action, at Fuentes D'Onoro, and if Bessières had shown greater determination and more desire to co-operate, things must have gone hard with the Duke. For Masséna had caught him badly, and Wellington himself said afterwards, 'If Boney had been there, we would have been damnably licked.'

But Marshal Bessières was a bad co-operator and, being a polished and ironical gentleman, he had evolved some neat little tricks for annoying Masséna. It was his engaging little habit to follow Masséna about, volunteering advice all the time, and inquiring most politely into the reasons underlying even the most trivial of the actions of the Commander-in-Chief. When Masséna, in front of Almeida, asked for the loan of cavalry and artillery, Bessières not only sent the barest minimum, consisting of a handful of foot-soldiers, one battery, and thirty spare gun-teams, but also turned up himself. 'I could have done with more men,' said Masséna furiously, 'and less Bessières.'

The result was that Wellington slipped out once again.

After Fuentes D'Onoro, Masséna, looking very old, very worn, very sad, departed for France with his dragoon-lady. Fuentes D'Onoro was his last battle, and on that day came to an end the fighting life of the man of Rivoli and Zürich and Genoa and Essling.

On his way home he found a chest of 300,000 francs at Salamanca, which had arrived for the army, and out of it he paid himself his own arrears of pay, amounting to 75,000 francs. Then, in somewhat better spirits, he proceeded on his way.

* * *

Neither the politically minded Soult nor the prematurely old Masséna had been a success against the

English, and so the Emperor tried a new type of leader, and called up Marmont, the great organizer, from Illyria. Marmont was delighted at the change from Dalmatia and Illyria. He had enjoyed very much his independence and his opportunities of building bridges and organizing tobacco monopolies and helping peasants to plough by lending them gun-teams, but he was beginning to feel that he was too far from Paris, and that he would be forgotten. Besides, there were no opportunities on the Adriatic for winning military glory. It was in a high good-humour, therefore, that the enthusiastic young Duke of Ragusa arrived at Salamanca to take command. He brought with him twelve cooks, three hundred pairs of boots, one hundred and fifty pairs of breeches, dozens of em-broidered coats, a host of flunkies in scarlet liveries and powdered wigs, and a massive silver dinner-service. The moment he arrived he set to work at reorganizing his army with a rapidity which upset all Wellington's calcula-tions. Marmont's first decision was to send home all senior officers who might make trouble, and to work the army with promoted brigadiers; only the black-bearded Montbrun remained till the end of the year as com-mander of the cavalry, as no substitute could be found for him. Marmont's kindness and consideration for his subordinates, the care he took of his men, and the splen-dour of his dinner-service, quickly made him immensely popular with all ranks, and the Army of Portugal, which Masséna had left a dispirited, exhausted, and half-fed rab-ble, was simmering, within a week or two, with zeal, discipline, and enthusiasm.

Once he had got rid of his grumblers, Marmont set his men to his favourite work of building bridges and roads and forts and entrenchments. It was also typical of him that, with the help of an armourer of an infantry regi-ment, he invented a hand-mill for the grinding of corn which was a great help in the ration supply, and he caused the utmost astonishment among the peasants in the neighbourhood of Salamanca by insisting upon paying for all requisitioned goods.

A great help to Marmont, at this time, was the recall of Bessières. The Emperor, who had been furious at the failure of Bessières to co-operate with Masséna, at last grew tired of his gloomy despatches and his perpetual complaints and criticisms of the conduct of the war. Poor Bessières was not the man, any more than Macdonald, for the war in Spain, and his command, the Army of the North of Spain, was not nearly large enough for its three tasks of supporting the Army of Portugal, watching the Spanish armies in the north-west, and suppressing an intensive guerilla warfare in a country of innumerable valleys and mountains and rivers, with the English fleet lying everlastingly behind it.

Almost the last act of Bessières was to advise Marmont not to march down to Badajoz to help Soult, and he gave this advice, not on strategical grounds, but simply because he detested the Viceroy of Andalusia. But Marmont was new to Spain and Spanish warfare, and he was much keener to help a colleague than the other war-weary Marshals, except Mortier, and to everyone's astonishment he led an army rapidly down to Soult's help. At this time Marmont did not know Soult. A curious series of chances had kept the two men apart. When Soult was in Portugal, Marmont had been in Dalmatia; Marmont was not at Austerlitz; when Soult was commanding the camps at Boulogne, Marmont's Corps was in Holland; at Marengo, Soult was in the Austrian hospital in Alessandria, and in the years before Marengo, Marmont was an officer of the Egypt-Italy Army, Soult of the Switzerland-Rhineland. They met for the first time in June, 1811, at Merida, and Soult was fulsomely flattering to his young colleague. But Marmont was much too shrewd to be taken in, and in a very short time became profoundly distrustful of the Viceroy.

The rest of the year was spent by Marmont in manoeuvring against Wellington, and he comments in his memoirs on the English Army:

Of all the infantry of Europe, its fire was the most murderous; while well-equipped and in a good state, better than any other. As soon as order vanished it disintegrated of its own accord. If it had had a month of what the French army had for four years, it would have ceased to exist before the end of the second month, without any fighting at all.

But in October his powers of manoeuvring against Wellington were fatally diminished by the order from the Emperor to despatch one-third of his army to the assistance of the French in Valencia. This order was the cause of Marmont's famous remark: 'Napoleon was at this period living in a non-existent world, created by his own imagination. He built structures in the air, he took his desires for realities, and gave his orders as if he was ignorant of the true state of affairs and as if the actual facts had been hidden from him on purpose.'

A new Marshal was created in 1811 when Louis Gabriel Suchet received a baton on July 8th, 1811. Suchet was the son of a silk-manufacturer of Lyons, and at the time of his promotion was forty-one years old. He first came into some sort of prominence in 1799, when he commanded the defence of the line of the river Var while Masséna was holding Genoa, but he made no real mark beyond acquiring a reputation of being a skilful commander of a division. Suchet's first big chance came when he was appointed in 1809 to command a corps which had just been battered to bits in the siege of Saragossa. The start of his command was unfortunate. He arrived to find 10,000 depressed, exhausted, and sulky men. Their pay was in arrears, their rations were only procurable by looting, and there was a general feeling that the rewards for the capture of Saragossa had all been given to Mortier's Corps. Worse was to follow very quickly. Within two days of reaching his headquarters, Suchet had to march out with this miserable body of men to meet the Spaniards, and on the 23rd of May, 1809, he had the mortification of seeing veteran Frenchmen panicking in front of Spaniards, and his new command being heavily defeated.

But this defeat was practically his only set-back in five years of fighting. In a very short time the new commander proved himself an able and resolute soldier in the field, a skilful and benevolent administrator, and a genial and popular leader. 'If Napoleon had had two Suchets,' said Madame Campan, 'he would have captured and kept Spain.'

General Suchet quickly cleared Aragon of brigands and guerillas, and settled down to govern. He abolished out-of-date taxes and lotteries and monopolies, suppressed corruption, refunded money that had been extorted (a record in the annals of the French in Spain), reorganized the Customs, protested vehemently against the Emperor's orders that all English produce should be burnt, and went on with the construction of the Imperial canal of Charles V in order to create employment. He started at once the rebuilding of Saragossa which his colleague Marshal Lannes had so efficiently destroyed, and designed fountains and parks and a new water-supply; he restored and re-endowed hospitals and orphanages; restored the bull-ring that had been destroyed in the siege; re-started the schools of drawing, architecture, and mathematics; and earned the profound gratitude of every Aragonese by flatly refusing to allow King Joseph to steal the famous Treasure of Nuestra Señora del Pilar from Saragossa. And finally, Suchet was the only Marshal, with the possible exception of Soult in easy-going Andalusia, to admit the Spaniards to a share in the government, and he won their hearts by ruthlessly suppressing all looting and plundering. By the end of the year the soldiers of the Army of Aragon, although completely isolated not only from France, but from the other French armies in Spain, were able to move about unarmed and singly among the very population which had risen against Moncey and so fanatically defended Saragossa. The peasants began to bring in food for sale; outlying villages sent in petitions for weapons to defend themselves against the guerrillas; and isolated French soldiers were frequently hidden from bandits by kindly cottagers.

Suchet's military operations, after his first defeat, were so uniformly successful that the Emperor transferred almost half of Macdonald's army of Catalonia to him, and told him that his Marshal's baton was waiting for him inside the walls of Tarragona. In June, 1811, General Suchet, by a rapid and skilful assault, captured Tarragona, and became a Marshal of the Empire with the title of Duke of Albufera.

***

During 1811 Davout was commanding the Elbe garrison and drilling his 50,000 men incessantly. As usual, the discipline of the garrison was strict and no officers were allowed to leave camp and enter any town without a special permit; courts-martial were frequent and looting non-existent. A contemporary records that 'chickens wandered about among the barracks without fear'. It was universally believed in Hamburg, and indeed throughout North Germany, that Davout was stationed there because the Emperor had promised him the viceroyalty of Poland, and that he would be marching into his new appointment at any moment. It is true that Davout himself told at least one officer of his staff that he had been promised the viceroyalty. But it is far more likely that he was kept at Hamburg to repress the activities of the English merchants, and, of course, to keep an eye on his old enemy, now firmly in the Swedish saddle as Crown Prince Charles. For already the late Marshal Bernadotte was making trouble by his old habit of sitting firmly on the top of the fence. Napoleon had offered him Finland as a reward for co-operating against Russia, but it was becoming clear that the Crown Prince, instead, wanted to get

hold of Norway as a reward for co-operating with nobody. It was also rather disquietening that he had been
overheard to say of the blockade of England, 'I do not
want to become a customs-officer for Napoleon.'

***

Far away to the south King Joachim of Naples was in
a bad temper. It was not so much fun being a king as he
had imagined, especially as he was strongly in favour of
trading with England. 'Am I only an advance-guard king?'
he exclaimed crossly when some particularly tiresome
despatch arrived from his formidable brother-in-law.

***

Masséna and Ney and Brune were all three in disgrace.
Augereau, Macdonald, Bessières and Jourdan had been
recalled as failures. The Marshals were rather under a
cloud in 1811.

***

All through that year the shadow of great events was
hanging over the Empire, and the preparations were
already on foot for the massing in the following year of
600,000 men on the frontier of Russia.

CHAPTER XV

MOSCOW

THERE was a dinner-party in the ancient red-brick town of Danzig in the end of May, 1812, and the diners were the Emperor, Berthier, Murat, and blunt Colonel Rapp, the Alsatian A.D.C. There was not much conversation. The shadow of the gigantic, imminent gamble lay across the table, and the Chief-of-Staff longed for his adored Visconti, and the Commander of the Reserve Cavalry longed for his sunny Bay of Naples. Suddenly Napoleon asked, 'How many leagues from Cadiz to Danzig?' The two Marshals discreetly said nothing. Colonel Rapp waited for his Seniors to answer, and then answered what was in their hearts.

'Too many, Sire,' he said abruptly, and silence fell again upon the group of doomed men.

The ultimate Madness was just about to begin. All through 1811 and the early months of 1812, the depôts and the stores and the magazines had been moving steadily eastwards, and the greatest soldier in the world, who for sixteen years had preached and preached, and practised and practised, the supreme military virtue – Concentration – was preparing to march one wing of his army to Moscow, while the other was hammering impotently at the gates of Cadiz.

The Marshals were distributed thus, on that sultry, windless day when the first troops crossed the Niemen into Russia:

Oudinot commanded the flanking, defensive corps on the immediate left of the Main Body, and Macdonald commanded another, in Courland, on the left of Oudinot. Neither of these honest, gallant, and clumsy fellows was to go to Moscow.

In the Main Army, which was the central French kernel in all that welter of polyglot strangers, were Murat and Berthier of course, and Davout. Berthier was on the worst possible terms with Davout, who had arrived with 70,000 men from Hamburg. It was their first meeting since 1809 when Berthier had bungled so badly in front of Ratisbon, and when first Davout, and then the Emperor, had pointed out his bungling in emphatic language. The two Marshals quarrelled violently from the beginning of the 1812 campaign, but Berthier, sitting day after day in the headquarter-office at the Emperor's side, had the interior lines, and Napoleon became cold and distant towards Davout. This was particularly unfair, as the painstaking genius of the Prince of Eckmühl had been working at its best during the last few months, and his Corps was completely organized with twenty-five days' provisions, innumerable vehicles of every kind, and a full strength of technical experts such as masons, bakers, tailors, shoe-makers, armourers, and fitters.

Ney was also with the Main Body, and the unfortunate Victor, who had been fetched from sunny, lazy, romantic Andalusia to that melancholy vastness of plains and pine-forests. When the march to Moscow started, Victor was left with the Reserve Corps, to advance as far as Smolensk if necessary. Bessières, as usual, commanded the Guard, and Mortier had the Young Guard. It is clear proof of the depression which was weighing so ominously on the spirits of the troops that even the optimistic, jolly Marshal Mortier was full of gloom. 'From the Niemen to the Vilia,' he told Napoleon, 'I have seen nothing but ruined houses and abandoned carts and equipment. Ten thousand horses have been killed already by the cold rains and by eating unripe rye which they are not accustomed to. The smell of the dead horses on the roads is perfectly horrible. But that is not so bad as the shortness of rations. Several of my Young Guard have already starved to death.'

Of the rest, Augereau was on garrison duty in Germany. Soult was dreaming of a kingdom in Andalusia, and scrupulously disobeying every order that King Joseph sent him. Marmont was busy, as usual, reorganizing the Army of Portugal and planning sensational coups against Wellington. Jourdan, hauled out of the retirement in which he should have been allowed to grow old gently, was doing his best to advise a fool of a King in Madrid, and to co-ordinate the movements of Marshals and Generals whose main ambition in life seemed to be to prevent their movements from being co-ordinated.

In the North, the Crown Prince of Sweden was busy negotiating with the Tsar. The invasion of Swedish Pomerania by Davout at the beginning of the year had infuriated Sweden, and the Tsar invited the Crown Prince to meet him at Abo, the capital of Finland, and offered him a Russian frigate to take him there. But Bernadotte, always the Gascon, insisted on crossing the Baltic in a Swedish frigate, even though it meant keeping the Tsar waiting for five days.

'He who knows how to win battles,' said Bernadotte proudly, 'is entitled to regard himself as the equal of kings.'

At Abo the foundations were laid of an alliance between Sweden and Russia which lasted long after the two men were dead. Bernadotte relinquished the Swedish claim to Finland; the Tsar, in return, promised to help in the Swedish conquest of Norway; Bernadotte, in his finest vein of rhetoric, promised to land 200,000 men on the coast of Brittany; the Tsar, in return, agreed that Bernadotte would be an admirable successor to Napoleon on the throne of the French Empire. On the other hand, the Crown Prince was firm against the proposal that he should divorce his vivacious little Marseillaise, Queen Désirée, and marry the Russian Grand-Duchess Catherine. Napoleon was not the only man in Europe who was thinking about his dynasty, and Bernadotte was anxious not to involve himself in complications.

***

Masséna, lucky old dog, was in disgrace at his château at Rueil, where, one-eyed though he was since the Emperor peppered him in the shoot at Fontainebleau, he could still see far enough to distinguish a pretty girl from a plain one, and a franc from a ten-centimes piece.

***

The army, 600,000 strong, of Frenchmen, Swiss, Austrians, Prussians, Poles, Illyrians, Rhinelanders, North-Italians, Neapolitans, Saxons, Bavarians, Westphalians, Portuguese, and Spaniards, crossed the Niemen on the 24th of June. There was a queer silence. Voices were hushed and there was no laughter or singing. On the other side there was not a living soul to be seen, save a Russian patrol which made a formal challenge, fired three musket-shots, and galloped off into the woods. There were no animals visible, or birds audible, and a thundery heat made the day stifling. Soon afterwards the heat was followed by storms of heavy rain. Day after day the enemy retired, and day after day the *Grande Armée* marched steadily eastwards in pursuit, through appalling clouds of dust. Witepsk was reached on July 28th, and it was there that Napoleon announced his determination to push on to Smolensk. Berthier burst into tears. He already hated Russia almost as much as he had hated Egypt in the old days.

The Main Body marched towards the east, shedding sick and stragglers every day. With a general sigh of relief it left the Jews behind at last, when the frontier of the Jewish Pale was crossed and Old Russia entered, but the relief was short-lived. For in a day or two everyone was regretting the absence of those strange, dark, inscrutable men who, grasping though they might be, at least had food and forage and vodka to sell, and at least spoke a semi-Germanic language which the veterans of the *Grande Armée* and the campaigns and cantonments of Germany could understand.

August 15th was Napoleon's name-day, and Murat and Ney celebrated it with a salute of a hundred guns, and were warmly reprimanded for wasting powder. They got over the difficulty by explaining that it was Russian powder which they had captured the day before, and the Emperor was delighted.

Three days later, Ney stormed into the blazing suburbs of Smolensk, and again, as at Witepsk, Napoleon had an opportunity of going into winter quarters and starting again for Moscow in the spring. But he refused to take it and pushed on, Ney commanding the advance-guard, and Murat scouring the countryside on his flanks. At the debouching out of Smolensk eastwards, there was a sharp engagement, and Gudin, one of Davout's three 'Immortals,' was killed.

Any doubts that the Emperor may have had in his mind about the wisdom of pushing on, were dissipated by the news from the north. Oudinot, the gallant but thick-headed Duke of Reggio, was commanding the mixed army of French, Swiss, and Bavarians which was guarding the left flank of the Main Body, and on August 17th he was attacked by the Russian Wittgenstein. Oudinot, according to his invariable custom, withdrew his artillery so far that it was practically out of range in order that it should not be captured, and himself proceeded to the front line of skirmishers, and was immediately wounded.

This was the best thing that could have happened to the Left-Wing Army, for Oudinot had to go to hospital, and he was succeeded by his second-in-command, General Gouvion St. Cyr.

St. Cyr was the strangest, most freakish, and least understandable of all the Marshals. He was the son of a tanner who had formerly been a butcher, and he was born at Toul in 1764. He was designated in his youth to be a civil engineer owing to an aptitude for drawing which he showed from an early age. He supported himself during his engineering studies by giving drawing lessons at Metz and later at Toul. But his love of drawing soon eclipsed his love of engineering, and at the age of eighteen he ran away from Toul and went to Rome to study art. He spent two years in Rome, but for some unexplained reason he never in after life would speak of his work there, his drawing-masters, his friends, or the studios in which he studied. Leaving Rome, he travelled in Sicily and in Italy, and went to Paris in 1784, where he worked in the studio of the painter Brenet. There was a brief interlude in his artistic studies when he was persuaded by the actor Baptiste to join his company at the Théâtre de la Cité, where the play *Robert, Chief of the Brigands* was drawing Paris. But St. Cyr, though handsome and the possessor of a beautiful speaking voice, was so shy that he soon abandoned the stage and went back to art.

In the Revolutionary Wars he first came into prominence as a staff-officer owing to the powers of observation and accurate memory which every painter must possess, and to his beautiful talent for map-making and field-sketching. He soon became a general, and rapidly acquired a reputation as a skilful mountain fighter, so that it became a proverb in the Army of the Vosges when distant artillery fire was heard, 'St. Cyr is playing chess again.' Moreau, the famous Republican general, remarked on one occasion, 'Desaix knows how to win battles, St. Cyr how not to lose them.'

In 1798 the ex-art-student was back in Rome commanding the Republican Army there, but he soon got
into serious trouble with the corrupt French officials.
For one evening he attended a ball and observed that the
wives of certain of these officials were wearing some
exceptionally fine diamonds. St. Cyr looked at the diamonds
again, and the eye of the artist and the sixteen-year-old
studies in Rome combined to tell him at a glance that
these jewels had been torn from the famous Monstrance
of the Doria family. As Commander-in-Chief, St. Cyr
insisted on their immediate restoration to the Dorias.

Brilliant though the young painter's career had been up
till now, a strange streak began to appear more and more
frequently in his character. Gradually he acquired the reputation of being a selfish and disloyal colleague in the
field. So long as St. Cyr was in sole command, he used
every iota of his cold, calculating, analytical genius for the
defeat of the enemy. The moment he was given either a
colleague or a superior, he withdrew into a shell of icy
contempt and aloofness. For instance, he commanded the
right wing at the disastrous battle of Novi in 1799 under
Joubert. In the right wing there was a newly arrived
division from Naples, and its commander, a foolish man,
begged for leave to attack an enormous mass of Austrian
cavalry. 'Do just as you like,' replied St. Cyr coldly, turning
away. His chief-of-staff, appalled at this decision exclaimed
that he would be overwhelmed. 'Yes,' replied St. Cyr, 'but
there is no harm in giving a few lessons to these lads from
the Naples Army.'

In 1800 St. Cyr was ambassador in Madrid, where he
helped to negotiate the sale of Louisiana to the United
States. But he hated diplomatic missions, and was soon
back in a military command, this time at Naples. But in
1803 and 1804 he made three fatal mistakes of policy:
firstly, he refused to sign the great address of congratula-
tion to the First Consul on his escape from the Pichegru
conspiracy; secondly, he refused to sign the petition begging

the First Consul to become Emperor; and thirdly, he refused to attend the coronation of the Emperor. As a result, he was in semi-disgrace until 1809, when he was appointed to the command in Catalonia. In that incredibly difficult campaign he displayed to the utmost all his first-class military talents, but was recalled to make way for Augereau, and was again disgraced for leaving his command before Augereau arrived.

There was one extraordinary habit that Marshal St. Cyr invariably indulged in. After winning a victory, instead of following up the enemy, or looking after his wounded, or making arrangements for subsequent operations, it was his custom to lock himself into the most secluded and remote apartment that he could find in his headquarters, and there play the violin for hours. He even took his violin on the Russian campaign and, after winning his brilliant victory at Polotsk (after Oudinot had gone to hospital), he enjoyed several happy hours with his beloved instrument. He received his Marshal's baton for this victory.

His men and his officers all detested him, but all admitted that he was the finest defensive soldier in Europe. He was universally known as 'The Owl'.

***

So the Main Body pushed on. Ney's Corps was exhausted after Smolensk and was replaced in the vanguard by Davout, an arrangement which was very unsuccessful. For Davout hated being under the orders of the flibbertygibbety King of Naples, and craftily resolved to show his disgust by an ostentatious show of correct procedure and discipline. He stopped writing direct to the Emperor, but sent all his reports, however urgent, to Murat, as his immediate superior, to be forwarded on to Berthier. As Murat was often liable to be galloping, gold wand in hand, on the heels of stray Cossacks, Davout's reports were often days late, and the Emperor became irritated. At last he ordered

Davout to resume his direct communications, adding, rather incautiously, that he could not always trust Murat's messages. Davout promptly seized this timely weapon, and refused to serve under a man whom the Emperor could not trust, and the distracted Emperor was forced to compromise by appointing them both joint and equal commanders of the advance-guard. A few days later the King of Naples, commanding the advance-guard, led a regiment of lancers into a desperately tight corner, and the artillery of the Prince of Eckmühl, also commanding the advance-guard, refused to fire a single round to get him out of it. This was going a bit too far and both commanders rushed off to Headquarters to complain. There was a furious scene.

Davout accused Murat to the Emperor of wasting the strength of the advance-guard by unnecessary manoeuvres, and said that he had no idea of how to handle infantry or artillery. 'Furthermore,' said Davout angrily, 'the King of Naples pays no attention to the time of day or the strength of the enemy. He rushes up among his skirmishers, makes himself hoarse by shouting orders, and dances about like a madman in front of the enemy line.' The result of all this peculiar behaviour, concluded the Prince of Eckmühl, was that the troops were under arms till after dark every day, and had to bivouac, find forage, rations, water, wood, and straw, all night in the pitch dark, and at dawn were under arms again. As for the cavalry, 20,000 men did not dare to dismount from their horses or to off-saddle for ten minutes, or to forage among the rye-fields, because at any moment the King of Naples might come pouncing down with some idiotic manoeuvre to perform. As a result the whole of the cavalry would soon be out of action.

Murat replied with equal violence that the way to defeat the enemy was to attack them as he did, and not to indulge in nice parade-ground drilling as Davout did. The harassed Emperor listened in silence, kicking

215

a Russian cannon-ball to and fro, and finally dismissed them with soothing compliments and a hope that they would behave better in future.

This hope was a vain one. On the eastern side of Viazma the Russians made a stand in a strong position at the back of a ravine. Murat put himself in person at the head of one of Davout's divisions, and started towards the ravine. Before the attack had proceeded far, Davout came galloping up, ordered the men to halt, and forbade his generals to obey Murat. Another violent scene followed, and Murat despatched his chief-of-staff to tell the Emperor that he must choose between the two. This time Murat got in first, and Napoleon sent a furious message ordering Davout to obey Murat as his military superior and to respect him as the Imperial brother-in-law. That night Murat sat in his tent brooding over the insult he had received on the field of battle, and the more he brooded, the angrier he became, until suddenly all his Gascon blood boiled over, and he seized his sword and started towards Davout's headquarters. Fortunately his chief-of-staff seized him and persuaded him not to be a fool.

It was not only among the Marshals that the ties of discipline were already beginning to slacken. Things were not well even among the Imperial Guard. One night at about this time the Emperor's Headquarters were behind a stream, and a detachment of the Guard was on duty at the only bridge over it. But the night turned cold, and the guardsmen destroyed the bridge and used the wood for a fire, and the next morning the Headquarter staff and the Emperor himself had to wait until a new bridge could be built.

Napoleon marched out of the east gate of Smolensk on August 25th, and on September 7th the armies at last met at Borodino. At 6 a.m. on this day the French Army numbered 130,000. No fewer than 470,000 men had thus been lost to the spearhead of the invasion by garrison duty, flank guards, and casualties without battle, and yet it was only seventy-five days since the frontier had been crossed.

The Russians were in a strong position, and had dug hard to make it stronger still. A redoubt, known to history as the Great Redoubt, some smaller earth-works, and the village of Semenovskoi, all looked so formidable that Davout shook his head thoughtfully and offered to lay his Corps, 35,000 men, secretly aslant of the Russian left wing during the night and have them ready to attack at 6 a.m. But the Emperor was in a ponderous, uninspired mood, and had no taste for anything but solid slogging. This was to be a second Wagram, not an Austerlitz, and the heavy work was to be done in the centre. On the day before the battle it had rained, a cold rain, and that evening the Emperor's ponderousness was increased by a severe chill, and he lost his voice. It was late before the Marshals got their orders, and the Guard, after several moves and counter-moves, was not in position till after midnight.

At 3 a.m. the Emperor was mounted and out, and between 5.30 and 6 a.m. the sun rose. 'The sun of Austerlitz,' cried Napoleon. But he was speaking as an adventurer and not as a gunner. For the brilliant sun was behind the Russians and in the eyes of the French, and the artillery advantage always rests with the guns which have the sun behind them.[1] Borodino was only the third out of all the great Napoleonic battles that was fought on an east-west alignment in the sunshine. At the first of these, Marengo, the artillery did not play a very decisive part. At the second, Austerlitz, the eastern army had all

---

[1] *This was the reason why, on the British front during the War of 1914-18, the German artillery was always more active in the morning, the British in the evening. The 'early morning strafe' was not due to a German passion for early rising, but to a professional desire to catch the sun.*

the advantage at the beginning of the day, and so it was at Borodino.[1]

The attack was led by Ney, Davout, and Murat. Ney went into action on a great white horse that was at once an inspiration and a target. Those near the red-headed Marshal were cheered by the ostentatious coolness with which he stopped from time to time for a fresh plug of tobacco to chew. Davout attacked on the right, advancing slowly across a terribly difficult ground, cut up by small ravines, and thick with bramble bushes, and his Corps was thrown into confusion by a rumour that the Marshal himself had been killed. A heavy shell had burst beside his horse, and when the smoke had cleared away there was no sign either of horse or rider, and it was not until half an hour later that Davout re-emerged from the chaos, wounded and somewhat shaken. Later in the day Murat led one of his most tremendous cavalry attacks. But the Russian infantrymen held firm, as they had done at Eylau, and it was not till the afternoon was well advanced that the Redoubt and the village were at last over-whelmed by the unceasing fury of the three Marshals. The line had been won at last. Now was the great Napoleonic moment, the crisis of the battle, like the instant in a tempest at sea when a towering wave seems to pause for a moment before it uncoils and hurls itself forward with a sweep and a thunder. The shock-troops, the storm-Marshals, had at last finished their work. The Russians were beaten, and the moment of pursuit had come.

But there was no pursuit.

Message after message was sent back to the Emperor, where he sat, impassive, silent, a mile in the rear, upon a black bearskin. But no reinforcement went up.

---

[1] *Eylau and Eckmühl were also east-west battles, but there was no sunshine.*

'For God's sake, send up the Guard,' implored the three storm-Marshals. For the Old Guard was intact. It had not been in action, and it was the pick of all the Army. The broken Russians could never withstand the slow, terrible tramp of the advancing Guard. But – it was the last dry cartridge in a gambler's magazine, and as the Emperor gazed out over the smoke and the carnage, and back at his untouched ranks of old moustaches, Marshal Bessières whispered in his ear, 'You are eight hundred miles from Paris, Sire.'

That clinched it, and the Guard did not go up, and the Russians retired in good order. But Ney, the faithful, the taciturn, the loyal, for the first time turned upon his master with a stream of furious words. 'What the blazing hell is he doing so far behind? If he is no longer a general, let him clear off back to the Tuileries and leave us to do the commanding for him.'

Both sides were utterly exhausted, except the indefatigable King of Naples. At ten o'clock that night, after more than twelve hours of almost continual fighting, with an ostrich-plume in one hand and a musket in the other, he was begging the Emperor to let him have the cavalry of the Guard for one more charge.

Fifty thousand men and thirty thousand horses were killed upon this day. Forty-three generals were on the French casualty list, and among the killed was Montbrun, the fourth of the young cavalrymen. Colbert had been sniped through the head at Cacabellos in Spain, Sainte-Croix killed by the stray shell from the English gun-boat in the Tagus, Lasalle brought down by almost the last shot at Wagram, and now Montbrun joined them. The Napoleonic fantasy was fast descending into the deep shadows.

From Borodino into Moscow Murat relieved the tedium of the long advancing by indulging in a cavalry skirmish almost every evening, which had no effect except to exhaust his men and horses unnecessarily. He himself was invariably in the front line of the skirmishers, and his astonishing costume, his total indifference to musket-fire or cannon-fire, and the magic immunity which seemed to protect him, made him almost a demi-god to the simple Cossacks, and when, on September 14th, he rode into Moscow, he was surrounded by admiring groups of them. The Cossacks, always lovers of the spectacular, were enchanted by the sight of the famous horseman, and indeed the King of Naples must have been a remarkable sight. For he had put on his best uniform for the entry into the Holy City, with a gold collar and gold belt on his tunic, pale pink riding-breeches (a new colour which he had adopted from Prince Poniatowski), and bright yellow leather boots. In his hat were not only four of his favourite ostrich-feathers, but an aigrette of heron's plumes as well. Gilded stirrups and a sky-blue saddlecloth embroidered with gold added to the gaiety of his appearance.

The eastern wing of the *Grande Armée* topped the Sparrow Hills on September 13th and saw below them the domes, the green and blue and golden domes of the two thousand churches of Moscow, and on the 14th the entry and the looting began. On that evening a fire broke out, somewhere on the Solianka, near the Orphanage. Another broke out by the Exchange, and the wind carried it to the Arcade, and on the next day, the 15th, many of the wooden houses were burning. On the 16th the Emperor had to escape through burning buildings to the Petrovsky palace outside the city, and that night it was possible to read within ten miles of the roaring furnace. The fire blazed till the first rains came at 3 p.m. on the 18th September, and in the evening the ruined city was acrid with the scent of wet smoke, and clouded with the fall of rain-loaded ashes.

The dull sun-setting made a queer reflected glow in the long, red drops on the branches of the lime-trees, and a silence fell upon the conquering, doomed army. It was a silence as strange, and as ominous, as that which had blanketed the first crossing of the Niemen on that sultry day in June.

On the 19th it rained all day, and the glow died down and the pungent smell of damp smoke increased.

Napoleon went back to the Kremlin and waited, while the indefatigable Murat rode out south-east again, towards Riazan, to pursue the ever-retreating enemy, and the Russian peasants sprang to arms with all the fanatical enthusiasm of the Spaniard. Our Lady of Kazan was as influential a recruiting-sergeant as Our Lady of Montserrat.

From September 14th till October 19th, 1812, the eastern wing of the *Grande Armée* remained in Moscow.

***

Ney, Duke of Elchingen, was created Prince of the Moskowa.

***

The year 1812 had opened badly for the Marshals in Spain, for the drain of troops for the Russian campaign was at its height in January. The Guard cavalry, with all its chasseurs, *grenadiers à cheval*, dragoons, and Polish lancers, had already gone, and the horse-artillery and the *gendarmes d'élite*. They were followed by the infantry of the Guard, the rest of the Polish regiments, and many other units, marching gleefully out of the hateful Peninsula. Their delight might have been somewhat tempered if they had been accompanied by a few trustworthy prophets.

Worse was to follow. Old Jourdan once again was dug out of his administrative work and despatched as chief-of-staff to King Joseph, who had just been promoted to the rank of Commander-in-Chief of all the armies in Spain. The Emperor was too busy with Russia to spare the time for devising any more strategical plans for the conquest of the Peninsula, and the task of co-ordination was assigned to Joseph and Jourdan.

Soult and Marmont, who had been independent of Madrid, the one for years, the other for months, were both furious at the new arrangement. Marmont, indeed, was already tired of Spain. A long-out-of-date, impracticable, strategical combination had reached him in the early part of the year from Napoleon, the only effective result of which had been that Marmont and Soult had stood firmly on their ground while Wellington neatly snapped up Badajoz from between them. 'A commander in Spain,' observed Marmont disgustedly, 'is like a shepherd who has to move his flock from the pasturage when it has eaten up all the grass,' and he wrote off to ask for a command in the Army of Russia. Luckily for him, his request was refused.

The first object of each French commander now was to keep open his lines of communication with Paris, not for any new-found military zeal, or in order to report progress to the Emperor, but simply in order to tell Madrid that they were in direct touch with the Emperor, and could not therefore obey Joseph.

In May 1812 the new chief-of-staff issued his first strategical orders to Marmont, Soult, and Suchet, who was commanding in Aragon. Nothing happened. All three calmly ignored them. Then Jourdan suggested that Andalusia, which had no strategical value whatsoever, should be evacuated. Instantly Soult set up a howl of rage and indignation. Abandon his beloved viceroyalty! Give up his quicksilver mines! Leave Seville the Beautiful! It was unthinkable, and he wrote off in hot haste to Napoleon. He was careful, however, to dwell less upon his own viceroyalty than upon the irreparable blow to the Imperial prestige which the evacuation, and the accompanying abandonment of the siege of Cadiz, would strike.

In 1812 there were 230,000 veteran French soldiers in Spain, and yet the offensive definitely passed into the

hands of Wellington during this year. The process was
accelerated by the events of July. Marmont and Wellington
had been doing some fine manoeuvring against each other
in the Kingdom of Leon and on the river Douro, and at
the end of July they were face to face near the town of
Salamanca, each with about 40,000 men. For some time
there was the extraordinary spectacle of the two armies
marching along, on parallel lines, in close order, within
gunshot of each other. The two Commanders watched
like hawks for a blunder. At last Marmont strung his divisions out too far, and Wellington pounced upon him. A
cannonball wounded Marmont at the beginning of the
action, and in half an hour the battle was lost and won. It
was many days before the wreckage of the Army of
Portugal could be reassembled into the semblance of a
fighting force.

On August 5th Captain Fabvier set out with Marmont's
despatch about the battle of Salamanca to ride with it to
the Headquarters of the Imperial Armies. It took him
thirty-two days to get there. For he reached the Headquarters on September 6th, in front of the village of
Borodino. The Napoleonic Theory of Concentration had
gone completely to the winds.

Salamanca shook Joseph and Jourdan, and it shook
even Soult. For when the wretched king, terrified at
Wellington's approach on Madrid, ordered the Viceroy of
Andalusia to abandon his province and concentrate upon
Valencia, to everyone's surprise the Viceroy obeyed. It was
the first order from Madrid that he had ever obeyed, and
it is fairly safe to say that if any single man by his self-
ishness and personal ambition ruined the French chances
of success in Spain, it was the Viceroy of Andalusia, the
Marshal-Duke of Dalmatia.

On the 26th of August, 1812, the Viceroy marched
out of Seville for the last time with a gigantic train of
wagons carrying the spoils of viceroyalty. In a specially
magnificent carriage rode *Les Maréchales*, two beautiful

sisters, one of whom was Soult's mistress, and the other had been Victor's up till the departure of the ex-drummer-boy-Marshal for the Russian campaign. Officers of the senior ranks were followed in the cavalcade each by a mistress on horse-back, and each mistress was escorted by a cavalry trooper.

On reaching Valencia Soult quarrelled so incessantly with Joseph and Jourdan that the harassed monarch despatched a certain Colonel Deprez to Moscow to appeal for Soult's dismissal. The Colonel rode from Paris to the Kremlin in twenty-six days, but it was labour in vain, for the Emperor paid no attention to the appeal.

The Emperor had other things to think about.

* * *

At Moscow the seasons were changing and October brought an autumnal chill in the air, especially after the brilliant sun had gone down in the evenings. The leaves had turned. The days were shortening. Ravens wheeled in great regiments round the church of Ivan Veliki, and their gloomy croaking exasperated the Emperor's nerves. Murat, at the outposts, reported an incessant wastage of cavalry horses, and a visible strengthening, day after day, of the enemy's horsemen. And still no word of negotiations came from the Tsar.

At last, on October 18th, the Emperor gave orders for the retreat, and 108,000 men and 569 guns started homewards. There were also several thousands of civilians with the Army, and innumerable carts and wagons and carriages of every sort and pattern. The gigantic column looked like a Mongol horde of nomadic tribesmen, rather than the disciplined ranks of the supremely victorious army of the age.

Mortier was left behind to blow up the Kremlin and other public buildings, a task which he characteristically omitted to fulfil. But during this final occupation of

Moscow he was forced to smash two thousand bottles of vodka to prevent the Young Guard from drinking itself into a coma. It must have gone to Mortier's jolly heart to do such a thing.

The story of the Great Retreat is too well known to need a long telling. At first the weather was warm, sunny, and without wind, and the *morale* of the troops was still sufficiently high to enable them to beat off Cossack attacks without difficulty. The first real shock to the *morale* was the appalling sight of the Borodino battlefield, where 50,000 bodies, naked, half-eaten, half-skeleton, lay on the devastated, shell-torn ground by the Redoubt and the village of Semenovskoi. Even the most war-callous veteran was chilled to the heart. No one stopped. The interminable column hurried on.

Davout was holding the rear-guard, but his love of method and orderliness was out of place in such a fearful task. He had no notion of irregular warfare, and wasted much valuable time in forming neat and elaborate squares, such as had proved so effective at Auerstädt against the Prussians. Against the wild Cossacks this parade-ground style was futile, and Davout, instead of marching three days behind the Main Body, soon dropped two whole days and was marching five days behind.

The land was very marshy, and the autumn rains had swollen the rivers and muddied the tracks.

On October 29th there were nine degrees of frost, and the first snow came down. On the 31st there was a strong wind and more snow, and on the first day of November the ground was white. On the 4th a regiment of the Guard marched across the ice of a frozen lake, and on the morning of the 5th there was a heavy rain which froze later in the day, so that many horses broke their legs and had to be destroyed.

During these first days of November Ney and his Corps took over the rear-guard from Davout, and the epic part of the retreat began.

The 5th of November was the last day of autumn, for late that night there came a terrible change. Out of the lowering, grey, foggy, over-clouded sky came down the Cold of Russia, and that grim morning of the 6th was the beginning of the tragedy.

The Army which went to Moscow was an Army of the South. There were a few Germans and Swiss, and a number of Poles. But the vast majority were Frenchmen, lovers of the sun and of wine and of laughter; and Prince Eugène had a corps of Italians; and there were three strong regiments of Portuguese which Junot had sent from Lisbon in 1807 for garrison work in the Baltic; and there were some unhappy Spaniards who had not managed to escape with De La Romana from Denmark in 1808. All these were men of the South, men of the blue sky and the olive-woods and the gay song in the vineyard, and on the early morning of November 6th they were struck with the deadly blight of thirty degrees of frost.

The Army withered in a day. It became as one of the hideous bodies on the field of Borodino, a thing of horror and decomposition.

One only, in all that reeling column, did not lose heart. Ney, the barrel-cooper's son, fought on, musket in hand, coolly, resolutely, and very silently. It is recorded of him that during this month he spoke very seldom.

The men of the steppes moved faster through the snow than the men of the vineyards, and the Russian armies began to appear not only on the flanks, but in front of the retreating army. The Cossacks harried stragglers, and grew bold enough to attack the Main Body itself.

From November 9th to 14th it was a little warmer, and 50,000 men reached what was supposed to be the blessed haven of Smolensk.

But Smolensk was a disaster. The famished troops, on seeing well-stocked magazines for the first time since they had left Moscow, completely lost their heads, and all discipline vanished. Some ate so much and so quickly that they died within a short time; some could find nothing to eat. Men shot or stabbed each other for a sack of flour. Some who looted a case of vodka ran into empty houses and hid, and were found dead next morning with the empty bottles scattered round them. The waste of stores was appalling, and it was discovered that the commissary who ought to have supplied the meat had sold a thousand oxen to the local Jews who had forwarded them to the Russian Army. The confusion at Smolensk, the disorganization, and the intense disappointment, struck a deadly blow at the Army, and although the Corps of Marshal Victor had arrived as reinforcement, nevertheless the men who marched out of Smolensk were weaker in every way than the men who had struggled in.

On November 17th the Emperor had still 50,000 men, but Ney with the rear-guard was apparently irretrievably lost. Napoleon waited as long as he dared, and then abandoned him and continued the westward march. He entered Orcha with 6,000 of the Guard which had started with 35,000. Davout had 4,000 left out of 70,000.

Ney had been cut off by overwhelming numbers. An attempt to fight through them was repulsed with great losses, but the Marshal even then did not despair. As night was falling he turned round and marched his survivors back towards Russia, and then wheeled northwards in the darkness and groped his way towards the river Dnieper. If the Dnieper was frozen, he might yet extricate himself. As he marched indomitably on, he heard the Russian artillery firing salvoes in triumph at the impending capture of an Imperial Marshal and his Corps. Ney at once ordered fires to be lit, as though he was bivouacking for the night, and pushed on again. At last he found the river. There was ice on it, enough to bear a man if he was careful and jumped from floe to floe. But a corps of armed men, however depleted, with horses and guns, in pitch darkness, was another matter. But it was the last chance, and the risk had to be taken.

Ney gave his men three hours' rest before attempting to cross. In these three hours the stragglers would close up, and the river might harden. He himself wrapped his cloak round him, and spent the three hours sleeping as soundly as a child on the bank of the river. At midnight the passage of the Dnieper began in single file on the precarious ice. The baggage and the guns were abandoned, but most of the men got across, and Ney rejoined the Main Body with about 900 men, and resumed his post as commander of the rear-guard. For the next two days he was harassed on three sides by 5,000 Cossacks, and on the second night he was caught asleep in a wood by Platov's mounted swarms. A panic set in and the rear-guard was beginning to disintegrate when Ney rushed forward, musket in hand, and ordered the trumpeters to sound the charge, as if the enemy's attack had been expected and the counter-attack was about to begin. The rear-guard immediately rallied, and the Cossacks fled.

When the Emperor heard that Ney had arrived at Orcha, he exclaimed, 'I would have given three hundred millions from my treasury rather than have lost him.'

The climax of the tragedy was reached at the famous crossing of the Beresina. Of all the famous generals of history few have been so badly treated by the weather as Napoleon. The fog helped him at Jena, and a snow-storm saved him for a moment in 1814. But against these two advantages must be set the snow-storms in the Great St. Bernard and the Guadarramas and at Eylau; the violent rains in the Danube valley in 1805 during the march to Austerlitz; the rain at Dresden; and, above all, the warmth during the third and fourth weeks of November 1812. The deadly cold of the 6th of November had gone, and in comparison the weather had become almost mild, and so the Beresina was not frozen. If those two weeks had been of normal Russian cold, the Emperor might have marched his men and horses and guns across at any point he liked. But the Beresina was not frozen, and the

Emperor was faced with the problem of building bridges across the river and covering the work with an army of 40,000 men, all the time surrounded on three sides by three separate Russian armies numbering altogether about 120,000 men. It was an insoluble problem, and yet Napoleon solved it. The river was not frozen, but a sudden small frost came during the night before the attempt was made, and froze the shallow marshes on each side of the river, and that helped the bridge-building. With a brilliant series of manoeuvres the Emperor bewildered the Russians. Victor put up a stubborn rear-guard fight. Oudinot, who had come down from the north, struck with 8,000 men so furiously at 50,000 Russians that he drove them back in confusion, and the time was gained to build bridges across the river on the 26th and 27th. Napoleon himself crossed at midday of the 27th with the Guard. But the bluffing and the manoeuvring could not last for ever, and the Russians arrived at the bridge-heads on the 28th, and attacked on both sides of the river. But Ney and Oudinot drove them back violently on one bank, and Victor kept them at bay on the other, till most of the army had crossed. But the stragglers, the non-combatants, the wounded, and many of the last rear-guard had to be left behind. At least 20,000 lives were lost during those three catastrophic days, but the military skill of the Emperor reached almost its highest point, and the Passage of the Beresina has increased, not diminished, his renown in history.

Larrey, the Surgeon-General, performed many operations at the roadside while the bridge-building was going on, and used a tree-trunk for his operating-table. He overheard one man, whose arm he had just amputated, remark as he rejoined the ranks, 'I am a long way from Carcassonne.'

That man was a good judge. The whole army was a long way from Carcassonne.

After the Passage of the Beresina, the cold increased again. But it was too late. The river had been bridged, at a cost of 20,000 lives.

On November 29th there were twenty-four degrees of frost, and then on the 2nd of December there was a terrible fall in the temperature to fifty-four degrees of frost. This appalling cold completed the disintegration of the *Grande Armée*, and the last remnant of discipline vanished, save only in a handful of the Guard and in the rear-guard.

Day after day the barrel-cooper's son fought on, marching, turning to form square or line, fighting musket in hand, turning again to plod westwards, many times a day for forty-two consecutive days.

At the village of Plaszczenitzy, Oudinot, lying wounded in an improvised casualty-clearing-station, was surprised by 150 Russian hussars and 400 Cossacks. The Marshal's escort fled, but the Duke of Reggio struggled up from his stretcher, barricaded himself into a log-cabin with seventeen survivors, and beat off every attack till the enemy retired in a panic. During the defence Oudinot was wounded again.

On December 5th the Emperor, who had refused to take the chance of escaping before the Beresina was crossed, saw clearly that he could do no more to save his Army in Russia. His place was now in the recruiting-depôts of the Empire. Handing over the Army, therefore, to Murat, and resisting poor Berthier's wail of appeal to be allowed to escape with him, Napoleon left Smorgoni on a sledge, and whirled away through the woods to the dull sound of thudding hooves and the swishing of steel sledge-runners.

On the following night there were sixty-three degrees of frost, on December 7th sixty-six. This was the coldest day of all the retreat. The last of the horses perished on that day, and even the crows and the ravens dropped down like stones from the stiff, frosted branches of the fir-trees.

But Ney fought on. He had with him as second-in-command a certain General Maison, and together they held off the pursuers. General Maison appears once more in this book, later on.

At Molodeczno they found Victor with 4,000 men. Ney's command was reduced to sixty men all told, and he had some reason to expect that Victor would take over rear-guard duty. But the Duke of Belluno, little chubby Beau-Soleil, intensely disliked the snow and the absence of good red wine, and he slipped away with his Corps during the night.

Ney galloped after him and implored him to return, implored him even to lend his troops if he did not wish to return himself. But Victor calmly refused, and Ney cursed him with every blasphemy that he could lay his tongue to.

Murat was utterly incompetent to control the rout, and a mass of ravenous, half-insane, blood-stained, ghastly wreckage swept like a grim tornado into Vilna. The glittering cavalryman lost his head at once, and nothing was done to defend the town except by Ney, who tried to reorganize a new rear-guard.

But Platov's floods of Cossacks came galloping down, and the fugitives staggered on to the frontier town of Kovno, on the Niemen, where Murat's first and only action was to order a precipitate retreat into East Prussia. But there was still the Niemen to be crossed and, for the fifth and last time in forty-two days, Ney started to improvise a rear-guard. Four had melted away in his hands, but he looked around for a fifth. He found a company of artillery and 700 Germanic recruits, and with them he manned the fortifications of the town. Murat and his men were tumbling pell-mell across the Niemen when, on December 14th, Platov launched the last Russian attack of the campaign, at the Vilna gate of Kovno. Ney rushed to the Vilna gate to rally his fifth rear-guard but it was too late. They broke and fled.

But Ney fought on. With four private soldiers he began to pick up and fire the loaded muskets which had been thrown away by the fugitives, and then he was joined by about thirty others. But a second Russian attack threatened to cut off their retreat, and at last Ney fell back.

At eight o'clock on the night of December 14th, 1812, the last French soldier out of all the 600,000 of the *Grande Armée* crossed the river Niemen, and left the soil of Holy Russia, and that last soldier was Michel Ney, Duke of Elchingen and Prince of the Moskowa.

An Emperor, two Kings, a Prince, eight Marshals, and 600,000 men had been defeated, all, all except the son of the barrel-cooper of Saarlouis.

CHAPTER XVI

LEIPZIG

IT was on December 5th, 1812, that the Emperor left Smorgoni. He had crossed the Niemen in June with 600,000 men. A thousand of the Old Guard came back with arms in their hands, and marching shoulder to shoulder. The rest had vanished. They had disappeared into eternity, or into Siberia, or they had deserted, or they were dying of starvation and disease and wounds. Many thousands were roaming Central Europe in wild, haggard bands, like wolves which a long frost has driven down from the hills to prowl round the villages. Of all that brilliant Army, only the thousand men of the Guard kept their ranks and their arms and their discipline to the end.

France had been fighting since 1792, since the day of Valmy, and after twenty years of it, had made her supreme effort and had seen it fail more disastrously than any effort in military history since the siege of Syracuse by the Athenians in 413 B.C. The game was surely up at last. The invincible genius was overthrown, more stupendously than anyone had dreamt of or dared to hope. France's Army was destroyed, and the Allies were stronger than ever. Russia was victorious, the Prussian nation was forcing its rulers to mobilize it against the tyrant, Sweden was a likely ally, Austria a certain one, and always, behind them all, there was the steady, relentless, immovable determination of the English oligarchy not to sheathe the sword, to use a phrase of our own times, until the military domination of General Bonaparte should be finally destroyed.

And yet the Allies hesitated – all except the Prussian people and the English aristocrats. Such was the magic of the Emperor's name, and the terror of his 'long boots', that it was some months before the Allies plucked up a concerted courage. In the meantime the Emperor was at work, just as he had worked before Marengo, or on the island of Lobau in 1809, and as he was to work once again before the end. He was raising an army.

At Smorgoni, in December 1812, there were eight Marshals and a thousand men of the Guard available to defend the eastern frontiers of France; in April 1813, four short months later, the French field-army on the Elbe and the Weser consisted of 226,000 men; the fortresses on the Vistula, the Oder, and the Elbe were heavily garrisoned; five hundred guns were in the field; the Emperor was commanding in person; and there were still 200,000 first-class fighting-men in the Spanish Peninsula. What a country! And what a man!

But the field-army had two serious defects. Firstly, it was terribly short of horses. There were only 15,000 cavalrymen altogether (Marmont's Corps consisted of 22,000 infantry and 200 horsemen, lancers of the Grand-Duchy of Berg), and the wide, open country of Saxony was a splendid place for cavalry work. The second fatal defect was the exhaustion of those of the Marshals who had made the Russian campaign. It is usually concluded by historians that the repeated defeats of the Marshals in 1813 were due to their incompetence as individual handlers of large masses of men. It is far more likely that mental and physical weariness had something to do with it. Ney, for example, was by this time not so young as in the days of the Sambre-et-Meuse when he was a dashing captain of hussars, and now, in 1813, he had just rounded

off twenty almost consecutive years of active service by
walking in a terrible mid-winter from Moscow to Kovno,
a distance of 550 miles, on quarter-rations, and fighting
personally with sword and musket every day. A little
exhaustion after such a climax to such a twenty years may
well be excused to a man of forty-three. During the campaign of 1813 Napoleon himself, also forty-three, was
seldom more than a shadow of the man of Austerlitz
or Wagram. To say that the Marshals longed only for
peace and an opportunity to enjoy their wealth and
honours, is to underestimate their sense of loyalty to their
Commander and their Profession. It would have been, for
instance, easy enough for Ney to have shirked the battle
of Bautzen in 1813, instead of galloping all over the battlefield with one leg in a silk stocking and slipper because
a wound prevented him from wearing a boot. Of all the
fighting Marshals, only Masséna was really skulking. For,
on being reappointed to the High Command in Spain, he
went as far as Bayonne, pleaded ill-health, and returned
home. The next nearest approach to skulking was Augereau,
who clung to his post as commander of a paper corps, far
behind the line, as long as he possibly could. The rest went
on stubbornly with the fatal work.

But there was a sense of gathering gloom. The shadows
were lengthening into the twilight, and all the gay
buoyancy of the old days was gone. Lasalle, Colbert,
Sainte-Croix, and Montbrun all were dead. The new
levies, marching in from France, were full of enthusiasm at
first, but they were soon sobered by realities, and in one of
their first pitched battles, at Bautzen, a sudden rain-storm
brought the whole thing to a standstill, just as if the Army
of France was a horde of Chinese with umbrellas. Nor
was there any longer the blind belief in the invincibility of
their Commander. Nor was Germany the pleasant, easy-
going campaigning-ground of the past. The people were
stirring, and the poet Körner was rousing strange emo-
tions with his fiery songs, and von Lutzow's Night Riders

were beginning to practise the arts which the Spaniards had perfected in long years of horror. No longer were faces at the roadside friendly; there was no welcome in the wayside billet; and the despatch-rider began to look fearfully over his shoulder as he clattered through the dark forests of Franconia.

***

The Marshals with the Army of Saxony at the opening of the campaign were Ney, Victor, Macdonald, Oudinot, Marmont, and St. Cyr, all commanding corps, Bessières with the Guard, Murat with the cavalry, and Berthier, as usual, in his office. Augereau was lying in reserve in Franconia with three paper divisions.

Murat's presence with the army was due to a curious accident. For months he and his dashing Queen Caroline had been intriguing with Metternich of Austria, and Murat was getting ready to transfer his allegiance at any moment to the other side. After he had extricated himself, therefore, from the Russian snows, he went down to his kingdom to continue the game. But his terrifying brother-in-law was soon on his heels, and a furious despatch ordered King Joachim up to Dresden. Very reluctantly he obeyed and set out for the north. On his way he met a courier from Metternich on the Campagna outside Rome, and stopped him. But the despatches which the courier was carrying from the court of Vienna to the court of Naples were in cipher, and Murat sent them on to Naples to be deciphered. They contained the news which he had been longing for, that Vienna would confirm his kingship if he changed sides. But the despatch went on to Naples, and the King rode on to Dresden.

Victor's main contribution to the campaign was an incessant flow of flattery and bad advice. According to Marmont, he spent such little wit and eloquence as he possessed in pleading causes that he knew the Emperor had already adopted, and in repeating over and over again that Europe was only waiting to see if Napoleon was going to sacrifice Danzig. In these days Napoleon jumped eagerly at anyone who would share his illusions, and during this crucial campaign it was to the stupid ex-drummer-boy that he turned most frequently for advice.

Davout, in Hamburg, received orders to march into Swedish Pomerania and occupy it if he thought there were enough boots in store in that territory to make the expedition worth while. Davout thought less about boots than about the opportunity of annoying Bernadotte, and he marched into Pomerania with great gusto.

* * *

The campaign which was to bring nothing to the Marshals but death, and defeat, and struggle without reward, opened tragically.

On the morning of the first day of May, Marshal Bessières, commanding-in-chief the cavalry pending the arrival of Murat from Naples, was in poor spirits. For a long time he refused to eat any breakfast, but was at last persuaded, saying gloomily, 'If I am going to be killed by a cannon-ball this morning, it had better not catch me starving.' He then burnt all his wife's letters, and mounted his horse and rode forward to the defile of Rippach, near Lützen in Saxony. An enemy field-gun fired a sniping shot from a forward position, and killed with a direct hit the Marshal's orderly, a Polish light-horseman of the Guard. The Marshal galloped away and returned with a burying-party. 'If the enemy advance,' he said, 'and find a soldier of the Guard on the ground, they will boast that they have driven back the entire Guard, and the Emperor will be angry.' At that moment the sniping-gun fired again and scored another direct hit, and the idol of the Guard went down. It was his own fault. No gunner would ever have ridden into the exact range of a laid gun. A few minutes later Ney came up, but fortunately for him the gun had retired. The stern rear-guard specialist gazed down at the body of the dead man, and after a while he said gloomily, '*C'est notre sort. C'est une belle mort*,' and rode slowly away to direct the storm.

Throughout his military life Bessières was understudy to Murat. Napoleon himself said that they were the two best cavalrymen in the Army, but that Murat was the ideal of an advance-guard man and Bessières the ideal of a cautious commander of reserves. He was adored by the veteran grumblers of the Guard, each man of which looked upon Bessières as his adopted brother, and the Marshal himself often said, 'I came from the ranks, and I am not going to forget it.' Indeed, all loved Bessières, except Masséna and Lannes, and the news of his death increased the sense of autumnal melancholy. 'He was one of our old companions of Italy,' said Marmont. More and more these men were looking back to the irresistible days of their youth, when the *Grande Armée* had never been thought of, and they were all young men together, and the Army of '96 was the magic Army of the world. Times were changing, and always for the worse.

The Emperor was in his most brilliant form at the beginning of the campaign, and he led off with the victory of Lützen. But he had so little cavalry for pursuit that the victory was an empty one, and the Army was still further depressed by the death of another of the companions of Italy. For Duroc, Grand-Marshal of the Palace, was mortally wounded as he galloped beside the Emperor. Duroc was no soldier, but a simple, straight, wise gentleman from the dark red plateau of the Auvergne. He had been a gunner-cadet with Marmont, and a sub-lieutenant in the garrison at Châlons in 1792, and he went to Italy and became A.D.C. to Bonaparte after the fight for the Bridge of Arcola.

The Emperor rode back after the battle and said, 'My Eagles were victorious, but my Star is setting,' just as after the victory of Dresden, he said to Marmont, 'Marmont, my game is going wrong.' The Star was setting. The game was going wrong, and there was not a man in the Army who did not know it. 'Take care of Vandamme,' wrote the Emperor to Davout; 'fighting men are getting scarce.' (Vandamme was captured a month or two later because of a bungle of the Emperor himself.)

There was a second victory, at Bautzen, in spite of the defective artillery ammunition (at least a third of the shells failed to explode), but again it was an empty one. For not only was there a shortage of cavalry, but the Emperor in these days found a strange new craving for sleep at the end of a battle, and the Marshals were dispirited and fractious. Ney went so far as to send in his resignation. Instead of launching a great pursuit after Bautzen, Napoleon signed an armistice.

The delay caused by the armistice was fatal. In August Austria joined the Alliance, and the Crown Prince Charles John of Sweden took a hand in the game. In July of 1813 an interesting reunion had taken place at Stralsund, when the guns of that fortress of Swedish Pomerania fired a salute in honour of a man who was landing from America on his way to join the enemies of France. The man who fired the salute was ex-Marshal Bernadotte, late of the French Army, and the man who received the salute was ex-General Moreau, late of the French Army. The two old friends of Republican days, one now a civilian, the other now heir to a throne, at once began to talk strategy, and it was Moreau who pointed out Bernadotte's faulty position, with his long line of communications between Saxony and Stralsund, and the famous Davout lying on his flank at Hamburg. Thirteen years of civil life had not blunted the judgment of the victor of Hohenlinden.

After this cordial greeting, the two friends went down to Silesia to fight against their country. At the Allied Headquarters they caused the gravest offence, at once, by making the brilliant suggestion that the Allies should everywhere attack when in the presence of a Marshal, and should everywhere retreat when in the presence of Napoleon.

'Are we not good enough,' cried old Blücher and the Russians indignantly, 'to beat Napoleon?'

'No,' replied the two Frenchmen kindly.

But the advice was taken, at any rate at the beginning, and the unfortunate Macdonald added to his consistent record of defeat by letting himself be caught by Blücher with the river Katzbach behind him. The battle was fought in a tremendous storm of rain, the river rose abruptly, and Macdonald lost every gun of his artillery and 18,000 prisoners. Later in life Marshal Macdonald achieved the singular feat of describing the battle of the Katzbach in his memoirs with only two casual references to the existence of an enemy, and with pages and pages about the rain and the mud.

Further north, Oudinot was caught in the same way, when he was out of the shelter of the Emperor's name, and driven back, and St. Cyr was besieged in Dresden. But St. Cyr, whom Marmont described as the finest defensive general in Europe, was able to hold out until help came up.

But in spite of the success of the policy of the two distinguished renegades, the Allied generals were still suffering from hurt feelings. They could not really believe that with 160,000 men they were not a match for Napoleon with 120,000, and so, on the 27th of August, they took their courage in both hands and attacked him at Dresden and were completely defeated. Murat led one of his most spectacular charges at the head of a mass of horsemen, and the Allied commanders, watching through their glasses his gay figure and irresistible dash, shook their heads gloomily and agreed that the new ally was over-acting his part. They did not know of the incident of the cipher on the Campagna, and were under the impression that Murat was biding his time to desert. On the evening of the second day of the battle the stage was set for yet another of those disasters to which Europe had grown so terribly accustomed during seventeen years, the rout into the twilight of an army and the pursuit of the Emperor thundering on its heels. But at Dresden the Allies were saved, for on that evening the Emperor was tired and he felt ill. He had no energy left either of mind or body, and he rode back slowly through the darkness and the drenching rain into Dresden. The next day, when the ladies of Dresden came trooping out in their best clothes to look at the battlefield, they found that the French Army had not advanced.

Melas had done the same thing at Marengo in 1800 when he had won the battle and thought that he had made an end of it. It cost Melas the campaign. At Dresden it may have cost Napoleon his throne. For a sweeping pursuit that night would have utterly destroyed the army of the Allies, and the world might well have thought that such a man was entirely invincible after all.

***

On October 17th, 1813, Prince Joseph Poniatowski, nephew of King Stanislaus of Poland, was made a Marshal in order to encourage the Polish contingent in the great battle that was about to be fought in front of Leipzig. Poniatowski was a Polish patriot, and like all Polish patriots, he welcomed enthusiastically the arrival of Napoleon in Warsaw in 1806, and had been appalled and disillusioned when France and Russia came together on the raft at Tilsit in 1807. A strong Russia meant a non-existent Poland. When, therefore, Napoleon and Alexander began to drift apart, no one was so delighted as Poniatowski. And when the *Grande Armée* crossed the Niemen in 1812, the Prince brought 36,000 Polish regulars to help in the invasion and provided another 65,000 for garrison work. He was wounded during the retreat from Moscow, but was ready to take the field again in 1813.

***

For three days the French Army lay in a vast semi-circle round Leipzig, and held back the Allies. But in the end, with two men for one, the Allies pressed steadily in upon them. On the night of the third day, October 18th, 1813, Napoleon at last gave orders for retreat, and instantly fell asleep. History is divided about the building of the pontoon bridges over the Pleisse and the Elster, the parallel rivers which lay between France and the French, at the back of Leipzig. Some say that the Emperor ordered their construction; others that he did not, and that Berthier stubbornly refused to take the responsibility for sending instructions to the bridging companies, covering himself behind a parrot repetition of '*l'Empereur ne l'a pas ordonné.*' However that may be, the only thing which affected those exhausted, powder-blackened, defeated men as they shuffled slowly through the winding streets of Leipzig and out by the single narrow western gate, was that no pontoon bridges had been built and that there was only one bridge across the Pleisse. And even this one bridge was blown up too soon, and 20,000 men were still on the wrong side. Napoleon had lost a second army within a year.

Of the Marshals, Berthier, Murat, Ney, Mortier, Marmont, Oudinot, Victor, Macdonald, Augereau, and Poniatowski took part in the battle of Leipzig. Marmont was wounded in the hand, got a bruised arm, a hat shot away, a bullet in his coat, and four horses shot under him. Macdonald escaped by swimming his horse across the Elster. Augereau escaped by the simple device of going away when things grew desperate. When, after the battle, Macdonald asked Augereau the meaning of a certain order of the Emperor's, the old swashbuckler burst into a foaming torrent of abuse against Napoleon: 'Idiot . . . coward . . . lost his head . . . do you think I am such a fool as to let myself be killed or taken for the sake of a Leipzig suburb? You should have done as I did, and run away.'

Marshal-Prince Poniatowski did not live long to enjoy his baton, for he tried to follow Macdonald's lead and was drowned in the Elster. He had been ordered to join Macdonald and cover the retreat through the suburbs. He collected about 2,000 Polish infantry, drew his sword, and exclaiming, 'Here we must fall with honour,' he counter-attacked the advancing enemy. He was immediately wounded in the arm (his third wound of the battle), but pressed on until it became obvious that the Allies were in such strength that his handful could effect nothing. Poniatowski, therefore, turned and rode his horse into the river Pleisse. Just as he reached the bank he was wounded for the fourth time, but managed to get across and scramble up to the opposite side. The horse was drowned, but the Marshal found another and, galloping through the garden of a certain Herr Reichenbach, he reached the steep bank of the Elster. Pursuit was close behind and the Marshal spurred his horse into the river. But both man and horse were exhausted and they were drowned within a short distance from the bank. Five days later the body of the Marshal-Prince was found by a fisherman and buried in Leipzig.

At Leipzig a spectacle that had electrified a hundred battlefields, and thrilled a million hearts, went at long last down the shadowy path that leads to legend and to saga. For the last time, huge armies, locked in the death-grapple, paused, almost without knowing it, in their work of manoeuvring and bayoneting and musket-loading and gun-laying and ramming home the shell, to watch, breathless, appalled, exalted, the glittering columns of the French cavalry go riding down to the attack, with the ostrich-plumes of Murat waving in front of them. It was the last charge of the innkeeper's son, Joachim Murat, Grand-Duke of Berg, Grand Admiral of France, King of Naples, and Commander of the Reserve Cavalry.

* * *

Some old friendships came to an end at Leipzig. It was the last time that Murat and Marmont fought side by side. They had been close friends ever since that night in Paris, eighteen years before, when General Bonaparte and Lieutenant Marmont, gunners both, waited anxiously hour after hour for Captain Murat to come back from the Sablons with some guns. They never met again after Leipzig.

Another pair who parted on the battlefield were the two renegades, for Moreau was mortally wounded at Dresden, and Bernadotte was the only mourner at his funeral. Later he settled a hundred thousand francs on Moreau's daughter.

***

St. Cyr was left with 26,000 men in Dresden. In spite of his habitual neglect of his men, and his consequent slackness in laying in supplies, he refused to allow any requisitioning from the inhabitants, even of wine, of which there was a vast supply in the cellars of the town. But 'The Owl' was a wise old bird and, ex-actor that he was, he knew the importance of playing to the gallery. And for Gouvion St. Cyr the goodwill of enemy civilians was going to be a lot more valuable in the deepening shadows than the rations of a handful of Napoleonic troops. He might be only a dreamy violinist, but he knew exactly to a decimal point how many beans made five.

In the north, Davout, Prince of Eckmühl, held fast to Hamburg. Davout knew not only how many beans made five, but how many men five beans would feed in a city which he was holding for the Emperor.

The remnants of the *débâcle* of Leipzig, 70,000 men, fought their way savagely and sullenly through an intercepting army, reached Mainz, caught typhus, and finally entered France. They were so exhausted that many of them got their feet frozen and gangrenous, although the temperature was warm compared with the cold of Russia.

Thirty thousand out of the seventy thousand died on their return.

The last time the *Grande Armée* had come home was the golden summer of 1808, when the men of Ulm and Austerlitz and Jena went swinging down to the Pyrenees through the exulting cheers of France.

＊＊＊

While the game was going wrong in Saxony, there were still 200,000 troops in Spain. Half of them at Leipzig would have shattered the Allied armies. A quarter of them would have turned the victory at Dresden into a devastating rout and saved the Imperial Throne. But they were in Spain, not in Saxony; they were fighting a losing campaign, not turning victories into routs; and the object of all their sufferings was not the preservation of the Imperial Throne but the occupation of a hateful and destroyed wilderness.

The strategical disposition of this army of 200,000 men in 1813 was characteristic of the unbelievable series of consecutive bungles which the Emperor had committed in Spain since that evening four years before, when the despatches from Paris reached him at Benavente and he galloped out of the Peninsula and never went back. There were two theatres of war in Spain in 1813; the eastern, Catalonian-Valencian theatre, which was quite unimportant, commanded by the brilliant Marshal Suchet, Duke of Albufera, who could conciliate or defeat Spaniards with equal dexterity and ease; and there was the all-important north-western sector, the line between Madrid and Paris, the key to the Pyrenees, the bottle-neck through which France must pass to invade Spain, and Spain to invade France. Against this sector the leopards of England were slowly creeping, under His Grace of Wellington himself, that master of the interminable stalk followed by the modified pounce, and the French Army against him was commanded by poor old Brother Joseph and his military adviser, Marshal Jourdan, who had won a battle nineteen years before and since then had won no other. For Soult had been recalled from Spain and was with the Army of Saxony.

Joseph and Jourdan contrived between them to make every military mistake possible, while Suchet had nothing better to do than build fountains and endow schools of medicine. Nearer and nearer came the leopards, until at last Joseph's divisional-commanders persuaded him to stand and fight, on June 21st, 1813, near Vittoria, with 65,000 men strung out in a grotesque disarray against 80,000 in an advantageous tactical position. Jourdan, on being told of King Joseph's decision, went to bed. After a series of tentative skirmishes, Joseph found that the English left wing was closing round behind him, where-upon the entire French Army bolted across the mountains to Pampeluna, leaving behind them 151 out of 153 guns, a million pounds sterling, and all the thousands of wagon-loads of loot which six years of steady and skilful looting had accumulated. Marshal Jourdan, who had got up to watch the battle, went back to bed again with the comment, 'Well, gentlemen, you would have your battle, and it seems to be a lost one.' A few weeks later he was dismissed, sent in disgrace to his estate near Orléans, and a month or two afterwards appointed to the command of the Military District of Rouen, a job at the desk from which he should never have been removed.

The effect of Vittoria was immense in Europe. It had two repercussions in Spain. Suchet had to evacuate Valencia and draw back towards France, while Soult came posting back from Dresden to take command in Spain and, if necessary, to arrest Brother Joseph.

The Command of the Army of Spain! All Soult's ambitions flared up again. In all the seven years of war in the Peninsula there had never before been an Army of Spain with one sole Commander-in-Chief. But it was too late.

The task of the new Commander was not to sweep triumphantly across the country, winning great victories and acting as Viceroy of each of the kingdoms until a real, statesmanlike, and at the same time military successor to the miserable Joseph should be found (someone with previous experience of being a Viceroy, say, in Andalusia). The time for all that was long past. The new Commander had to reorganize a broken and dispirited army and prepare to defend the very soil of France itself, and that in the face of a victorious enemy.

Fortunately for the Duke of Dalmatia, the Duke of Wellington, as usual, had limited his pounce. The pursuit after Vittoria was a feeble affair, and Wellington, according to his usual practice, blamed the failure upon his men. Meanwhile Soult's energy put new life into the Army of Spain. Within thirteen days of his arrival he was able actually to launch an exceedingly dangerous offensive. But as Wellington said, 'Soult did not quite understand a field of battle. He was not so good as Masséna.'

The offensive soon petered out, and through the summer and autumn of 1813 Soult was fighting incessant defensive actions, and being pushed steadily back towards the frontier. (At the engagement of Sauroren on July 27th–28th, the difference between the English and the French temperament was brought out in a startling form. For no human imagination can picture Murat riding into action as General Sir Thomas Picton did in this battle, wearing a blue frock-coat, a top-hat, and carrying, instead of a sword or riding-whip, a neatly rolled-up umbrella.) San Sebastian was stormed at the third attempt by the English and, though an Allied city, heartily sacked, and in October the Allied Army reached the line of the Bidassoa.

The last two Marshals in Spain kept up the five-year-old tradition to the very end. Soult at one end of the mountains, and Suchet at the other, exchanged a long and tortuous correspondence during these months, each protesting the utmost confidence in each other, each offering to co-operate loyally, and each secretly determined to see the other damned before he served with him, let alone under him.

On October 7th, 1813, the Allies advanced to the assault of the line of the Bidassoa and, by the evening of that day, were standing upon the soil of France. Save for Pampeluna which fell three weeks later, and the retreat of Suchet, the War in the Peninsula was over. It had lasted exactly six years, for it was on October 18th, 1807, that Junot led the Corps of the Gironde across the frontier on its way to Lisbon.

How many regiments, how many gay horsemen, how many rattling guns, and what high hopes of glory, had travelled that westward road that runs from Bayonne through Vittoria and Burgos to Madrid. And after what sufferings and diseases and wounds, what tortures and cruelties, what sackings and burnings, what heroisms of men and women, what courage and what infamy, did that handful of men recross the Bidassoa under Soult. Fifty thousand men under Soult, Duke of Dalmatia, and twenty-five thousand under Suchet, Duke of Albufera, were all that was left of those magnificent armies with their high sonorous names: the Corps of Observation of the Gironde, the Corps of Observation of the Ocean Coast, the Corps of Observation of the Pyrenees, the Army of Aragon, the Army of the North, the Army of Portugal, the Armies of Andalusia, of Catalonia, of Valencia, and finally the remnant Army of Spain.

Of the twenty-six Marshals, only Kellermann, Pérignon, and Sérurier – all three long since retired from active service – and Davout, Bernadotte, Oudinot, Brune, and the unfortunate Prince Poniatowski, did not serve in Spain. And only one, Suchet, achieved enough distinction to earn a Spanish title.

CHAPTER XVII

THE ABDICATION

ALL the world, except one man, knew that the game was up.

Germany had risen after Leipzig, just as Spain had risen after Baylen, not by a *levée en masse*, or royal proclamations, or votes in Parliaments, but with the irresistible awakening of the soul of a people. The poet Körner was dead, killed in action, but his songs lived on. Bavaria suddenly abandoned the French alliance and went over. Holland went over. King Joachim of Naples hastily dropped the little gold stick that he used to carry into battle and, picking up his sceptre, resumed negotiations with Austria, and all the time the Duke of Wellington was pushing further and further, though at no dazzling speed, into France. Bordeaux was getting ready to welcome the Duke of Angoulême and hoist the white cockade of the Bourbon. And France itself was passionately longing for peace. Two great armies had been utterly destroyed in two succeeding campaigns at the end of twenty years of warfare, and the country was exhausted.

There was no money in France, and no industry, no commerce, no army, no navy, no horses, no munitions, while advancing to the Rhine and crossing it were

Russia, Prussia, Bavaria, Saxony, Austria, and Sweden, and England was already north of the Pyrenees.

But the greatest brain of the age, alone among men, either could not or would not grasp the situation, and the struggle went on. For the first and only time in his life, the Emperor had to fight a defensive campaign. He had shown the world that he was the supreme master of the attack; in 1814 came the necessity to experiment with an art that was new to him.

Seven Marshals were with him when the invading columns had groped their way across the Moselle and the Meuse, and reached the Marne: Berthier, Ney, and Mortier of the original eighteen; and of the later creations Victor, Oudinot, Marmont, and Macdonald. Augereau was down at Lyons with 25,000 men. Soult was facing Wellington between Bayonne and Toulouse, and Suchet from the Catalan frontier was posting off every man he could spare up to Augereau. Davout was holding stoutly on to Hamburg, Bernadotte was invading his native country, and Murat was intriguing against it. Moncey and Lefèbvre were in Paris. The rest were dead or scattered.

But even the seven veteran Marshals had only a small hand in the startling events that took place in the pleasant valleys of the Marne and Seine during the spring. The campaign of 1814 belongs to the Emperor and no one else. He started slowly. For a fortnight, the last week of January and the first of February, he was the man of Borodino, or of Dresden, sluggish, indecisive, lethargic. On February 1st his mixed army of veterans and boys was heavily defeated at La Rothière, and only a heavy snowstorm prevented Blücher from following up his victory. It was the only time that snow helped the Emperor. It had held him up in the Great St. Bernard in 1800 when, as First Consul, he was silently pouring the Army of Reserve across the mountains to cut off Melas from Vienna and reconquer Italy in a single day; it had turned Augereau's attack into the fatal slant at Eylau; it had blocked the

Guadarramas at Christmas-time in 1808, so that Sir John
Moore got an extra day's start in the long-distance race to
Corunna; and it had played a part in the affair of 1812. But
at La Rothière the snow changed sides at last.

For a week after the defeat Napoleon seemed to understand what everyone else understood, that the game was
up; and then on February 8th, 1814, he sprang to life,
and showed the world a sight that had not been seen during eighteen years, had been half-forgotten, had been
obscured by vast events, the sight of the young gunner-
general of 1796 handling an army of 50,000 men. For
twenty-six days Napoleon wore his 'long boots', whirling
his little army up and down the valleys, striking blow
after blow, now flinging Blücher back in rout, now
appearing miraculously upon the Austrian flank and sending Schwartzenberg spinning back towards the frontier,
now cutting off and almost annihilating a Russian Corps.
Châtillon-sur-Marne, Montmirail, Château-Thierry, Vau-
champ, Champaubert, Nangis, Montereau, all were victories in these bewildering days in the country round the
little town of Brienne, where Cadet Bonaparte had studied the theory of war four years before the mob tore the
Bastille down.

The pace was terrific. But could it last? Could 50,000
men, plus the greatest captain of the age at the very dazzling pinnacle of his form, really be a match for 400,000
odd? There was one chance, and only one. If Augereau
with his 25,000 men came tumbling up from Lyons and
cut the line between the Austrians and home, it was a safe
wager that Schwartzenberg, the Austrian Commander, who
was already wobbling, would do what every compatriot of
his had done for twenty years. He would lose heart on
finding his communications cut. And once Austria was out
of it, who knew what might not be done with the Tsar or
Bernadotte? And Blücher's army had been so knocked to
pieces that it was out of action for a time at least. So it all
rested with Augereau. The Marshal-Duke of Castiglione

got his orders on February 13th, but did not move. On the 16th Napoleon wrote again, urgently, vehemently. 'If you are still that Augereau of Castiglione,' he cried, and the 'old moustache' muttered in reply, 'Give me the men of Castiglione,' and he made no move until February 28th, and then it was too late. It was not that the last card was a failure. The last card was not in the pack.

On March 9th Ney, for the first time in all these years, led the Old Guard into action at Laon; but Marmont, whose heart was beginning to fail him, made a pitiful bungle and left all his guns – he, a gunner – to be surprised and captured. 'The Emperor would have been justified in cutting him down,' cried Berthier, 'but he is so fond of him that he leaves him in his command.' And why should he not be fond of Marmont, his earliest comrade of old gunnery days? Marmont was a man he could trust, like Victor who had been with him at Toulon, and Berthier who had never left his side since '96, and faithful, dog-like Ney, and solid Oudinot, and the too-little trusted Macdonald, and good-natured Mortier. These men would stick to him for ever.

And yet – would they? After the victory at Champaubert Napoleon cried exultantly, 'Another day like this and I shall be on the Vistula,' and neither Berthier nor Marmont answered a word. Was the sacred fire really extinct? Augereau's treachery was disquieting – but then Augereau had always been a cunning, sly rascal. There was nothing new in Augereau behaving badly. But – where were the men of Castiglione? Where were the men who rushed the bridge at Lodi, and held the plateau of Rivoli, and swarmed up into the Carnic Alps with Masséna in front? and . . . out there, in this year of grace 1814, on the hillsides of the Marne, the men did not know how to fight like the old rascals. But how should they? What was that story of Marmont's – he had asked a boy at Champaubert why he did not fire, and the boy had answered that he would fire as well as anyone if he knew how to load.

And at Craonne, a division of the Young Guard was only twenty days old and had stood in close formation for three hours under fire because it did not know how to deploy. The Young Guard! And he had himself seen old Drouot, Commander of the Artillery, showing gun-layers on the field of Arcis how to lay their guns. Imagine Sénarmont giving gun-drill when Ney was storming into the streets of Friedland in '07. Imagine Marmont teaching his men how to load those last five guns at Marengo, while Desaix was forming up for the counter-attack and young Kellermann was waiting with his handful of cuirassiers among the mulberries. Imagine Murat halting at Eylau to teach a regiment how to form line of squadrons in the snow-storm. Imagine – but it was no time for imagining. 'Long boots,' and one more victory, and 'I shall be on the Vistula again.'

* * *

But the swift victories were barren and all the high strategy useless. Old Blücher suddenly had a vision, a rare thing for one of his race, of the truth, and he saw that the wheeling, darting, pouncing handful of Frenchmen was only a thing of straw, and when the Emperor played his last brilliant card and raided the Allied communications, Blücher ignored him and went straight for Paris. The bluff was called, and the Emperor came back to defend his capital.

Only Berthier, Ney, Mortier, Marmont, Oudinot, and Macdonald were with him now; for Victor had been ignominiously deprived of his command for utter incompetence. But the gallant Moncey brought up the number of the Marshals to seven again by marching out of Paris with the National Guard and a handful of students from the Polytechnic School to help in the defence. Augereau was in the full swing of his treachery, and Murat had actually taken the field in Italy against the Viceroy Eugène. In

distant Hamburg the iron Davout held on and waited for
help that he knew would not be coming.

But all was useless, and at last the seven faithful Marshals
knew it. On April 4th six of them stood on a terrace at
Fontainebleau and watched the Emperor review the Guard.
Marshal Lefèbvre, Duke of Danzig, the stout old Alsatian
ranker with the washerwoman wife, joined the group.
Seven Marshals out of twenty-six, and Berthier in his
office was the eighth. They had fought beneath the walls
of some capitals, of Lisbon, Madrid, Rome, Milan, Turin,
Berne, Venice, Antwerp, Munich, Naples, Berlin, Dresden,
Warsaw, Cairo, Jerusalem, and Moscow, and at the end
they were fighting beneath the walls of their own capital.
By what means the subject was broached, or by whom the
first word was spoken, will never be known. Probably it
was Ney, the bluntest of them all. Ney had been acting
very strangely since that first wild outburst against the
Emperor on the day of Borodino. There was a sort of des-
peration, almost hysteria, about him, which in modern
days would have been labelled shell-shock; and when the
Marshals, standing on the terrace, suddenly decided to
send a deputation to Napoleon that very afternoon, it was
Ney who volunteered to act as spokesman. Lefèbvre and
Moncey agreed to go with him.

Berthier was with Napoleon when the three came into
his room at the palace that afternoon and demanded that
there should be an end of the fighting and an end of the
Emperor's reign. Napoleon, calm and dignified, delivered a
lucid description of the new stroke that he was about to
launch, counted up the reserves that were hastening to
Fontainebleau, and spoke of a national uprising against the
invaders. The deputation listened in deadly silence. Not even
Berthier murmured a word of agreement. Then Oudinot
and Macdonald came in to report the arrival of their troops.
Napoleon repeated his description. Again there was that
deadly silence. Then Macdonald said, 'We are resolved to
make an end of all this.' Napoleon made a third and last

appeal, but Ney, the Ney of Borodino, cut him short, him, the terrible Emperor: 'The Army will not march.'

The Emperor for the only time in the interview spoke loudly. 'The Army will obey me.'

'The Army will obey its Generals,' replied Ney, and no more words were spoken.

That night the Emperor signed an Act of Abdication in favour of his son, the King of Rome. The Marshals had ended his reign, but they were not going to end his dynasty.

Ney and Macdonald took the Act of Abdication and rode to Tsar Alexander's quarters in Paris, calling in on Marmont's headquarters on the way, to take him with them. At one o'clock in the morning on April 5th, 1814, the Tsar received them and listened with respect to Ney, the one man out of 600,000 whom neither the Tsar's Cossacks nor the Tsar's climate had been able to shake, when he appealed that the Abdication should be accepted and the dynasty maintained. The Tsar promised his support and asked the delegates to return at nine o'clock. With Alexander's word the day was as good as won.

But nevertheless it all failed, and the dynasty was not maintained, and the Bourbons came back, because, between that first dead-of-night meeting with the Tsar and the second meeting at nine o'clock, the Army Corps of Auguste Frédéric Louis Viesse de Marmont, Duke of Ragusa, gunner-cadet of Brienne, old companion of Italy and Egypt, deserted to the enemy at the orders of its commander. Then the Allies saw that the game was more completely in their hands than they had known, and they struck out the dynasty from the Act of Abdication, and on April 26th, 1814, Louis Stanislas Xavier, brother to the late king, old and fat and gouty, landed at Calais to inherit the Eagles of Marengo and Austerlitz.

Marmont was the oldest friend of the Emperor.

***

As Napoleon was driving south on his way to Elba, he saw near Valence, for the first time in twenty-five years, French soldiers wearing the white cockade, and a little further down the road he met, also wearing the emblem of the Bourbons, their commander, Marshal Augereau, Duke of Castiglione. Napoleon stopped, alighted, pulled off his hat, and embraced him. The Marshal kept his hat on and returned the salute. 'Thou hast behaved badly to me,' said Napoleon without bitterness. The hawk-nosed gutter-boy burst out, speaking in the second person singular with which he had addressed, once, long ago, General Bonaparte of the Army of Italy when he himself was, for a few absurd months, General Augereau of the Army of the Rhine.

'It is thine own insatiable ambition,' he cried. 'Thou hast sacrificed everything to it, even the happiness of France. I care no more for the Bourbons than for thee. All I care for is France.' Upon this Napoleon said nothing, but turned sharply away, and then, lifting his hat again, he went back into his carriage. The Marshal-Duke put his hands behind his back and nodded a casual farewell. It was only a few days since he had proclaimed to his Corps that they were released from their oaths by the abdication of a man who, after having sacrificed millions of victims to his ambition, has not known how to die like a soldier.'

The story of the Marshals during the first Restoration is soon told. They wanted peace and they saw that the return of the Bourbons meant peace. Furthermore, there were no confiscations or cancellations. The titles and the castles were left alone, and the coopers' sons and brewers' sons and fruit-women's sons were admitted to the Peerage of Rohan, Luxembourg, Montmorency, de la Tour-du-Pin-Gouvernet, Château-briand, Suffren St. Tropez, and all the great names of French history. But then they themselves had made some contribution to French history since the Cannonade of Valmy.

Moncey, as one of the oldest of the Marshals and also as Inspector-General of Gendarmerie, went to meet Louis at Calais. Ney, Augereau, and Macdonald joined the Council of War; Soult, now a keen Royalist, went to command in Brittany, and indulged his queer passion for erecting monuments by putting up one to commemorate the dead of the battle of Quiberon Bay. Later in 1814, he came back to Paris as Minister for War, by a route which shows very clearly how quickly the soldier of Moreau's old Repub-lican Army of the Rhine had acquired the Bourbon technique. For Soult's favourite A.D.C., General Brun de Villeret, had married the niece of the Comte de Bruges, and the Comte de Bruges was a great favourite of Monsieur, brother of the King, and the Comte de Bruges had two secret and consuming ambitions. He wanted to be a Lieutenant-General, although his experience of han-dling large bodies of men was less wide, say, than cabin-boy Masséna's, and he wanted to be Grand Chancellor of the Legion of Honour. So it was all arranged, and Soult became Minister for War in place of Dupont, *le capitulard* of Baylen, and a dark shadow was lifted from the con-science of France. For, after all, whatever the route by which the Duke of Dalmatia had reached office, at least he had stood beside Masséna at Zürich in '99, and stormed the Pratzen hill at Austerlitz. Whereas Dupont had dragged the Eagles into the dust and, by his folly and his cowardice, had sent 8,000 Frenchmen to die of starvation upon the desert island of Cabrera.

Marmont, Duke of Ragusa, had already enriched the French language with a new word, for *raguser* quickly be-came the fashionable expression for 'to betray'. At the welcoming of Monsieur at the barrier of Paris on April 12th he alone wore the Tricolor, and next day he wore the White. A few days later he went with Ney to Compiègne to meet the King, and listened to Ney's speech of wel-come (Ney was becoming a great talker), and was relieved to hear the courtly Bourbon describe the White as the

Panache of Henri IV. But Marmont, oldest friend and deadliest traitor, was a gunner at heart, as everyone is who has ever served those fascinating and fearful engines of destruction, and he was appalled to find that he had betrayed his master for a man who could, eleven days after returning to Paris, sign away in a moment fifty-four strong places in Poland, Italy, Germany, and Belgium, with ten thousand guns that belonged by right to the gunners of France.

During this time Marmont indignantly refused to subscribe to Soult's Quiberon monument.

Jourdan, the old Republican victor of Fleurus in 1793, hoisted the White over his headquarters at Rouen. Vittoria had cured him of any lingering desire for strife.

Pérignon emerged from his obscurity and was appointed to a Commission which was verifying the claims to Royal favour of *émigrés* officers.

Masséna, at home at Rueil, got a letter from his lifelong friend Lucien Bonaparte:

'MON TRÈS CHER MASSÉNA – Voilà donc enfin le drame terminé! Tant de gloire perdue par la plus lâche fin. Bon Dieu! Que de souvenirs. Que de regrets.'

Que de souvenirs! Que de regrets!

Bernadotte, all success and suavity, tried to gloss over the less happy incidents of the last few years, and coined the soothing phrase, in talk with Marmont in Paris, 'When one has commanded in ten battles as you have, one is of the family of Kings.' His three years of Scandinavianism had done nothing to soften his Gascon accent.

Berthier, in those last painful hours, had asked Napoleon for leave to visit Paris. 'He will not return,' was the Emperor's calmly disdainful comment. Nor did he.

All the Marshals, except Davout, received the Grand Cross of the Order of St. Louis from the Bourbon.

After the Abdication was formally signed at Fontainebleau and the main hostilities were over, there were still three Marshals of the Empire in the field. Suchet was in the Lusignan with his Army of Aragon (in five years of flawless command he had captured 82,000 officers and men, and 1,415 guns), and Soult was facing Wellington at Toulouse. The galloping couriers from Fontainebleau brought both to an armistice. So only one was left. Davout, Prince of Eckmühl and Duke of Auerstädt, was holding Hamburg.

It was in May, 1813, that Bernadotte, commanding the Swedish Expeditionary Force, retreated from Hamburg on the plea that it was a comparatively 'open' city, and therefore undefendable. Soon after, Davout marched in and at once set to work with all his energy and meticulousness to accumulate stores and improve the fortifications.

After the catastrophe of Leipzig in October, 1813, Hamburg was completely isolated. Typhus and fevers broke out; English cruisers came up the Elbe and bombarded the town; the hostile population was three times as large as the garrison; and a large army of besiegers lay all round. Davout's position was the same as that of General von Lettow-Vorbeck in East Africa from 1914 to 1918. There was no chance of rescue, and yet no thought of surrender.

In April, 1814, the Allies sent word to the indomitable Prince of Eckmühl that the Emperor had abdicated and that he must surrender. 'The Emperor would not send me orders by the mouths of Russian officers,' replied the Prince. At last a curt note arrived from Dupont, Minister of War, simply announcing that General Gérard was to supersede him and that an armistice had been declared, and Davout's invincible garrison marched out with their arms in their hands. But the Marshal was not allowed to lead his men back to France. He was ordered to return alone, and, on arriving, was forbidden to live in Paris, was officially disgraced, and was instructed to be ready to stand his trial on three charges: that he had seized the Bank of Hamburg; that he had destroyed houses in the suburbs in order to make a defendable glacis; that, by his severity, he had rendered odious the word 'French'.

None of the Marshals, except Oudinot, liked Davout, but all felt that he represented much of the glory of the Empire, and Oudinot was chosen by them to ask the King to reinstate him. Oudinot failed, and then Ney tried and he too failed.

Bernadotte went back to Sweden very soon after the Abdication. He had not been at all happy in Paris, in spite of the Tsar's tentative suggestion that he might succeed Napoleon on the throne. Talleyrand had killed the suggestion with a sentence, 'If we want a soldier, we still have the finest in the world of our own.

Bernadotte's position in Paris had been very awkward. He was a conqueror of his own compatriots, and it required all his Gascon suppleness and blandness to explain away the two squadrons of Cossacks who guarded his lodgings in Paris. It was common talk that old washerwoman Lefèbvre, the Duchess of Danzig, had called him a traitor to his face, and people were still laughing at the story of the armistice at Stettin. Bernadotte had ridden, during the armistice, close to the walls and had been fired on by a sentry. Protests were made and the French commander had replied, simply, 'A French deserter was in sight, and naturally the guard shot at him.' So on the 1st of May the Crown Prince of Sweden slipped away. He never set foot in France again. Within a few weeks of returning to Stockholm he marched his veteran army into Norway and in a very short time demolished Norwegian resistance and forced the union of the two countries through the Norwegian Storthing. This was his last campaign, and there were no casualties on either side.

The other Royal Gascon, Joachim of Naples, had a much more difficult time in 1814 than his brother of Sweden. For although Metternich, on behalf of the Austrian Emperor, had signed a treaty on January 11th of peace and alliance with King Joachim, nevertheless there

were strong forces of Legitimacy who wanted to put the
miserable Ferdinand Bourbon back on the throne that he
had soaked in blood. But Metternich had put his hand to
the treaty and it could not be repudiated. And besides, he
was enjoying the charms of Caroline, Queen of Naples,
and he was anxious to oblige his mistress with a little tri-
fle like a kingdom. So Murat maintained a precarious
position throughout the year, and Europe watched him
uneasily.

Masséna, Prince of Essling, came out of his retirement
sufficiently to accept the command of the district of
Marseilles.

* * *

During the first Restoration the Bourbons contrived to
make themselves distrusted, despised, and detested in an
incredibly short space of time. The blunders which they
committed in those few months were really remarkable.
For example, the Household Corps of Louis XIV was
revived with its 6,000 pretty youths as officers, and its
annual cost of twenty million francs for elegant silks and
satins, while the Imperial Guard, renamed the Royal
Grenadiers, was removed from Paris to make way for the
gallant 6,000, and the half-pay ran into arrears. No one
had grudged Murat his feathers and gold and diamonds,
for at least they always glittered in front of the attacking
cavalry. The popinjays of the Household Corps fought
their great battles in the drawing-rooms of Paris.

The Legion of Honour was lavishly flung to civilians,
and the Order of St. Louis became the only military
order; on the Star of the Legion, Henri IV and the Three
Lilies were substituted for Napoleon and the Eagle; an
archbishop was made Chancellor of the Legion, and after
him a civilian duke; the Duke of Angoulême entered Paris
in an English uniform and insulted several of the
Marshals; an ordinance established the atrabiliar gloom

of the English Sunday; Monsieur gave a dinner to the Marshals at the Tuileries, and used Napoleon's gold dinner-service with the Imperial monogram upon it; and when Soult became Minister of War he ordered all his old half-pay comrades-in-arms to leave Paris, and awarded pensions to everyone who had been wounded in defence of the Bourbons in the long-ago rising of the Vendée.

The discontent came to boiling point over a trifling incident, as so often happens when people are simmering with dumb anger. A dashing cavalryman, General Excelmans, a leader somewhat in the style of the great Lasalle, refused to obey Soult's order to leave Paris. The Duke of Dalmatia lost his temper and, by a ludicrous display of melodrama and violence, turned Excelmans into a national hero in a single night. And Excelmans was an officer of that man who had been sent away by the almost universal will of the French People only nine months before, so swiftly can a Bourbon move in getting rid of goodwill and popularity.

On January 25th, 1815, General Excelmans, late cavalry leader of Napoleon, was acquitted at Lille on a charge of insubordination, a charge of which he was palpably and admittedly guilty, and France roared its approval.

***

On March 1st, 1815, Napoleon landed at Cannes.

CHAPTER XVIII

THE EAGLE FLIES TO NOTRE DAME

THE news from Cannes filled the Marshals with despair. Although a year of Bourbonism had disgusted and saddened all except Soult and Marmont, those most persistent of place-hunters, and although the Eagles and the Tricolor and the memories of great days had been spat upon, and trampled upon, and humiliated, by fat old cowards and pink young cowards, yet there was peace in France, and those tired fighting-men felt that they had earned some peace. It was getting on for twenty-three years since that first affair at Valmy. And it was not as if they themselves were neglected or on half-pay. It was true that the proud ladies of the Court, who had run away from the storm once and were quite ready to run away again, were carefully impertinent to the Marshals' wives. But the husbands themselves were all, except Davout, treated with the utmost deference. They had nothing to gain by a change of regime, and everything to lose if they took the wrong side. And yet, there was something damnably magical about the little wizard in his old green coat. And if there were going to be some more victories, it would be a pity not to be there. And if the People rose for Napoleon, to resist him would be to provoke a civil war, the greatest of all crimes. To and fro went

263

the struggle in the perplexed and bewildered hearts of each of these men.

Masséna had to decide first, for Cannes lay in the military district of Marseilles, where he was making a show of commanding. The cautious old hero took no risks. He began by despatching a body of troops to intercept the adventurers, and a consignment of ammunition to the Duke of Angoulême at Nîmes. So far, perfectly correct. But when the Duke was captured and expelled from France by Grouchy, the Prince of Essling began to scratch his head. The affair was not so easy after all.

His next step was to call out the National Guard, and to issue ammunition to a volunteer battalion and despatch it after the Emperor. But no one knew better than the Prince of Essling what chance a battalion of volunteers had of catching the 'Long Boots', and he was able to return to Marseilles with the satisfying knowledge that he had done his duty without harming the Emperor a single jot. As soon as the news came south that the Eagle had reached Notre Dame, Masséna sent his son to make his peace with Louis, and within a month of the landing at Cannes the Tricolor was flying at every flagstaff in the whole command of Marseilles. Then, having dismissed all Royalist officials and imprisoned the prefect of the Var, Masséna repaired to Paris to plead that he was too ill for a command in the field.

The next was Ney, Commander of the Royal Grenadiers, Lieutenant-General of the King, and he drew his sword in defence of the throne and swore to bring back the monster to Paris in an iron cage, and rushed off to the south.

After Ney, the next to be actively embroiled was Macdonald, the Duke of Taranto. He too decided to throw in his lot with the Bourbons and he hurried to Lyons, the second city of France, to stiffen the ebbing resolution of the Royal Princes, Monsieur and the Duke of Orléans, and to organize the defence. The troops were already showing a difficult temper, but they brightened on the arrival of the Marshal. To brighten on the arrival of a Napoleonic veteran, however, was a less cheering omen than it appeared at first sight, and when the Marshal-Duke of Taranto harangued the corps in the Place Bellecœur on March 10th in pelting rain, and wound up with repeated shouts of *'Vive le Roi!'* there was a disconcerting silence. It was broken at last by the sound of horses' hooves, and a courier galloped up. 'The advance-guards have met in the Guillotière suburb.'

'Are our outposts driving them back?'

'No. They are drinking with them.'

The Royal Princes went pale. When they joined the Army of France as Corps-Commanders, the last thing they had expected to be called upon to do was to fight. After all, it was hardly their business. So they turned and bolted for Paris, leaving their troops, their city, and their honour behind them. They were never court-martialled for desertion or cowardice.

Macdonald waited a little longer and then bolted after them.

Augereau, the traitor of 1814, turned his coat twice more in rapid succession. He issued a proclamation to his troops in which he said, 'The Emperor's rights are unassailable. Never were they more sacred to us.' He then retired to his country-house, abandoning Louis, Napoleon, and his men with a fine impartiality.

St. Cyr hoisted the white cockade at Orléans. His troops tore it down, and the ex-actor vanished like a pantomime demon.

In Paris there was quiet confidence. The brave Princes of the Royal House would bar the way at Lyons, and the invincible Prince of the Moskowa was on his way south to finish off the job with his iron cage. A few edicts about arrears of pay were published in order to please the soldiery, and Soult was dismissed on suspicion of treachery. But the 'escapade' was not treated seriously.

The news from Lyons was a nasty jolt. Worse was to follow. The iron cage seemed to have been somehow mislaid. The Prince of the Moskowa took it as far as the Inn of the Golden Apple at Lons-le-Saulnier, and there, late at night, two muffled strangers in civilian clothes were admitted to his room. They were officers of the Imperial Guard, and they brought a message scrawled on a sheet of paper: 'Meet me at Châlons. I shall receive you as I did after the Moskowa,' and it was signed with a single letter, a capital N. Ney spent a sleepless night, struggling desperately with his loyalty to France, his loyalty to Louis, and his loyalty to the Emperor. It never occurred to him to do what scores were doing all round him and simply resign his command. 'I was in a storm,' he said afterwards, 'and I lost my head.' Next morning, looking wild and haggard, he paraded his three thousand men and started to read a proclamation which he had written during the night. He was only allowed to read the first nine words, 'The cause of the Bourbons is lost for ever.' All else was drowned in a thundering *'Vive l'Empereur.'* That night he gave a dinner-party at the Golden Apple and sat like a skeleton at the feast. On the 14th of March he joined the Emperor.

Paris fell into the wildest alarm. The confidence melted away like the Royalist armies. On March 16th King Louis asked his Deputies and Peers if they could suggest a better finish to his life than death in defence of his country. 'We will all die in defence of the country,' cried Deputies and Peers, and on the dark, rainy night of March 19th King, Court, Household Corps, Deputies, and Peers, all bolted for their lives, and it must have been with a singular pleasure that General Excelmans led the pursuit. With the King went Marmont, who seemed unwilling to stay and welcome his oldest friend, and Macdonald and Mortier and Berthier. A contemporary has recorded that Macdonald seemed intensely amused by the whole business, and caused great irritation among the nervous courtiers by his hearty laughter.

At Lille the fugitives paused for a brief rest, and the Marshals held a military conference. But it was interrupted by the Prince of Condé, who was anxious to know if the King was going to perform the Maundy ceremony as usual on the next day. An earlier Condé would have preferred, perhaps, to join the Marshals in their conference.

At the frontier of Belgium, Macdonald and Mortier, both honest, loyal men, halted. They had escorted their master to safety, and now their duty was to their country. So they returned to Paris, Mortier to serve once again as a Marshal of the Empire, Macdonald to retire more prudently into the obscurity of civilian clothes. Macdonald was better even than Masséna at maintaining a footing in both camps. Berthier, who was on duty as Captain of the Royal Bodyguard, had to go on as far as Ghent. From Ghent he went to Bamberg to meet his family and bring them back to France. Poor Berthier was in terror of being taken for an *émigré* who was flying from the Emperor, and told Macdonald over and over again that he was coming back.

After Berthier's departure, only Marmont was left, and he remained with his new friends a little longer. At Ghent he inspected a battery of English horse-artillery and met the N.C.O. who had laid the gun at Salamanca that wounded him. There could be no mistake about it, for it was a single shell, fired a little while before the main battle began, and aimed at the French General Staff. Marmont, gunnery expert, was greatly impressed by the simplicity of construction of the English gun. Later on, the type was introduced in France. It is not known whether this chance meeting reminded the Duke of Ragusa of his wound, or whether it was just a coincidence that he suddenly said *au revoir* to his corpulent and gouty friend at Ghent, and went off to Aix-la-Chapelle, 'to recuperate from his Spanish wounds'.

Victor, the silly drummer-boy of Toulon days, who was still a silly drummer-boy, vanished with the White Cockade, and so did Pérignon.

***

On the 19th of March Napoleon arrived at the Tuileries. The last desperate play of the cards had begun.

Of the twenty-five Marshals of the Empire, Marmont, Victor, Macdonald, Pérignon, St. Cyr, had declared for the Bourbon. Augereau and Berthier had retired. Bernadotte was in Sweden, Murat in Naples. Lannes, Bessières, and Poniatowski were dead. Jourdan, the Republican of Fleurus, who had become an Imperial Marshal, and had hoisted the White Cockade in the first Restoration, went back to the Emperor and was made a Peer of France at last, and appointed Governor of Besançon. Moncey, Lefèbvre, and Sérurier were too old and too incompetent for active command. Brune was almost as bad, but there was a shortage of officers and Brune was sent to command the Army of the Var, the river between France and Italy. Masséna pleaded illness. Oudinot was at his estate in Lorraine, and no one knew on which side he would come down. Soult, just dismissed by the Bourbon, was free to join his old master. Suchet joined immediately and was given a corps.

At nine o'clock on the morning after Napoleon's arrival at the Tuileries the vast, surging, excited crowd, outside in the Place Carrousel, burst into a frenzy of cheering as a new arrival drove up in a carriage. It was Davout, the only one of all the Marshals who owed neither allegiance nor gratitude to the Bourbon. The Emperor embraced him. It was their first meeting since that dark, icy night at Smorgoni on December 5th, 1812, when Napoleon's sledge galloped off to the west to raise the new armies and repair the catastrophe. Two hours later they were alone together in the Tuileries and the Emperor asked the Marshal to take the Ministry of War. Davout declined. 'Listen,' whispered Napoleon in his ear; 'they all think that I am acting with the Emperor of Austria, and that my Empress and my son are already on their way to join me. It is not true. I am alone, alone against all Europe. Will you desert me?'

'I accept the Ministry,' replied Davout.

But the Emperor was not entirely alone. It would have been far better if he had been. For he had an ally, a single ally, and that ally was a fatal one. There was a chance, a dim chance perhaps but nevertheless a possibility, that a war-sickened Europe would not take arms against the apparently inexhaustible genius and resilience of the greatest captain of the age. The Allied Sovereigns might have shrugged their shoulders and kept the peace, if Napoleon showed no signs of aggression. But even that dim chance was extinguished when King Joachim of Naples made his last *volte-face* and deserted his new Austrian friends. As soon as the news of the landing at Cannes reached him, Murat acted with wild and reckless precipitation. Without waiting to hear from Paris, he abandoned his hectic round of festivals and balls and gaiety, and flung his army against the Papal States, captured Rome and Florence and Bologna and reached the line of the Po. But his troops were not the Reserve Cavalry of the *Grande Armée*. They were Neapolitans, of whom their old king had said, 'Dress them in blue, or red, or green, they'll run away just the same.'

Murat met the Austrians on the Po, and his men ran away; and the greatest cavalry leader in the world escaped in disguise by sea and landed at Toulon without a penny. The wheel had turned all the way round, and the inn-keeper's son from Cahors was poorer in 1815 than he had even been as a lad, when he was studying his books for the priesthood that the Talleyrand family had offered him.

From the moment that Murat began his mad enterprise, war was a certainty, and Davout had to set to work to make an army. His first task was a painful one. His ancient friend, almost the only man he had ever loved, whom he had called 'thou' in official despatches, Marshal Oudinot, wrote from Lorraine and declared himself against Napoleon. With instant and characteristic iciness, Davout severed the friendship of twenty years and in a stern, impersonal message ordered Oudinot to retire to his estates. There was no room in Davout's heart for two loyalties.

* * *

On April 17th, 1815, the last Napoleonic baton was awarded when Emmanuel, Marquis de Grouchy, was created a Marshal. A pre-war aristocrat, de Grouchy became an ardent Radical when still a young man, and on the outbreak of the Revolution eagerly joined the Republican armies as Citizen Grouchy. He was second-in-command in the unsuccessful expedition which sailed in 1796 under Hoche to Bantry Bay, and later on was sent to command cavalry in Italy. He came into prominence with Pérignon at the battle of Novi in 1799, when these two gallant generals were in such a hurry to surrender that they were mistaken by the enemy for an ambush. After some pleasant years spent on parole near Graz in Austria, Grouchy returned to the *Grande Armée* and commanded heavy cavalry in Spain, Russia, and elsewhere. In the retreat from Moscow he led the handful of officers who formed themselves into the Emperor's bodyguard. But between 1792 and 1815 he held no really important independent command of cavalry, nor any command of infantry at all.

There was something about Grouchy's character which did not endear him to his colleagues. For example, in 1814 he was dining with Marmont during the campaign in France, and seeing on the table the handsome sword of Prince Yurusov, whom Marmont's Corps had just captured in a night attack, he begged for the sword to replace his own heavy sabre. The sabre, he said, was chafing an old wound. Marmont immediately gave him the sword, and was somewhat annoyed to read later in the *Moniteur* that General Marquis de Grouchy had captured the sword of Prince Yurusov and had presented it to the Empress. Four days before Napoleon left Elba, Grouchy had been decorated with the *Cordon Rouge*, and had renewed his protests of fidelity to King Louis and the Royal Family. His conscience, however, was singularly elastic. For the first task assigned to him by Napoleon, some ten days later, was to go to the Midi and oppose the Duke of Angoulême. Grouchy, in view of his recent oath, should either have refused this mission or should have insisted on a guarantee of safety for his late patron. He not only did neither, but finding that a guarantee had already been signed by a subordinate, he tore it up and seized the Duke.

***

On June 1st, 1815, another of the Marshals died, the senior of them all, Alexandre Berthier, Prince of Neufchâtel and Wagram, wizard of the maps, old veteran of Lafayette and Rochambeau and half-forgotten battles on the banks of the Ohio river. After parting from Louis XVIII and Marmont at Ghent in the flight from Paris, he had hurried to his family at Bamberg, intending to bring them back to France. But at Bamberg his heart sank, and he hesitated, and was lost. He was too old. He was tired. He was done with wars. And so he decided he would not return to the famous maps that he had pored over for so many arduous and glorious years. He threw away his compasses. He would not need them again. But on that day in June, the street in Bamberg below his window was filled with old familiar noises, the tramping of boots on the cobblestones, and the rattle of artillery-wagons, and the staccato shouts of the officers, and Berthier looked down and saw that they were Russians marching to the attack on France.

271

The Emperor would be out again with the Eagles, and the maps would be spread in the travelling-carriage, and the Chief-of-Staff would not be there. In an agony of remorse the Prince of Neufchâtel and Wagram flung himself from the window into the street and was instantly killed.

***

On June 12th the Emperor started for the north-eastern front. His army was in five corps, commanded by D'Erlon, Reille, Vandamme, Gérard, and the Count of Lobau. No Marshal led a corps, for Suchet had been transferred to the Army of Italy. Soult was chief-of-staff, and Grouchy commanded the Reserve Cavalry. Mortier rode from Paris with the troops, but dropped out with an acute attack of sciatica at Beaumont.

A civilian accompanied the Army, alone, in a hired farmer's trap. It was Ney, with bitterness in his heart. He was still in semi-disgrace, for Napoleon had not forgiven him for the iron cage. At Beaumont Ney abandoned the trap and bought two of Mortier's horses, and he was a little encouraged when the soldiers cheered him as he rode past the foot-columns, and when he heard them call out, 'Things are hotting up. There goes *le rougeaud*.'

The last great Imperial attack thundered up the Charleroi road while Wellington was writing to a friend, 'Bonaparte's departure is not likely to be immediate, and I think we are now too strong for him here,' and Ney came upon the Emperor, sitting at a table outside an inn above the Sambre, studying a map. The disappointed civilian dismounted and hovered near a group of staff-officers in the hope of getting some employment, however humble. The Emperor looked up and saw him. Within thirty seconds Ney had been appointed to the command of the First and Second Army Corps, to which were added two regiments of light cavalry of the Imperial Guard and eight regiments of Kellermann's heavy cavalry, in all some

50,000 men and seventy-two guns. It was a strange and casual appointment.

* * *

The story of the Waterloo campaign is soon told. It is a story of blunders. The utter defeat of the Emperor's last army was due entirely to the mistakes of the three Marshals, Ney, Soult, and Grouchy. Ney's attack at Quatre Bras was a muddled, ill-judged, ill-planned operation, but that was by far the lesser of his two blunders on that day, June 16th. His other one ruined the campaign and destroyed the Empire. For when Napoleon was hammering Blücher at Ligny, he sent for Ney's Reserve Corps to come up on the Prussian flank. D'Erlon, commanding the Reserve Corps, marched towards Ligny. Ney, in a wild tempestuous outburst of the temper which he had shown on the field of Borodino, cursed and swore at the Emperor and countermanded the order, and D'Erlon, obeying his immediate superior, marched back towards Quatre Bras. The fighting at Quatre Bras was over before he arrived, and his Corps, 20,000 strong, fired not a shot all day. If D'Erlon had come to Ligny that afternoon, bringing a strong fresh corps across the right flank of the hammered Prussians, Blücher's army must have been utterly destroyed and Grouchy's 33,000 men would have been under Napoleon's hand and Wellington could not have stood at Waterloo without being disastrously beaten. Ney's counter-order to D'Erlon ruined all.

At Aix-la-Chapelle Marmont, in the intervals of remembering his Spanish wounds, watched with mixed feelings the headlong arrival of several thousands of his new Prussian allies who had come pelting back from Ligny.

* * *

At Waterloo the Emperor reverted to the methods of Austerlitz and Borodino. After making the general dispositions he left everything to Ney, just as he had left the tactics of the other two battles to the Marshals. There were none of the brilliant improvizations of Friedland or Wagram, when the Emperor himself formed the giant batteries and organized the storming columns. At Waterloo it was all Ney, and Ney had never recovered from 1812. The wildness of shell-shock was upon him, and he had lost the unerring quality of his tactical judgment. His matchless courage never deserted him, but coolness and judgment would have been more valuable. During the chaos and turmoil of the French cavalry charges, an English officer saw the Commander of the French Centre, his uniform blackened, his epaulettes shot away, his helmet lost, madly beating an English cannon with the flat of his sword. A telescope, a writing-pad and a pencil would have been more effective weapons.

Soult was a failure as chief-of-staff. It was sixteen years since he held that position to Masséna in Genoa (in Spain he had been Joseph's adviser rather than chief-of-staff), and he had forgotten the technique, while the third Marshal, Grouchy, could not have dallied away the precious hours more surely if he had been an Austrian instead of a Napoleonic Marshal.

Late that evening the Marshal-Prince of the Moskowa led his last attack. He had led the first infantry assault up the slopes of St. Jean; he had led the great charges of the heavy cavalry against the British squares, and now for the last time he drew his sword, dismounted from his horse, and went up the hill once more, and behind him marched the veteran soldiers of the Imperial Guard.

But those dense columns had never before met the rippling musketry of the English Line, and the Guard recoiled and the last English counter-attack dashed the tottering Empire to pieces. D'Erlon rode back amid the rout, and as he went he caught a glimpse of Ney standing beside the road, raging at the fugitives who would not stand with him. At last Ney saw an unbroken brigade that was retiring in good order, and he forced his way through the press towards it and roared at it to halt and turn about. 'Come and see how a Marshal of France can die,' he shouted, brandishing the stump of his sword that had snapped against the bayonets of the British Guard. But no bullet or bayonet struck him, and soon even that unbroken brigade would not stand, and the Marshal was left alone once more. Then he found three squares of the Old Guard near La Belle Alliance, and he fought with them until they too dissolved into chaos, and at last there were no more men for him to lead. So he turned and trudged slowly back in the darkness towards Genappe.

***

Louis XVIII went to a Te Deum service for the victory in the Cathedral of St. Bavon in Ghent. He was attended by Victor, the old companion of the siege of Toulon, the Marshal-Duke of Belluno.

CHAPTER XIX

THE END OF THE STORY

THE triumph of the Allies was all but complete. One man
alone remained to be dealt with. The Marshal-Prince of
Eckmühl was still at his post at the Ministry of War, and
he demanded an amnesty for all political opinions that
anyone had held during the Hundred Days. The demand
was refused. It was suggested in some quarters that it was
hardly the moment for a Napoleonic officer to be de-
manding anything. But Davout was immovable. He sat at
his desk and reiterated his demand. Marshal Macdonald
was asked to see him and find out what his intentions
were. 'I have 150,000 men and 30,000 horses and 750
guns,' said Davout, 'and I will march them across the Loire
and carry on the war, unless an amnesty is given.' No
threat of that stern man's was ever an idle threat, and
Macdonald, though an indifferent commander, was a Celt
and therefore a sensitive man, and he knew it. The Allied
generals signed the amnesty and Davout handed over his
last command. The Marshal-Prince of Eckmühl and Duke
of Auerstädt was undefeated to the end.

On August 2nd, 1815, another Marshal died, victim of
a hateful, cowardly mob-cruelty. For a scum of hooligans
at Avignon tore Marshal Brune out of his carriage and
kicked him to death and threw his mangled body into the

Rhône. The poor ex-patron of literature, Jacobin printer, and doggerel poet, had a military record of almost unrivalled ineptitude, but the manner of his death was not justified by that. Even his poetry was no excuse for such a deed. It was the twenty-three-year-old story that killed Brune, the story that he had been present in the old days of the Terror at the savage murder of the Princesse de Lamballe. All those years the story dogged him, and it pulled him down in the end.

Lannes, Bessières, Poniatowski, Berthier, and Brune were dead. Two more followed swiftly and violently.

On October 13th, 1815, Joachim Murat landed at Pizzo in Calabria, where six years earlier he had pitched his royal Pavilion, in a wild endeavour to raise his former subjects and recapture his kingdom. He was arrested and shot that same afternoon. It was a twelve-year-old crime that killed Murat, for he had been Governor of Paris when the Duke of Enghien was shot in the moat of Vincennes, and the Bourbons never forgot the names of anyone who might have been even remotely connected with that dark act.

So ended in a dirty Calabrian village, at the hands of a miserable, corrupt, and cowardly government, the most dazzling and picturesque figure that ever led a charge of cavalry.

Murat was a vain and stupid man, mentally dishonest, unstable of judgment, and under the thumb of his brilliant and treacherous wife. For his personal character there is little to be said, but he has left behind him a great series of military exploits, and a record of personal courage that was equalled in the higher ranks of the Emperor's army only by Ney and Lannes and Oudinot, and surpassed by no one. He had the surest eye of all for the slopes of ground, and the curves and gradients of hillsides, and folds, and ravines, and sunken roads, and all the peculiarities of 'terrain' that make or mar a cavalry attack, and he had an unfailing instinct for the exact moment at which to give an order to his massed columns to advance to the assault. The Napoleonic armies contained many brilliant cavalrymen, but Joachim Murat was the greatest of them all, and his fame is still spoken of when the merits of horsemen are compared.

Murat was followed very soon by Ney. The Bourbons came back to the first Restoration exuding an odour of benevolence and goodwill. They came back to the second Restoration in a great rage. They had been frightened out of their wits, and they had bolted with ignominious promptitude. The famous Household Corps with its 6,000 expensive young officers had made itself the laughing-stock of Europe. They were elegant on parade, but they had found it convenient to leave the actual battle against the Corsican usurper to be fought by Englishmen, Dutchmen, and Prussians. In a word, the descendants of the great and ancient military houses of France had made cowardly fools of themselves, and they knew it. So the moment they came back they began to clamour for blood, and the first on their list was the man who had lulled them into security with his talk about an iron cage, and had then gone over so tamely to the enemy. On the 3rd August, 1815, Ney was arrested, and all aristocratic Paris, except only the fat, good-natured King, was delighted. The King was in despair and told Marmont how bitterly he regretted the folly of Ney in letting himself be caught. On the 21st of August, Marshal St. Cyr, who had succeeded Davout as Minister of War, ordered that Ney should be tried by court-martial, and in order to embroil as many of the Marshals as possible, he arranged that Moncey should preside and that Masséna, Augereau, and Mortier should be among the members of the court. Moncey refused to serve. St. Cyr repeated the order. Moncey wrote to the King himself, again flatly refusing in a letter so gallant that it is worth quoting. Moncey was no military genius, but he was a man of honour.

'Is it for me to pronounce upon the fate of Marshal Ney? But Sire, allow me to ask Your Majesty, where were his accusers while Ney was fighting on so many fields of battle? Did they follow him, did they accuse him during twenty years of toil and danger? If Russia and the Allies cannot pardon the conqueror of the Moskowa, can France forget the hero of the Beresina? At the crossing of the Beresina, Sire, in the midst of that awful catastrophe, it was Ney who saved the remnant of the Army. I had in it relatives, friends, and finally soldiers, who are the friends of their chiefs. And I am to send to death him to whom so many Frenchmen owe their lives, so many families their sons, their husbands, their relations! Excuse, Sire, the frankness of an old soldier, who always holding aloof from intrigues has known only his duty and his country. He believes that his voice, which spoke in disapproval of the wars of Spain and Russia, may likewise speak the language of truth to the best of kings, to the father of his subjects. I do not disguise from myself that this might be a dangerous course with any other monarch. Nor do I fail to see that I may thus draw down upon myself the hatred of courtiers, but if, as I go down to the tomb, I can say with one of your own illustrious ancestors, "All is lost but honour!" I shall die content.'[1]

For this expression of honesty and nobility of character, Moncey was expelled from the Chamber of Peers and imprisoned in a fortress. His place was taken by Jourdan. Masséna made a typical effort to shuffle out of the whole business by pleading that his quarrel with Ney in Portugal in 1811 made him a biased judge, but the other members overruled him, unanimously resolving that so lofty a character and so pure a nature as the Prince of Essling would be utterly incapable of bias. Augereau, companion of Italy of the old days, who had competed with Swindler Masséna a hundred times for loot, must have thoroughly enjoyed the wording of this resolution.

But Ney had got it into his head that to be tried by court-martial would be fatal. 'They will kill me like arabbit,' he kept on saying, and he demanded to betried

---

[1] Translation from A. Hilliard Atteridge.

by the Chamber of Peers. Davout, though no longer in office, moved heaven and earth for a court-martial. 'No one could condemn such a man,' he cried over and over again. 'No one. Not even Ragusa.' Not even Ragusa! That was the depths to which Marmont had sunk in the eyes of his brother-Marshals. But Ney, with fatal stupidity, persisted. The Court-Martial jumped at the loop-hole that would get it out of the responsibility of trying an old comrade, and voted that it had no jurisdiction, and referred the whole matter to the Peers.

Ney was taken back to the Conciergerie Prison, and during the next few weeks his wife wrote to the Duke of Wellington and called his attention to the little matter of the amnesty which Davout had forced out of the Allied commanders. The Duke had been one of the parties to the signature of that amnesty, but with characteristic ingenuity he shuffled out of his responsibility by saying that he could not bind the King of France in dealing with his own subjects. In other words the amnesty was a simple fraud. The Marshal himself also wrote to Wellington and received the same ingenious answer from that somewhat honourable man. Wellington, of course, was perfectly safe in repudiating his word, for Davout had carried out his part of the bargain, and the French Army was being disbanded.

At this time Wellington was practically supreme in Europe.

The chief witness for the prosecution at Ney's trial was a General de Bourmont, a gentleman with a singular record of loyalty. He had fought for the King in the Vendée in the old days, and had afterwards abandoned the Bourbons for Napoleon. In 1814 he went back to the King, and during the Hundred Days rejoined Napoleon. He was given the command of a brigade in the Waterloo Army and deserted to the Prussians at the first opportunity. The chief witness for the defence was Davout, who gave evidence that he would never have signed the amnesty had he not been firmly convinced that the amnesty clause covered such cases as Marshal Ney. This evidence was rather awkward for the prosecution, so they got over it ingeniously by getting it ruled out of order.

At two o'clock in the morning on December 7th, 1815, the Peers recorded their votes. A hundred and thirty-seven voted for the death penalty, and seventeen for deportation. There were five abstentions, and one, de Broglie, voted 'Not Guilty'. Among the hundred and thirty-seven there were five Marshals: Kellermann, the old Duke of Valmy, Sérurier and Pérignon and Victor and Marmont, the Duke of Ragusa, who had by now given himself up to a perfect ecstasy of betrayal. 'Raguser' was already a household word, and Davout had been wrong. There were also fourteen generals among them. One was Dupont, who had saved his skin in Spain by surrendering his army at Baylen; another was Maison, who had fought side by side with Ney in the retreat from Russia, and whose life Ney had saved at Pleszczenitsky; Lauriston was among them, the Scottish gunner, who had commanded the Grand Battery at Wagram; and La Tour-Maubourg, the cavalryman. The last to sign the judgment was a Count Lynch, a Franco-Irishman who had betrayed Bordeaux to the Duke of Angoulême in 1814. Count Lynch was the only one of the Peers who voted for the guillotine. The rest of the hundred and thirty-seven were descendants of ancient and famous houses. The rattle of Ney's firing-party was probably their one and only experience of gun-fire. On the next day the Prince of the Moskowa was shot in the Luxembourg Gardens. One of the firing-party aimed at the top of the wall, high up and wide. A Russian officer rode out to see the sport and was instantly cashiered by the Tsar. Bernadotte was so horrified at the news of the execution of his old comrade that he invited Ney's son to accept a commission in the Swedish Army. But neither the Tsar nor the Crown Prince of Sweden lifted a finger to save Ney's life, and the Tsar, as Commander-in-Chief of the Allied Army, was responsible for the signature of the amnesty. His gesture, therefore, of cashiering the spectator-officer, would have carried more weight as an honourable gesture if the Tsar had not already somewhat tarnished his honour by repudiating his signature.

Soult had narrow escapes of sharing not only the fate of Murat and Ney, but also the fate of Brune. After Waterloo he had to bolt for his own country, Albi and the Tarn valley, but it was a matter of life and death that he should not cross the line of his 1813–14 retreat from the Pyrenees to Toulouse. For throughout that broad strip of country he was execrated by the peasants, who regarded his resistance to Wellington as the source of all their loss of money and cattle and grain and wine that had been requisitioned or looted by the two armies. Soult, once almost a king, had to disguise himself as a farm-hand and slip home to Soultberg by circuitous routes.

But the peasantry were not the only people who were after the blood of the Duke of Dalmatia, and General Robert Wilson wrote an urgent line to Lord Grey, 'I have just heard that Soult is to be on the first list, and that the Princes are going to do all they can to get him shot. I am writing to warn Soult.'

General Wilson, who does not appear to have possessed his Commander-in-Chief's capacity to kick fallen enemies, sent off his warning, and Soult fled with a faithful friend, the owner of a post-chaise, and escaped to the territory of Berg, where once Murat and his Caroline had ruled.

The two Marshals who played the most prominent part in the early days of the Second Restoration were Macdonald and St. Cyr. True to traditional form, they detested each other, and had done so ever since the disastrous battle of the Trebbia in 1799, when Suvorov gave Macdonald such a hammering. Macdonald always maintained that St. Cyr had left him in the lurch on the three days of that battle, and had never forgiven him.

Shortly after the last flight of Napoleon, Davout marched the Army across the Loire, and handed over the command to Macdonald; while Masséna, acting-Governor of Paris, after expressing his opinion that Paris was not so easy of defence as the triple-ringed town of Genoa, handed over his command to St. Cyr.

St. Cyr, as Minister of War, ordered the demobilization of the Army, and Macdonald, as Commander-in-Chief carried out the order. Macdonald did everything in his power to make the demobilization as easy as possible for his old comrades-in-arms, and took a surreptitiously active part in thwarting the Bourbon proscriptions. Orders for arrests mysteriously kept on going astray at Headquarters; arresting-agents were detained by military police owing to unfortunate misunderstandings, and only released when the birds had flown; and somewhere or other there was an extraordinary leakage of warnings to the Imperialist officers whose names were on the lists.

By the end of 1815 the demobilization, thanks entirely to the tact, sympathy, and firmness of Macdonald, had been carried out without leaving too great a bitterness behind.

***

Davout, who alone of the Marshals owed no allegiance to the Bourbons, wrote to Gouvion St. Cyr and pointed out that many officers on the proscribed list had only obeyed his, Davout's, orders during the Hundred Days. He offered, therefore, to stand trial himself in return for the lives of Generals Gilly, Excelmans, Drouot, Clausel, Delaborde, Alix, Dejean, and Marbot.

The offer was refused.

***

Marshal Victor was appointed to trace down the actions of his former colleagues during the Hundred Days, and report the names of those who should be proscribed. Little 'Beau-Soleil', the Waterloo Te Deum ringing triumphantly in his ears, threw himself with gusto into the task. He was especially severe when he came across any of the old companions.

On the first day of 1816 the new Royal Guard was formed. It was commanded in rotation, for three months at a time, by Marmont, Victor, Oudinot, and Macdonald. The two last were becoming more and more popular with the Bourbons, and even the firmness with which Macdonald gave evidence at the trial of General Drouot in favour of the accused man, did not diminish the esteem in which he was held.

On the other hand, Gouvion St. Cyr, that strange, independent, brilliant man, abruptly resigned his Ministry of War, refusing point-blank to have anything to do with a Government that proposed to cede French territory.

In June, 1816, Augereau died, the Marshal-Duke of Castiglione, at his château of La Houssaye. The picturesque gutter-boy had changed his coat too often in the difficult years, and at the end was trusted neither by Imperialist nor Bourbon.

Less than a year later he was followed by the other divisional commander who had waited in Nice in '96 for the little gunner-general to come and take over the Army of Italy. For Masséna died on April 4th, 1817. He left forty million francs, amassed through long years of thrift and looting, and the illicit sale of trading-licences, so he could well spare the three millions which the Emperor stole from the Livorno bank. Before he died, the Marshal-Prince of Essling met Wellington at Soult's house, and they talked about old days in Portugal when they had watched each other like hawks for so many months, and neither had dared to make the semblance of a slip in the face of the other.

During this year Marmont, always restless, always looking for something to organize or to build or to design, launched out as an experimental farmer. His two main contributions to the science of agriculture were the construction of three-storied pens for his sheep, and the manufacture of neat little leather coats for them in winter. But he lost money and soon gave it up, and returned to the more congenial task of suppressing Bonapartism whenever and wherever he found it.

Macdonald, as Grand Chancellor of the Legion of Honour, was asked to sign the award of the cross to his ex-gardener, who had spied upon him and helped him to grow beetroot when he was in disgrace in the early days of the Empire. 'The Legion is still the Legion of Honour,' said the Grand Chancellor, 'and the profession of spy to Fouché is not a very honourable one.' He refused the man the cross, and gave him a handful of money instead.

In February, 1818, King Charles XIII of Sweden died, and the Crown Prince, once a sergeant-major, signed for the first time his new name: 'We, Charles John, by the grace of God, King of Sweden, of Norway, of the Goths and of the Vandals,' and on the 11th of May, 1818, he was crowned by the Archbishop of Upsala.

Pérignon died on Christmas Day, 1818, and Sérurier almost exactly a year later.

In 1819 there was a change of policy. It was becoming more and more difficult even for a Bourbon king to ignore the plain fact that France numbered among her citizens a body of soldiers who were more famous than any other soldiers in the world, and that she could not keep them permanently in disgrace. So in 1819 an amnesty was declared, and the outlawed Marshals came back to their estates, their titles, their orders, and their peerages.

Soult, whom the Bourbons had distrusted, was included at the urgent pleading of St. Cyr; but it was a stern, cold, proud man who returned to France. 'Let me present a comrade of Waterloo,' said a friend, introducing an officer.

'I was not aware,' replied the Duke of Dalmatia, 'that I had any other comrade at Waterloo than Marshal Ney.'

Honest old Lefèbvre retired with his washerwoman-duchess to their country estate at Combault, and the splendid old pair devoted the rest of their lives to helping ex-service men. When he felt that his time was up, and that his lifetime of duty was at an end, the Marshal-Duke of Danzig went to Père-la-Chaise and chose a tomb beside Masséna, near Pérignon and Sérurier.

Kellermann, Duke of Valmy, the connecting-link between the incredible days of '92 and the glories of the Empire, died on September 12th, 1820, and two days later old Lefèbvre followed him.

In 1820 Suchet ought to have been one of the witnesses at the birth of the Duke of Bordeaux. But unfortunately he was so punctilious about putting on the correct uniform when he was awakened for the event at three o'clock one morning, that by the time he arrived the royal baby had been born.

Suchet had settled down to a quiet, unambitious life in Paris; and it is recorded of him that he used to give many musical parties, and was greatly distressed at the chatter of the guests through the music. The soldier who had made short work of the *guerillero* bands of Aragon, could not cope with the fashionable ladies of Paris.

***

On May 5th, 1821, the Emperor died.

On his deathbed he exclaimed in a strange, half-conscious, half-delirious paean of ultimate triumph, 'I shall meet my brave warriors in the Elysian fields, Kléber, Desaix, Bessières, Duroc, Ney, Murat, Masséna, Berthier.'

In his will he wrote: 'I have been defeated by the treachery of Marmont, Augereau, Talleyrand, and Lafayette.'

***

In 1823 there was trouble once more in Spain. The so-called Liberals with their Constitution, their absurd demands for reasonably good government, and their attitude towards monarchy, were being a source of grave alarm to all the reactionaries of Europe; and it was decided that a French army should invade the Peninsula in order to re-establish the forces of reaction. Victor, Duke of Belluno, was Minister of War, and he soon brought down upon himself a volley of scorn from Marmont for his ludicrous arrangements. Knowing nothing whatever of army administration, the Duke of Belluno gave orders that each infantryman of the Army of Spain was to carry eight hundred cartridges. 'If you can carry sixty,' commented Marmont, 'you may think yourself lucky, but I doubt if you can even manage that.' Marmont had just come back from a visit to Holland, where he had found, to his great chagrin, that his beautiful Marmontberg of 1804 had been built upon sand and had entirely vanished.

The command of the Army of Spain was given to a Prince of the royal blood, the Duke of Angoulême. But as the Princes of the royal blood were apt to understand very little about war, Marshal Oudinot and Marshal Moncey were sent with him to supply the professional touch. Curiously enough, Oudinot was one of the very few Marshals who had not campaigned in the Peninsula before.

The war of 1823 was a very different one from the war of 1808–14. There was no popular rising against the invaders; there were no assassinations and torturings. The people of Spain displayed an astonishing lack of memory, and they greeted the French Army as warmly as if there had never been a siege of Saragossa or a sack of Cordova. Madrid was soon captured, and a decisive battle won at Trocadero, and the war was over.

Macdonald, presiding over a special commission of inquiry, fearlessly exposed the corruptness of the administration of the Army of Spain under the Royal Duke, and the Duke never forgave him.

Davout died in 1823. Since the amnesty he had lived alone in the country in strict seclusion, and never once visited the Tuileries to pay his respects to the King. And that stern and silent man was as lonely in death as in life. For only a handful of officers followed the coffin of the Marshal-Prince of Eckmühl and Duke of Auerstädt, one of the greatest soldiers that France has ever had. He was buried in Père-la-Chaise near Masséna and Ney.

In 1826 Suchet died, and Marmont received his last important appointment. For he was sent as special Ambassador of France to Petersburg, to represent the King at the coronation of Tsar Nicholas. On his way to Petersburg he met Wellington, who was on his way back, and they had a friendly talk. After the ceremony of the coronation, Marmont went down to visit the field of Borodino (this was Marmont's first visit to Russia), and spent many hours examining it with the famous book of the Count Philippe de Ségur in his hand. He identified the Russian earth-works and the site of the Great Redoubt, wandered round the village of Semenovskoi, and found the place on which Napoleon's black bearskin had been laid, where Bessières whispered his decisive words into the Emperor's ear. From Borodino Marmont followed the fatal route, beside which so many thousands of his fellow-soldiers were buried, into Smolensk, and passed the walls and towers of Boris Godounov, until he came to the bridge-head at Borissov, where Oudinot with his 8,000 drove back the 50,000 Russians, and the ford at Studianka where the bridges over the Beresina were built.

It was in this same year, 1826, that Soult returned to public life, and almost at once found himself plunged into controversy. For the Austrian Government suddenly decided not to recognize the Imperial dukedoms which had been taken from Austrian or Italian soil. Accordingly the Austrian ambassador gave a big reception at the Embassy, at which the flunkeys announced the Dukes of Dalmatia, Treviso, Ragusa, Reggio, and Taranto, as Marshal

Soult, Marshal Mortier, Marshal Marmont, Marshal Oudinot, and Marshal Macdonald. Instantly French public opinion was roused to a fury at the insult. The great days of the Empire, and the great soldiers who had carried the Eagles throughout Europe, were already being lifted above the bickerings of party politics, and the Marshals were almost legendary figures. Victor Hugo, shortly after the insult at the reception, published his *Ode à la Colonne* amid the wildest enthusiasm. At the next Austrian reception there were no Frenchmen present at all, and the Austrian Government, after one attempt to save its face, climbed down. The attempt consisted of offering Soult, in exchange for the Dukedom of Dalmatia, the Dukedom of Soult-Austerlitz. There had been a time when Nicolas Jean-de-Dieu Soult would have given his right arm for the title of Soult-Austerlitz, but that time was past, and the only man from whom he would have accepted it had been dead for nearly six years.

In 1830 took place the revolution which drove the Bourbons out of France once more. The Duke of Ragusa, who had been summoned from his retirement by Charles X and appointed Governor of Paris, remained as loyal as ever to his Bourbon friends, and put himself at the head of the Swiss Guards, and organized the defence of the Tuileries and the Louvre. But he was quickly driven out, and had to fly the country.

Soult was down in his native district of Albi when he got the news of the revolution, and the prefect of the department sent over an urgent message to ask the great man's advice. 'Tell him,' said Soult, 'that I have nothing to give him. From this moment Marshal Soult draws his sword and throws away the scabbard,' and with that he drove to Paris and put himself at the disposal of the provisional government. Soon after he became Minister of War, and worked eighteen hours a day at the reconstruction of the Army.

There was an unfortunate incident between the new Government of France and the Government of Sweden.

The White Cockade of the Bourbons had been replaced by the Tricolor once again, and the young Prince of the Moskowa, son of a famous father, arrived in Stockholm with a letter from the one king to the other, and hoisted a huge Tricolor flag on the balcony of the French legation before King Louis-Philippe had been recognized officially. So far had the King of Sweden travelled from his early days, when he had done precisely the same thing himself in Vienna and defended his flag with a drawn sword on the steps of his own Chancery, that he insisted on the flag being pulled down, and he refused to receive young Ney.

Marmont, after flying from France, took refuge in London where he found much to interest him. He was greatly impressed by Brunel's tunnel under the Thames, and by John Nash's new Regent Street with its colonnade, but not in the least by Westminster Abbey. The Duke of Wellington visited him and arranged for him to see the arsenal at Woolwich. It was to have been an unofficial visit, but Marmont was delighted when he arrived to find a full-dress review in his honour. By a strange coincidence, at this review he met once again the gunner who had fired the shot at Salamanca. The man was now the caretaker of a magazine in the arsenal, and had lost an arm at Waterloo. 'Ah, *mon cher*,' said Marmont, 'we all have our turn.'

From London Marmont went to Vienna, and there he met the son of his oldest friend, a youth who was now called the Duke of Reichstädt, who had once been called the King of Rome, and who might have been, but for Marmont's treachery in 1814, the Emperor of the French. For the next three months the Duke of Ragusa spent two and a half hours three mornings a week, describing the great campaigns to the son of Napoleon, and being very careful to moralize, at the express wish of Metternich, upon the disasters to Europe which the campaigns had caused and the impossibility of ever attempting to repeat them. Once again the Duke of Ragusa had a congenial task.

In 1830 Gouvion St. Cyr died at Hyères.

Macdonald, by now sixty-five years old, was finding the gout too much for him (it had attacked him at Figueras in the Catalonian campaign as far back as 1809), and in this year he retired from the Chancellorship of the Legion of Honour. He had devoted the last fourteen years to the care of old soldiers of the Emperor and their wives or widows and their children. He was succeeded in the Chancellorship by Mortier.

In 1832 King Louis-Philippe appointed Soult to be Prime Minister of France. His ministry lasted for two years and he was succeeded by Mortier. But the good-natured Duke of Treviso was no politician, and he soon resigned.

Marmont was wandering restlessly and unhappily through Europe. In 1833 he left Vienna and went travelling in Italy. He visited Lodi and gazed for a long time at the bridge. Near the bridge he found a number of low, overgrown banks which he recognized at once. They were the emplacements behind which he had rallied a hussar regiment and then led it against the Austrian artillery thirty-seven years before. At Castiglione he hunted about among the rolling slopes of downland till he found the exact spot where he had massed the horse-artillery to support Augereau's desperate work, and at Arcola he identified the place where he and the others had pulled the little gunner-general out of the ditch when the infantry attack came reeling back under the Austrian fire. '*Que de souvenirs. Que de regrets,*' as Lucien had written to Masséna.

Jourdan, once a pedlar in haberdashery, and never quite reaching the Dukedom of Fleurus, died at his post as Governor of the Invalides in 1833, and was succeeded by old Moncey.

In 1835 the Marshalate of the Empire lost, for the eighth and last time, a Marshal by violence. Three had been killed on the field of battle, one had committed suicide, one had been lynched, and two executed. On July

28th, 1835, a man called Fieschi threw a bomb at King Louis-Philippe. The King was not hurt, but the bomb killed Mortier, who was in attendance.

Soult, hearing the news down at Soultberg in the Tarn valley, was deeply moved by the death of his old colleague, whom everyone had loved. 'Last year it would have been me," he said, and then he added, pointing to the sky, 'I begin to hear them sounding the Recall up there.'

Only three of the original creation were left – Bernadotte, Soult, and Moncey – and five of the last eight – Victor, Macdonald, Oudinot, Marmont, and Grouchy.

Up in Stockholm King Charles XIV was mellowing into a Constitutional Monarch. The old bitterness had gradually passed with the years, and the reconciliation between the King and his native country, begun by the magistrates of Pau, spread to Paris. When the Arc de Triomphe was completed in 1834, Bernadotte's name was given its rightful place, and his portrait was put in the Gallery of the Marshals at Versailles. And, on the death of Mortier, the message of sympathy which came from Stockholm was not from a king but from an old comrade-in-arms.

On June 28th, 1838, the streets of London were packed with dense, cheering, enthusiastic crowds of loyal subjects. For the Queen had just been crowned, and the coronation procession was passing through the streets. Each representative of the foreign powers was duly applauded by the hospitable Londoners, but a storm of spontaneous cheering welcomed, on every yard of the route, the Representative of France, the white-haired old Marshal-Duke of Dalmatia. Louis-Philippe had given him a specially built carriage, in the shape of a gondola, in blue and silver, with silver wheels, and ducal coronets on the lamps, and the ducal arms in jewels upon the panels, and the old enemy of the Pyrenees and Waterloo made a fine show. Soult had an interview with the Queen, at the end of which Wellington came softly up behind him and clapped him suddenly on the shoulder with the words, 'Aha, I've got you after all these years.'

On the 15th of December, 1840, in a snow-storm, as it might have been upon the Guadarramas, or at Eylau, or on the great retreat, the ashes of the Emperor came home to the Invalides. Only Soult and Moncey and Oudinot and Grouchy out of the twenty-six of the Emperor's Marshals were there to meet him. For Macdonald had died earlier in the year at his country home at Courcelles-le-Roi, and Victor would not come, and Bernadotte was in Stockholm, and Marmont was drifting unhappily from Saxony to Bohemia, and from Bohemia to Syria, and from Syria back again to Italy. Surgeon-General Larrey, seventy years of age, put on his uniform of a General of the Imperial Guard and walked all the way from Courbevoie through the bitter cold and the snow to the gate of the Invalides, to meet the ashes of his old master.

Victor died in 1841 and Moncey in 1842. Oudinot succeeded Moncey as Governor of the Invalides. He was already Grand Chancellor of the Legion of Honour.

$$* * *$$

A whole nation mourned the death, in 1844, of the soldier who came straight from European battlefields and laid the foundations of the 'Scandinavian Peace.'

For thirty years no gun had been fired in anger in the north, and the peace has lasted ever since.[1]

On the 8th of March, 1844, King Charles XIV of Sweden died, the King who had once been the Prince of Ponte-Corvo, Marshal of the French Empire, Commander of the First Corps of the Army of the Coasts of the Ocean, refugee in the forest of Sénart, Minister of War,

[1] *The Prussian attack on Denmark in 1864 was no fault of the Danes.*

Ambassador in Vienna, Divisional Commander in the Armies of Italy and the Rhine, and Sergeant-major in the Regiment Royal-la-Marine.

***

Oudinot and Grouchy died in 1847. The thirty-four wounds which Oudinot had received did not prevent him from living to the age of eighty-one.

In that same year, 1847, Soult was created Marshal-General of France. In all the sunlit history of France, from the days of the earliest kings, there have only been four Marshal-Generals – Marshal Turenne, Marshal Villars, Marshal Saxe, and Marshal Soult.

The Duke of Dalmatia had become a legendary figure. He was the Veteran Soldier of France. It was five-and-forty years since he had stood over against the Pratzen heights at Austerlitz and had told the Emperor that twenty minutes was all he wanted. Men were fifty years of age who had been in their cradles when Soult was helping Masséna to hold Genoa for the Republic, and standing beside him in the bastion of Switzerland when Suvorov was plunging up the pass from Bellinzona. And there were few men in the whole of France who could remember the days of the Sambre-et-Meuse in which Captain Soult had made his mark, and fewer still were alive who had seen a parade of the regiment of Royal-Infantry with Sergeant Soult at the head of his file.

The old man spent all his time now at Soultberg, among the art treasures that he had loved for so long. His favourite picture was kept covered with a double curtain of serge and green silk which was only drawn back in the presence of the Marshal-General himself or the Curator of the Louvre. It was a Conception of the Virgin, by Murillo, and after Soult's death it was sold for 563,000 francs. Another of his favourites was a Raphael, an Ascension of the Virgin, for which he had had to pay, as he delighted to explain, the lives of two monks. They had been sentenced to death in Spain, and had been bought off by the local patriots with the Raphael. There was also a reliquary of which he was very proud. It contained a lock of hair of the Cid, which had been brought from his grave in Burgos.

But the old veteran was hearing the Recall more insistently than ever, and he began to build his tomb in his little village of St. Amans-la-Bastide where once be had aspired to be the village baker. On one side of the tomb he placed a part of the bronze bas-reliefs from the celebrated column of the *Grande Armée* at Boulogne. The column had been pulled down, and an art-dealer had picked up one of the bronze figures and Soult had bought it for two hundred and fifty-three francs, grumbling, as he did so, that he had already paid for it once.

On the 26th of November, 1851, the Marshal-General of France died at the age of eighty-two. His coffin was heaped with his blazing stars and orders. Conspicuous among them was the Swedish Order of the Seraphim which Bernadotte had sent him, and the Order of the Golden Fleece of Spain, conferred on the Commander-in-Chief of the Army of Spain by King Joseph.

One only of the Marshals of the Empire was left, Auguste Frédéric Louis Viesse de Marmont, Duke of Ragusa, the oldest friend, the traitor of 1814, the man of whom the Emperor had spoken as *'mon fils, mon enfant, mon ouvrage'*.

Unhappy and alone, exiled from his country, despised and outcast, Marmont died in Venice in 1852. It was exactly sixty years since he had been a gunner-cadet at Dijon, and fifty-six years since he had ridden with Murat and Berthier and General Bonaparte to the Army of Italy in the splendour and the strength of their youth.

Que de souvenirs! Que de regrets!

BIBLIOGRAPHICAL
NOTE

I am profoundly suspicious of almost all bibliographies. Nothing is easier than to hire someone to visit the British Museum and make a most impressive list of authorities, which will persuade the non-suspecting that the author is a monument of erudition and laboriousness.

I propose therefore, to confine myself to the simple statement that every single detail of this book has been taken from one or other work of history, reference reminiscence or biography.

My chief regret is that the book was in the press when the highly important last volume of the memoirs of the Baron de Caulaincourt, Duke of Vicenza, Grand Écuyer of the Emperor, was published in Paris for the first time.

A.G.M.

INDEX

and the abdication, 261;
Napoleon's return, 264;
Ney's trial, 280;
death, 285-6
Metternich, Prince, 236, 260-1, 292
Moncey, Marshal, 18;
background, 21;
title, 135;
Peninsular War, 139, 141, 142, 146, 159;
campaign of 1814, 253;
first Restoration, 257;
Ney's trial, 279-80;
death, 294
Montbrun, 219
Moore, Sir John, 152, 153, 155, 157, 251
Moreau, Marshal, 50, 56, 60, 82, 239-40, 244
Mortier, Marshal, 94, 182;
background, 42;
title, 135;
Peninsular War, 184, 193, 197;
Russian campaign, 208-9, 224;
Napoleon's return, 267, 272;
death, 293
Moscow, 207, 220-21, 224
Murat, Marshal, 52, 77, 95-6, 97, 105-7, 151, 180, 191, 193, 205, 249;
background, 8, 10;
in Egypt, 30-1;
Aboukir, 34;
coup d'état, 57, 60-1;
marriage, 82-3;
Elchingen, 91;
uniforms, 102, 122, 132, 133, 148, 220;
Jena, 109;
Pursuit of the Three Marshals, 115-7;
in Poland, 120, 122-3;
Eylau, 125, 126;
Peninsular War, 139-41;
Russian campaign, 207, 211, 214-6, 218, 218-9, 221, 224,

230, 231-2
Saxony campaign, 236, 240, 243-4;
campaign of 1814, 253;
and the abdication, 260-1;
and Napoleon's return, 269-70;
death, 278-9

Napoleon II, King of Rome, 255, 292
Nelson, Admiral, 25, 30
Ney, Marshal, 51, 94, 181-2;
background, 42, 78-81;
Elchingen, 91, 135;
Jena, 108-9;
Pursuit of the Three Marshals, 113-14;
in Poland, 121, 122, 124;
Friedland, 129;
Peninsular War, 143-4, 146, 148, 149, 150, 153, 156, 186-9, 198-9;
Russian campaign, 208, 211, 214, 218, 219, 225-31, 234-5;
Saxony campaign, 236, 238, 239;
campaign of 1814, 252;
and the abdication, 254-5;
First Restoration, 257-8;
Napoleon's return, 264, 266, 272;
Waterloo, 273, 274-5;
trial, 279-83
Novi, 40

Oudinot, Marshal, 28, 88, 96, 128, 295;
Swiss campaign, 42, 48;
Wagram, 171;
background, 176-7;
title, 178;
Russian campaign, 208, 211-2, 229, 230;
Saxony campaign, 236, 240;